THE ENVIRONMENTAL STATE UNDER PRESSURE

RESEARCH IN SOCIAL PROBLEMS AND PUBLIC POLICY

Series Editors: William R. Freudenburg and
Ted I. K. Youn

Volume 1: 1979

Volume 2: 1982

Volume 3: 1984

Volume 4: 1987

Volume 5: 1994

Volume 6: 1997

Volume 7: 1999

Volume 8: The Organizational Response to Social Theory – edited by Stephanie W. Hartwell and Russell K. Schutt, 2000

Volume 9: Environmental Risks: Perception, Evaluation and Management – edited by G. Böhm, J. Nerb, T. McDaniels and H. Spada, 2001

RESEARCH IN SOCIAL PROBLEMS AND PUBLIC POLICY
VOLUME 10

THE ENVIRONMENTAL STATE UNDER PRESSURE

EDITED BY

ARTHUR P. J. MOL
Department of Social Sciences, Wageningen University, The Netherlands

FREDERICK H. BUTTEL
Department of Rural Sociology and Institute for Environmental Studies, University of Wisconsin, USA

2002

JAI
An Imprint of Elsevier Science

Amsterdam – Boston – London – New York – Oxford – Paris
San Diego – San Francisco – Singapore – Sydney – Tokyo

ELSEVIER SCIENCE Ltd
The Boulevard, Langford Lane
Kidlington, Oxford OX5 1GB, UK

First edition 2002

Library of Congress Cataloging in Publication Data
A catalog record from the Library of Congress has been applied for.

British Library Cataloguing in Publication Data
A catalogue record from the British Library has been applied for.

ISBN: 0-7623-0854-0
ISSN: 0196-1152 (Series)

∞ The paper used in this publication meets the requirements of ANSI/NISO Z39.48-1992 (Permanence of Paper).
Printed in The Netherlands.

CONTENTS

LIST OF CONTRIBUTORS

Olga Aksenova	Institute of Sociology, Russian Academy of Sciences, Moscow, Russia
Tim Allmark	Environmental Sociology Research Group, Imperial College at Wye, University of London, Kent, UK
Bianca Ambrose-Oji	Environmental Sociology Research Group, Imperial College at Wye, University of London, Kent, UK
Peter Buckley	Environmental Sociology Research Group, Imperial College at Wye, University of London, Kent, UK
Bindi Clements	Environmental Sociology Research Group, Imperial College at Wye, University of London, Kent, UK
Dana R. Fisher	Visiting Scholar, Institute for Social and Economic Research and Policy, Columbia University, New York, USA
Pekka Jokinen	Department of Regional Studies and Environmental Policy, University of Tampere, Tampere, Finland
Graeme Lang	Department of Applied Social Studies, City University of Hong Kong, Kowloon, Hong Kong
Allan Mazur	The Maxwell School, Syracuse University, Syracuse, NY, USA
Arthur P. J. Mol	Department of Social Sciences, Wageningen University, Wageningen, The Netherlands

Valeriy Nedelkov	Engineering Center "ArtEco", Zosimovskaya, Vologda, Russia
Dara O'Rourke	Department of Urban Studies and Planning, Massachusetts Institute of Technology, Cambridge, MA, USA
David N. Pellow	Departments of Ethnic Studies and Sociology, University of Colorado at Boulder, Colorado, USA
Rauno Sairinen	The Centre for Urban and Regional Studies, Helsinki University of Technology, Finland
Allan Schnaiberg	Department of Sociology, Northwestern University, Evanston, IL, USA
Gert Spaargaren	Department of Social Sciences, Wageningen University, Wageningen, The Netherlands
C.S.A. Van Koppen	Department of Social Sciences, Wageningen University, Wageningen, The Netherlands
Adam Weinberg	Department of Sociology and Anthropology, Colgate University, Hamilton, NY, USA
Eric W. Welch	Department of Public Administration, University of Illinois, Chicago, USA
Douglas C. Wilson	Institute for Fisheries Management and Coastal Community Development, North Sea Centre, Hirtshals, Denmark
Graham Woodgate	Environmental Sociology Research Group, Imperial College at Wye, University of London, Kent, UK

THE ENVIRONMENTAL STATE UNDER PRESSURE: AN INTRODUCTION

Arthur P. J. Mol and Fredrick H. Buttel

THE EMERGENCE OF THE 'ENVIRONMENTAL STATE'

Environmental quality has traditionally been perceived as a common or public good which cannot readily be provided via the market, and thus the state has been assumed to be the principal actor in environmental protection (albeit with great variations in the processes and efficacy of state environmental management institutions across nation-states). It is worthwhile noting, however, that the presumption of state responsibility for ensuring environmental quality is a relatively recent phenomenon. Particularly during the early years of nature protection at the turn of the twentieth century it was generally not the state, but rather civil society groups, that took the initiative in safeguarding natural areas and protecting the habitats of endangered species (Hays, 1987). The growing middle class was the key driving force behind the notion of preserving national parks and endangered species. Ultimately, though, states played growing roles in codifying these notions of nature protection in the form of government regulations and establishment of state-protected natural areas (Andrews, 1999).

In the industrialized countries of North America, Europe, and Oceania the institutionalization of environmental tasks in state policies and politics – and

The Environmental State Under Pressure, Volume 10, pages 1–11.

ISBN: 0-7623-0854-0

thus the emergence of what we can label an "environmental state" – generally dates back to the 1960s. From the 1960s through the 1980s the state rapidly expanded the span of its activities and powers in environmental protection and occupied a "comfortable" and unquestioned position in dealing with environmental problems. Scholars and other observers, of course, pointed out repeatedly at the time that government responses to environmental problems, challenges, and crises were very uneven and often inadequate (e.g. Rosenbaum, 1973). But during the heyday of the environmental state, concerns about the limited successes of government natural resource and environmental protection policies invariably led to calls for more rather than less state activity and intervention in the economic processes of investment, production, and even consumption. The nearly universal reaction among environmental management professionals and scholars was that there was no realistic alternative to assigning to the state the key role in ensuring environmental "public goods." There was also broad consensus that the only way to realize societal demands for high environmental quality and minimized environmental risks was for a stronger state to better counterbalance the power of capital. Even where the capitalist economy was seen as one of the major causes of environmental deterioration, more active intervention of the nation-state in the essential economic decisions in the private sector was believed to be the only plausible remedy. This consensus behind the necessity of an interventionist environmental state was cemented further by the more general view in the 1960s and 1970s, particularly in Europe, of the desirability of developing an activist welfare state.

In the 1980s, however, the comfortable state of affairs of a constantly expanding environmental state came under serious scrutiny and pressure for the first time. The conservative regimes of the 1980s – especially those in the United States (Reagan) and the United Kingdom (Thatcher) – were heavily inspired by neo-liberal scholars who argued for and legitimized strong deregulation and privatization programs. These neo-liberal tendencies affected a wide range of policy fields, including the environment (cf. Simon, 1982; Vig & Kraft, 1984). In addition, Reaganism and Thatcherism indirectly but substantially influenced the political cultures and regimes of a variety of countries around the world and led to similar deregulatory demands elsewhere.

In various developed countries the 1980s witnessed attempts by conservative governments to achieve "regulatory relief" – or, in other words, to reduce the role of the state in regulating the environmental performance of the productive sectors – with varying degrees of success. In the U.S., for example, the first Reagan Administration achieved a very substantial setback of environmental state activities and influence, as indicated by the fact that major American state environmental agency expenditures declined in real (1997) dollars from $24.4 billion in 1980 to $18.2 billion in 1984; as late as 1998 environmental agency spending in constant 1997 dollars remains below the 1980 pre-Reagan expenditure level (Vig & Kraft, 2000, p. 396). While the environmental deregulatory impulse was particularly strong in the U.S. and the U.K. and had considerable influence abroad, its impacts were quite variable internationally. Environmental policies in the Netherlands, for example, were hardly affected by the wave of deregulation and privatization of the 1980s.

NEW DEBATES ON THE ENVIRONMENTAL STATE

In the early 1990s the main currents of neo-liberalism, deregulation, and privatization seemed to have lost some of their sharpness – and arguably also their political impact in the environmental field – particularly on account of the rise of environmentalism on the public and political agendas at that time (Dunlap & Catton, 1994). The conservative neo-liberal environmental deregulatory programs in the U.S. and the U.K. lost some of their luster, and were tending to be balanced or supplanted by more progressive, "state-friendly" governments which were beginning to replace conservative regimes (e.g. Clinton, Blair). Even so, debate concerning the role of the state in environmental protection not only continued, but also widened considerably in three ways. First, the debate became broader and more sophisticaed, moving away from simple deregulation and privatization arguments, and toward the issue of political modernization (more commonly known as "reinventing government" in the U.S.; see Rosenbaum, 2000, for a useful discussion of "reinventing EPA"). Second, in addition to the ongoing debate on the environmental state within national boundaries, the processes of and political debates on globalization have led to new challenges to the viability of the (nationally ordered) environmental-regulatory state. Third, the debate has widened geographically, from Europe and the North American continent to the Central and East European countries undergoing transitions away from centrally planned economies with all-dominating states, and to states in the so-called South. We will elaborate shortly on these changes in the debate on the environmental state.

State Failure and Political Modernization

Jänicke's influential 1986 book *Staatsversagen* (published in the U.S. as *State Failure*; Jänicke, 1990) set the tone for a less ideological and more progressive critical analysis of how alternative modes of (environmental) governance and reform can be identified, and how the welfare and regulatory apparatuses can rely less heavily on a bureaucratic state. Rather than a debate organized around the simple dichotomy of centralized state-regulation versus privatization-deregulation, these analyses focused on new modes of environmental governance and on new instruments in environmental policy making such as voluntary agreements and market-based instruments (with all their growing pains of implementation and effectiveness). Jänicke's analyses were focused heavily on the environmental arena, and featured observations of new tendencies regarding relations between state and polluters (e.g. a move from adversarial to more consensual or negotiated rule-making), new divisions of tasks between central and local environmental authorities, and shifts of environmental tasks to parastatals, public-private partnerships, or even private companies. Jänicke has also written more broadly about the growing role of the state as arbiter and facilitator between different interests instead of the state as protector of common interests or of those of the powerless, while Ulrich Beck has been influential in analyzing the emergence of environmental-subpolitical arrangements beyond the traditional state institutions of parliaments, political parties, and bureaucracies (Beck, 1994).

In the more positive evaluations, these new state structures and practices are often referred to as "political modernization," and in terms of the renewal of the environmental state by taking better into account the changing character of modern society. In an era of reflexive modernity, with growing complexities, uncertainties, and information flows, the state can no longer be expected to design and prescribe the way society and economic interactions should be organized. More pessimistic evaluations interpret these changes in terms of the growing ability of capital to circumvent the regulatory capability of the state.

Globalization and the Undermining of Environmental Sovereignty

In the 1990s the growing intellectual preoccupation with globalization strongly reinforced the idea that the nation-state was losing control in the field of environmental protection. Wapner (1996) is one of the more visible proponents of this point of view. Wapner has argued forcefully that the emergence of various supra-national and global political and economic institutions and mechanisms diminishes state sovereignty and further reduces the capacity of nation-states to intervene in those economic activities of production and consumption that degrade the state's territorial environment. These limited possibilities for management and control are not only related to those global environmental problems that transcend the national level, e.g. ozone layer depletion, loss of biodiversity. In addition, the declining autonomy of national-state regulation in spheres such as import restrictions and export bans (of hazardous waste) also affects the state's ability to manage more routine or "normal" environmental problems. The strong push for a "level" playing field in the global investment system, which was one of the claims made for the original plans for the Multilateral Agreement on Investment (MAI), would have meant a major weakening of the nation-state vis-à-vis transnational companies in environmental politics.

National environmental regimes are also believed to fail due to the growing organizational and technical complexity of globalizing production and consumption systems that stretch beyond the nation-state's territory, for several reasons. First, the high speed and wide-ranging character of social and economic transformations are difficult to integrate into rather static or slowly changing national environmental regimes. Second, the state is faced with vast flows of new information on the causes and consequences of, and the disruptions resulting from, environmental problems. Rising expectations from citizens that these information flows be used adequately in environmental policy programs, and that environmental protection regimes should be refined and fine-tuned according to local physical and social/economic conditions, lead to legitimacy problems. As Lash and Urry (1994) argue in analyzing the changing relationship between nature and society in the era of globalization, contemporary nation-states now tend to be too small for the large problems, such as "high-consequence risks," and too large for the small problems, which need local fine-tuning and close collaboration with local actors.

Perhaps one of the most telling indicators of how environmental issues have led to new lines of thought about state practices and capacities is the fact that Peter B. Evans, who has built his scholarly reputation on analyses of macro-political processes (e.g. Evans, 1995), has recently shifted his attention to local-level embedded-autonomy practices and to the factors that shape "urban sustainability" and "livable cities" (Evans, 2002).

It is also the case that while the field of international environmental politics has traditionally been the monopoly of nation-states, other organizations and institutions are playing growing roles. One the one hand, international and supranational organizations themselves are increasingly competing with, and often supplanting, the role of the nation-state, as these international organizations develop their own interests, cultures, logics, and rationalities. On the other hand, non-governmental actors and decentralized authorities increasingly appear on the stage of transnational environmental policy-making, having a major impact on the state's ability to remain control over environmental policy-making. The Brent Spar case was telling in the way Greenpeace, and finally also Shell, undermined the position of the U.K. government in environmental policy-making (Dickson & McCulloch, 1996).

The Environmental State Beyond the West

While many of these developments are valid for most states, though with variations in magnitues and time frames, the environmental state in developing countries is a critical arena requiring more attention for both practical as well as intellectual reasons. In most of the nation-states of the South the environmental state is of quite recent origin, and its character often diverges to a considerable extent from the environmental states in Europe and the North American continent. Faced with different development paths from, for instance, the European countries, the articulation of environmental interests in civil society and within the political institutions and arrangements in the South can be quite different from those in the Northern political democracies. The relations between central and subnational authorities, the profile of the environmental movement, the democratic vs. nondemocratic character of political processes, and the relations between economic and political elites typically differ strongly as well. In addition, the nation-states of the South are confronted with actors – particularly various fractions of capital, but also party, bureaucratic, and other elites – who can undermine particularly forcefully the environmental tasks, priority-setting activities, fiscal allocations, and goals of environmental regulatory agencies. In addition to the pronounced role played by transnational corporations, international official development assistance, multilateral banks, and international financial institutions are major actors in influencing environmental regulatory agendas. In addition, international environmental NGOs (e.g. WWF, IUCN, Friends of the Earth, and Greenpeace) have a much stronger influence on these environmental states in-the-making than on the environmental states in the North.

Although the actors, institutions, and mechanisms that put the environmental state under pressure differ between developing countries and industrialized societies, we can also witness similarities in the sociological analyses and the political debates involving the environmental states in distinct social contexts and geographical regions. Globalization, as introduced above – but also the global exchange of ideas, theories and analysis in academic institutions – contributes to partly identical debates on the actual and necessary transformations of the environmental state. This volume gives evidence of such similarities in environmental state analyses in diverging geographical regions.

ANALYZING THE ENVIRONMENTAL STATE: CONTRASTING PERSPECTIVES

The issues just discussed take a central place in the twelve papers which have been grouped together in this book. Overall, the 12 articles leave little doubt that the contemporary environmental state is indeed faced with major new challenges as we enter the new century. The state is under persistent pressures from different sides, and experiences both significant changes and major continuities in its main strategies and performances with respect to environmental problems. Various analytical frames and social theories are now being applied to understanding and evaluating the nature of these social processes, transformations, and continuities. While there is a considerable diversity of theoretical perspectives among the 12 articles, in this introduction we emphasize two contrasting views of the changing nature of the environmental state at the turn of the century – the treadmill-of-production and the ecological modernization perspectives – that are given particular stress in this volume.

The theory of the treadmill of production has been one of the most durable perspectives in environmental sociology, and has been closely associated with the work of Allan Schnaiberg and associates. The treadmill of production has its roots in neo-Marxist thinking and stresses the continuity in the relation between capital and the state with respect to environmental deterioration and reform. The core idea behind the treadmill of production is that there are powerful tendencies within both the capitalist market system and the state toward capital-intensive expansionism which results in "additions" (essentially pollution) and "withdrawals" (essentially depletion of renewable and non-renewable resources). The compelling character of this expansionism, and the great difficulty of identifying alternatives to capital-intensive, environmentally destructive growth, has led Schnaiberg and his associates (particularly Kenneth Gould, Adam Weinberg and David Pellow) to label it a "treadmill." In addition, while recognizing that the nature of capital accumulation processes change and the environmental state seems to mature, the treadmill of production perspective suggests that the overall tendency is more so the continuity in the marginal successes of the environmental state in regulating "additions" and "withdrawals" (see Schnaiberg, 1980; Schnaiberg & Gould, 1994; Gould et al., 1996) rather than fundamental changes in the direction of sustainability (Weinberg et al., 2000).

The ecological modernization perspective is a more eclectic one, drawing on the ecological modernization literature in environmental science and on political-sociological concepts such as reflexive modernization, subpolitics, and state failure. The ecological modernization theory is most closely associated with the work of Northern European scholars such as Joseph Huber, Martin Jänicke, Arthur Mol, and Gert Spaargaren (see Mol, 1995; Mol & Sonnenfeld, 2000). In contrast to the treadmill of production view, the ecological modernization perspective emphasizes the institutionalization of environmental interests in the state (and in economic processes and institutions), and stresses the discontinuities in this regard from the 1970s to the present. Ecological modernizationists recognize that the pressures on the environmental state may lead to a diminution of the autonomy of the environmental state in environmental politics, and to a marginalization of the environmental state vis-à-vis capital. But the ecological modernization perspective argues that these tendencies are counterbalanced reflexively by major state reforms, new modes of governance, new relations between state and economy – or, in other words, by what ecological modernization adherents would label political modernization and environmental subpolitics.

These contradictory perspectives and evaluations of the 'environmental state in transition' are introduced in some detail in the first two articles, by Schnaiberg et al. and Mol and Spaargaren. The two articles represent a dialogue, in that both detail the differences between and commonalties of the two perspectives discussed above. These two perspectives are drawn on in a number of the other contributions which focus on various aspects of the role, logic, and dynamics of the environmental state in actual processes of (failing) environmental reform. Rather than aiming to verify or falsify either of the two perspectives on the basis of one case or country study, most articles show the (sometimes limited) relevance of these perspectives in understanding the state in environmental conflicts.

OVERVIEW OF THE VOLUME

The contributions to this work are a selection of the papers presented at the conference "The Environmental State under Pressure," organized by the International Sociological Association's Environment and Society Research Committee (RC 24). On 6–7 August 1999 some 50 scholars gathered together at the downtown Chicago campus of Northwestern University to present and discuss over 30 papers on the challenges and transformations states are undergoing in dealing with the environmental crisis. Both the countries of origin of the authors as well as the topics and theoretical perspectives dealt with by these scholars were wide-ranging. Given the impossibility of including all the presented papers, the papers were selected for publication in order to recognize the variety of perspectives that exist on the environmental state.

A geographical accounting of the articles indicates that the scope of the papers is quite wide-ranging, allowing for comparative insights. Of the 10 papers that follow the theoretical introductions, only one deals explicitly with the environmental state in the North American continent (Mazur and Welsh), while three analyze the environmental state in Western Europe (van Koppen, Sairinen and Jokinen). No less than five papers provide detailed analyses of the successes and failures of environmental states outside the so-called triad of the EU, the NAFTA area, and Japan. Two articles focus on African states (Ambrose Oij et al. and Wilson), two on Asian countries (Lang and O'Rourke), and one deals with the so-called transitional economies in Central and Eastern Europe, in casu Russia (Aksenova & Nedelkov).

Following the two theoretical introductory articles by Schnaiberg et al. (on the treadmill of production perspective) and Mol and Spaargaren (on ecological modernization), Dana Fisher complements the first section on theorizing the environmental state. She aims to interpret and understand the differences between the two perspectives, using a Habermasian framework.

The second section of the book contains several analyses of Northern states. Allan Mazur and Eric Welsh start with a quantitative analysis of air pollution abatement policies in the United States of America. In a quantitative empirical assessment of the reductions of emission in sulfur and nitrogen oxides, Mazur and Welsh observe that stringency of state regulation has little direct relationship to reductions in emissions. Both Sairinen and Jokinen analyze the successes and failures of the Finnish environmental state, albeit from distinct perspectives and with regard to different environmental issues. Rauno Sairinen applies the Foucauldian notion of governmentality in analyzing the regulatory reform of the environmental state, particularly with respect to environmental impact assessments, carbon taxation, and the emergence of voluntary environmental agreements. Pekka Jokinen examines agri-environmental regulation, focusing on the dialectic between national and supranational (EU) environmental state formation. The typical, closed policy domain of national agricultural politics is challenged and opened by the emergence of both environmental interests and the process of Europeanization. Kris van Koppen continues the analysis of European states, by looking into the debates around major infrastructure projects in the Netherlands and Portugal and the role the state is claiming and is given. These often controversial projects, and the related debates, show a continuing strong role of the state: vis-à-vis supranational structures (the EU), vis-à-vis expert systems, and vis-à-vis market actors and other non-governmental organizations. It is especially the high levels of uncertainties linked to these mega-projects and to the complex decision-making structures which give states pride of place.

The third section looks into the South, more particularly into the successes and failures of African environmental states in regulating the "withdrawal" of natural resources. Bianca Ambrose-Oji and her colleagues of Wye College, University of London deal with forest conservation in Cameroon, especially looking critically into the frequently-expressed desire for participation of local communities. In discussing forest conservation practices and discourses in West Cameroon, the article especially focuses on the role of the environmental state in terms of the contradictory imperatives of creating favorable conditions for economic capital accumulation and maintaining legitimacy by protecting the ecological capital and the needs of communities depending on the forests. Doug Wilson addresses the challenges the Tanzanian state faces in regulating Nile perch fisheries on Lake Victoria, in a situation where global markets, transnational companies, and the EU set the boundaries of the playing field, as well as some of the rules of the game, for local fishermen. Wilson's paper is focused on the issue of how it is that the Tanzanian state manages the environment in such a complex policy environment.

Finally, attention shifts to the so-called transitional economies, in which the relations among state, economy, and society are perhaps most in flux. Graeme Lang analyses the relations and contradictions between the central Chinese government and the local governments in the struggle to balance demands for water control, resource conservation, and economic development, against the backdrop of heavy flooding and extensive logging. While the principal initiative to control floods by banning logging comes from the central government in Beijing, the decentralization of power since the late 1970s has worked against an effective environmental state. The legitimacy of the central government in China to take strong action relies heavily on its economic performance; so it will be especially motivated to do so if and when banning logging stimulates the conditions for continued economic growth. In developing his notion of complaint-driven regulation in Vietnam, Dara O'Rourke analyses the role of communities in motivating a conflicted environmental state to take action against major polluters. He provides two detailed case studies that shed light on the factors that make such a system work, without being over-optimistic on the general applicability of such mechanisms inside and outside Vietnam. Finally, Olga Aksenova and Valeriy Nedelkov analyze how decentralization and privatization (or self-organization) processes in Russian environmental policy are a logical consequence of the failures and the near-disappearance of the national environmental state. In a situation where traditional actors vanish and rules of the game change, there is a vacuum in environmental policy-making. New actors and new unorthodox and un-Russian rules are now emerging to fill this vacuum, and these practices are not too far away from ideas of ecological modernization the authors suggest.

REFERENCES

Andrews, R. N. L. (1999). *Managing the Environment, Managing Ourselves.* New Haven, CT: Yale University Press.

Beck, U. (1994). The reinvention of politics: towards a theory of reflexive modernization. In: U. Beck, A. Giddens & S. Lash (Eds), *Reflexive Modernization: Politics, Tradition and Aesthetics in the Modern Social Order* (pp. 1–55). Cambridge: Polity.

Dickson, L., & McCulloch, A. (1996). Shell, the Brent Spar and Greenpeace: a doomed tryst? *Environmental Politics*, *5*(1), 122–129.

Dunlap, R. E., & Catton, W. R., Jr. (1994). Struggling with human exemptionalism: the rise, decline, and revitalization of environmental sociology. *The American Sociologist*, *25*, 113–135.

Evans, P. B. (1995). *Embedded Autonomy*. Princeton, NJ: Princeton University Press.

Evans, P. B. (Ed.) (2002). *Livable Cities*. Berkeley: University of California Press.

Gould, K. A., Schnaiberg, A., & Weinberg, A. S. (1996). *Local Environmental Struggles*. New York: Cambridge University Press.

Hays, S. P. (1987). *Beauty, Health, and Permanence*. New York: Cambridge University Press.

Jänicke, M. (1990). *State Failure* (Staatsversagen [1986]). University Park, PA: Pennsylvania State University Press.

Lash, S., & Urry, J. (1994). *The Economies of Signs and Space*. London: Sage.

Mol, A. P. J. (1995). *The Refinement of Production*. Utrecht: Van Arkel.

Rosenbaum, W. A. (1973). *The Politics of Environmental Concern*. New York: Praeger.

Rosenbaum, W. A. (2000). Escaping the 'battered agency syndrome': EPA's gamble with regulatory reinvention. In: N. J. Vig & M. E. Kraft (Eds), *Environmental Policy* (4th ed., pp. 165–189). Washington, D.C.: CQ Press.

Schnaiberg, A. (1980). *The Environment*. New York: Oxford University Press.

Schnaiberg, A., & Goiuld, K. A. (1994). *Environment and Society*. New York: St. Martin's Press.

Simon, J. (1982). *The Ultimate Resource*. Princeton: Princeton University Press.

Vig, N. J., & Kraft, M. E. (1984). *Environmental Policy in the 1980s: Reagan's New Agenda*. Washington, D.C.: CQ Press.

Vig, N. J., & Kraft, M. E. (2000). *Environmental Policy* (4th ed.). Washington, D.C.: CQ Press.

Wapner, P. K. (1996). *Environmental Activism and World Civic Politics*. Albany: State University of New York Press.

Weinberg, A. S., Pellow, D. N., & Schnaiberg, A. (2000). *Urban Recycling and the Search for Sustainable Community Development*. Princeton, NJ: Princeton University Press.

PART I:

CONCEPTUALIZING AND THEORIZING THE ENVIRONMENTAL STATE

THE TREADMILL OF PRODUCTION AND THE ENVIRONMENTAL STATE

Allan Schnaiberg, David N. Pellow and Adam Weinberg

THE INITIAL LOGIC OF THE TREADMILL

The *treadmill of production* (TOP) is a concept first introduced in 1980 by Schnaiberg, arising from two observations. First, a major change appeared in the impact of production processes upon ecosystems in the last half of the 20th century. Second, social and political responses to these impacts were quite variable and volatile. While some people rebelled against this modern production system, others embraced new technologies as their best hope for solving environmental problems.[1]

Ironically, we have returned to this theoretical ambivalence at the end of the twentieth century. Among environmental sociologists, proponents of ecological modernization (EM) have postulated that there is a growing independence, or 'emancipation,' of the ecological sphere from the political and economic spheres in state and industry policy-making (Mol, 1995; Spaargaren & Mol, 1992). Thus, within each of the spheres, there are significant environmentally-induced institutional transformations, which leads firms to employ new technologies to reduce environmental impacts of production. Contrarily, our own model falls within the range of political economy perspectives that view recent political and economic trend as minimizing – and often undermining – progress on both the social and ecological goals. Proponents of political economy models urge

The Environmental State Under Pressure, Volume 10, pages 15–32.

ISBN: 0-7623-0854-0

increased mobilization and opposition to socially and ecologically oppressive actions by state and private sector actors.

In this paper, we outline the model of the treadmill as a political-economic context for the so-called *environmental state*. Contrary to many assumptions of ecological modernization theory, we find that economic criteria remain at the *foundation* of decision making about the design, performance and evaluation of production and consumption. This primacy of economic criteria still tends to overshadow most, if not all, ecological concerns. Further, the state also shares this orientation, despite its own political interests, and often cedes a great deal of power to private sector actors. We view this as highly problematic for creating conditions for sustainability and ecological responsibility.

Schnaiberg argued that one major element of change in the U.S. production system during the Post World War II era was the changing status of workers, moving from a working to a middle-class, albeit within a society still marked by considerable poverty (Rubin, 1996; Reich, 1992). Workers gained new income and occupational opportunities through the post-1945 expansion of production and trade. In three books, Schnaiberg and his collaborators outlined a new production system that had changed its relation to the environment in two fundamental respects (see Schnaiberg, 1980; Schnaiberg, Watts & Zimmermann, 1986; Schnaiberg & Gould, 1994):

- First, modern factories needed greater material inputs. The modern factory was capital-intense, and hence, more energy was needed to run machinery. Likewise, the machinery was designed to vastly increase production levels, thus requiring far more raw materials. This feature of this new production system helped explain why ever-greater levels of *withdrawals* from eco-systems were required. These ecological withdrawals led to one set of environmental problems, natural resource depletion.
- Second, modern factories used many more chemicals in the new production processes. The modern factory used new "efficient" energy/chemical intensive technologies to transform raw materials into finished products. Thus, workers were increasingly engaged in managing energy and chemical flows, and directing their flows through the complex machinery, to create marketable products. This feature led to a second set of environmental problems, pollution – which Schnaiberg termed *additions* to the ecosystem.

In a later series of empirically-grounded works (Gould, Schnaiberg & Weinberg, 1996; Schnaiberg, 1994; Gould, 1991, 1992, 1993; Weinberg, 1997a, b; Weinberg, Schnaiberg & Pellow, 1996; Gould, Weinberg & Schnaiberg, 1995), this earlier concept of the treadmill was further elaborated, as Schnaiberg was joined by a succession of students, including: Gould, Weinberg and Pellow. Together they depicted a political economy driven by the following goals:

1. **Economic expansion**. Economic expansion is generally viewed as the core of any viable social, economic, or environmental policy. Economic expansion is thought to increase the profits that corporate managers and their investors require for capital outlays. Workers are believed to benefit from these outlays because they lead to increased production, which creates new local employment opportunities. Capital outlays also lead to higher levels of productivity, a precondition for rising wages. Government agencies need to ensure that national production generates sufficient profitability to: (a) induce investments by capital owners; (b) provide enough additional market values to maintain a level of wages adequate to sustain consumer demand; and, (c) generate enough tax revenue to cover the state's social expenditures. Governments believe that tax revenues from the accelerating treadmill will rise more rapidly than citizen demands. Thus, government officials and agencies increasingly share a stake in the economic expansion of the private sector.
2. **Increasing consumption**. If economic growth is to come about through increased production of the amount of goods, consumers need to have the disposable income to purchase the goods. Therefore the state, along with private capital, works to make low-interest loans available to consumers for the purchase of homes and other items. This ensures a continued cycle of production and consumption.
3. **Solving social and ecological problems by speeding up the treadmill**. Social and ecological problems are thought to be best solved "through the market." Thus, there is an untenable, almost magical, sense that any type of economic expansion will reduce social and ecological problems. Poverty will be reduced by a growing economy because there is an expanded job base and increased wages at the bottom. A growing economy also supports government social expenditures (for education, housing, and other needs of the poor) and provides the source of funding for technology development that could address environmental ills.
4. **Economic expansion via large firms**. Economic expansion is seen as fostered primarily through the growth of large firms, the Fortune 500 or "core firms." Large firms are thought to be the driving engine of the economy. Their growth creates the most demand for jobs, and it creates secondary demand for supplies, which fuels the growth of smaller entrepreneurial firms. The wages paid to the large labor pools provide consumption capacity among consumers who keep mainstreet American

merchants in business. The earlier popular slogan "What's good for General Motors is Good for America" captures this thinking.

5. **Alliances among capital, labor, and governments**. The post-1945 political economy was largely held together by an implicit contract. Private capital's need for a reliable labor force aided in the development of strong trade unions that could collectively bargain for wage increases and safer working conditions. Workers' need for jobs and their general satisfaction with unprecedented material gains led to a "no strike" pledge with management. The state played its part by expanding public education in order to produce a higher quality labor force, while also expanding consumer credit to make sure that domestic demand for goods kept pace with the increase in production.

Throughout these papers, we noted that as early as the 1960s in the United States, the treadmill had already begun to undergo significant changes (Gordon, 1996; Reich, 1992; Rubin, 1996). With increasing international competition, investors and managers became concerned about the existing pact between management and labor, which ensured a relatively high rate of return to workers, as workers accommodated the treadmill. In part this reallocation of profits had occurred because of rising rates of unionization, and the growing agreements between unions and investors/managers. However, beginning in the mid-to-late 1960s, and increasingly in the 1980s and 1990s, managers began to undermine unions. Their tactics ranged from union-busting, to mobility from unionized to non-unionized areas within the United States (e.g. from north to south), and then increasingly to off-shore production facilities. The state did nothing to prevent these shifts, and indeed accepted the argument that higher corporate profits would lead to further national economic expansion.

With the growth of global investment and production patterns in recent decades, these anti-labor trends have accelerated sharply. Among other indicators, there has been well over a 50% decline in union membership in the United States, frequently and inaccurately attributed merely to changes in the composition of the workforce, from blue collar to white collar. Yet most de-unionization has in fact been the result of union busting campaigns (Bluestone & Bluestone, 1994). To some extent, the earlier form of the treadmill had followed the "high road" to development (Harrison, 1994), allowing workers a greater share of material gains. But after the 1960s the treadmill began to shift to the "low road", in which labor costs were to be reduced to ensure higher profits. Arising from this shift, negative ecological and social outcomes emerged. We noted that this shift can be attributed to a convergence of technological and political changes that made it possible for firms to act on their historical desire to minimize labor costs.

First, ever more of the production process shifted to energy- and chemical-intensive forms, using these elements to replace human labor and simpler machinery. Second, a smaller share of the work force was involved in the production process, much as had happened in earlier decades within agricultural production. For example, in Chicago's Ford Motor Company Plant on the city's Southeast Side, production workers were downsized from over 5000 to under 2500 in a decade. In Dearborn, Michigan's River Rouge Ford plant, the reductions were even more dramatic. Third, those workers remaining in the plants were increasingly deskilled, relying on automation for the execution of many tasks previously done by human beings (Edwards, 1979). Again, the state was passive with regard to these changes, in part because of the growing involvement by firms in campaign financing, which escalated substantially (Beeghley, 1995). Moreover, the corporate-framed ideology of modernization, "growing world competitiveness", and "free trade" rationalized these shifts as well.

Yet the state became caught in a double bind. With increasing displacement of the labor force from production, there were growing demands for social safety nets, to cushion displaced workers and their families. Under these pressures, the U.S. state moved in an uncritical fashion to further support the expansion of the treadmill, now under the rubric of "free trade." Implicit in this statement was the hope that the new accelerated treadmill would resolve the very community problems that the previous state of the treadmill had created.

"But the old communities implied safety and stability that the new corporate communities cannot offer. They provided continuity and relationships across the generations, rules that didn't change no matter how often we broke them, and leaders, trusted men and women, who had the interests of the community at heart. The continuity is gone, the rules keep changing, and somehow the downsizing captains of today's corporations are one's idea of trusted community elders" (Longworth, 1998, p. 112).

SOCIAL vs. ECOLOGICAL ELEMENTS OF THE TREADMILL

Two forms of a "treadmill" emerged in this new system. As firms made more products using more efficient technologies, they also garnered rising profits, which could be invested in still more productive technologies. This suggested a kind of *ecological treadmill.* Profits were thus invested in new technologies that would support still greater production expansion. This expansion required greater inputs (raw materials and energy) and hence greater withdrawals of natural resources. It also led to greater additions (toxic chemical pollution and other forms of liquid and solid waste). The implications of this model were that ecosystems were increasingly becoming used as sources of raw materials and as "sinks" for toxic wastes, thereby increasingly degrading ecosystems while enhancing profit levels.

A second form of the treadmill was *social*. After each cycle of production, a growing share of profits was allocated to upgrading the technological "efficiencies" of the firm. Workers (in some ways analogous to ecosystems) were helping to sow the seeds of their own displacement. By generating profits in one cycle, they would help set in motion a new level of investment in labor-saving technology, ultimately leading to their removal from the production process (Rifkin, 1995).[2] Despite these trends, some workers gained opportunities in this process, as skilled technological workers (Wellin, 1997).

Moreover, as this treadmill expanded, it created new sources of revenue for governments. Some of this revenue was used to give displaced workers social and economic compensation (e.g. income supplements and alternate employment). Thus, there were losses and some gains as the treadmill expanded, replacing earlier forms of production, natural resource utilization, and employment.

In its initial formulation, therefore, the treadmill was more than a model for ecological impacts of production. Inherent in its logic was a necessary and simultaneous shift in social relations in production, and social relations between producers and other institutions. Thus, from its inception, the treadmill's focus has been both *within the firm* and *within the society in which the firm is embedded*. This is a primary distinction between the theory of the treadmill of production and the theory of ecological modernization. Moreover, a core of this differentiation between models is the emphasis within the treadmill model of **social distributional** features. Social distributional features of the treadmill include the changing nature of the workforce, the relationship between social inequality and environmental quality, the growing autonomy of firms from control by local and national governments, and the growing dependency of governments on treadmill organizations for fiscal and political support. So for example, in recent decades, the rising tide of global investments and geographic shifting of production has intensified competitive pressures on ever more workers in industrial societies (Longworth, 1998), leading to down-sizing and increasing bifurcation of global labor forces, outsourcing of production, and a decline in real wages for more workers (Rifkin, 1995). Furthermore, ecological risks within communities and workplaces have increased markedly (Erikson, 1994), while nation-states have ceded significant policy-making authority to corporate-run global trade organizations.

In a series of recent works, we have used empirical data on recycling (Weinberg, Pellow & Schnaiberg, 2000; Pellow, Schnaiberg & Weinberg, 2000; Schnaiberg, Weinberg & Pellow, 1998), green businesses (Weinberg, 1998;

Pellow, 1999; Gould, 1999), and social movements (Pellow, 2000; Weinberg, 1997) to make sense of these changes. Considering recycling programs in the U.S., it becomes clear how the practice of substituting larger forms of physical capital for human labor had permeated every aspect of this industry. From billing and accounting, to collection, processing, labeling and shipping, the recycling industry has wholeheartedly adopted labor-saving technologies, robotics, and expert systems. The commodification of recycling also fundamentally represented a failure of the environmental movement, which had earlier emphasized its use-value potential. Additionally, the anticipated employment and revenue gains for communities and governments never materialized and when municipalities contracted with private industry, the same trends prevailed. Furthermore, despite recycling's local image, markets for post-consumer waste are much more volatile and global in scope than previously expected. This double-bind that governments face is a typical dynamic produced by the modern treadmill of production. We address this topic further in the following section.

GOVERNMENT ENVIRONMENTAL POLICIES AND THE CONSTRAINTS OF THE TREADMILL

From a conceptual perspective, we might characterize an "environmental state" as encompassing the following feature: whenever it engaged in economic decision-making, considerations of ecological impacts would have equal weight with any considerations of private sector profits and state sector taxes. Put this way, most industrialized nation-states fall far short of this standard. Indeed, it is increasingly true that any **environmental policy-making** is subject to more intensive **economic** scrutiny, while economic policies are subject to less and less environmental assessment (Daynes, 1999; Soden & Steel, 1999)[3].

One way of expanding our example of the government double-bind in recycling is to consider the broader limits to state environmental protection policies. The brief outline of the central tenets of the treadmill noted previously indicates that unlimited expansion of treadmill production is a goal of treadmill proponents. Therefore, it would appear that **any** state environmental protection is experienced as a form of **scarcity**, which limits treadmill producers from reaching their desired state of indefinite expansions of production or profits. In like manner, at first blush all **firms** embodying ecological modernization appear as countercases for the diffusion of the treadmill logic, as such firms hypothetically are equally concerned with environmental and economic goals.

Two features of the American political-economic landscape affirm the tensions inherent in state environmental policy-making. The first is that generally, treadmill organizations resist environmental regulation with all their substantial means at their disposal. For example, prior to the advent of recycling regulations and programs, container firms fought all forms of "bottle bills", spending perhaps U.S. $50 million opposing such bills, and succeeding in about 2/3 of the states. Yet even these bottle bills were only indirectly constraining firms. Legislation did not directly mandate a refillable container, but only the imposition of a deposit on all containers. Yet refunding mechanisms for the deposit put some cost burdens on non-refillable container manufacturers and/or users. Thus, in recent years in New York state, bottlers have refused to repurchase stockpiled refunded containers. They have let these accumulate at brokers and large retailers, seeking thereby to mobilize opposition to the bottle bill system. For the remaining 2/3 of states, container manufacturers and bottlers have simply encouraged recycling, and have kept feedstock prices low, and labor costs for refilling containers also low.

Second, where direct resistance against any environmental legislation becomes infeasible, under pressures from environmental NGOs, firms first dilute the legislation to minimize its impacts on their operations. Then they wait for opportunities to further lighten their regulatory load, whenever the political climate shifts and/or NGOs are elsewhere engaged. In the recycling arena, this has been commonplace. Affected industries have continuously shifted their campaigns to avoid mandatory direct controls on their production and distribution activities. All U.S. government regulations have avoided mandating firms with a "life cycle" responsibility for their own generation of post-consumer wastes, as has occurred in some European states. Instead, governments had introduced fairly weak mandates for firms, requiring higher "recycled content" of their production. Firms have responded by including post-production waste recycling (a standard economic practice for decades) as part of post-consumption recycling.

On a broader level, the major types of state environmental policies have been largely restricted to regulating ecological additions (pollutions of various types). They have largely avoided regulating ecological withdrawals (depletions of various ecosystems). There is some confusion over this, because American environmental legislation has also included some protection of specific ecosystems – e.g. regulating logging in national parks, in old-growth areas, for example. But even in these cases, which represent a rather small share of national and state environmental legislation, there is no prohibition of the general treadmill expansion into a variety of **other** ecosystems. That is, the most the state has done is to restrict this expansion in a small set of publicly-owned lands, to protect a limited range of ecosystems. The same is true for other legislation such as the Endangered Species Acts, which has put somewhat ineffective controls over specific habitats of a small number of particular species.

Yet is leaves unprotected all manner of national and transnational habitats to resource extraction – and even to certain "protective" extractions from delicate ecological reserves, such as oil fields in the Alaskan Reserves. Thus, in general, the state has allowed private firms to extract a great deal of ecological withdrawals on publicly-owned lands.

After spending many years analyzing political and social conflicts around environmental policies, we are nonetheless startled to realize how very limited a role the state has played in protecting natural habitats in the United States and throughout the world, especially the developing world. It sometimes appears to us that treadmill organizations and their states have accepted a tradeoff: permit firms relatively unlimited access to the world's biotic and mineral reserves, and the states are politically permitted to tinker with "end-of-pipe" controls over a limited range of pollutants, to maintain their political legitimacy with other constituents.

Treadmill organizations seem to be arguing: do not attempt to control national and global expansion of production, through limiting economic access to ecosystems, or we will undermine your agencies. Perhaps the most interesting case is in global warming, where states **appear** to be moving into the atmospheric "habitat" and restricting expansion of the treadmill. Neither the Rio UNCED ("Earth Summit") nor the Kyoto ("Climate Change") conferences have actually undermined the expansionism of the treadmill, though, especially within the United States, but also even within Europe. This is because, for the first time, national governments, under the auspices of transnational organizations such as the United Nations, having begun to consider regulations that still **indirectly** restrain treadmill expansion. And while expressions of accommodation and good will seem present, treadmill organizations are nonetheless baulking at these national and transnational efforts.

A more recent example is the President's Council on Sustainable Development (PCSD).[4] The PCSD was an effort by U.S. Vice President Al Gore to bring private sector, federal government, and NGO leaders together to move forward on an ecological modernization agenda. From 1993–1999, the PCSD was a central hub of environmental activity for the Clinton Administration. Two major reports were issued (PCSD, 1993, 1999) which outlined a vision and an action plan. This culminated in a May 1999 National Town Meeting in Detroit, where private sector and federal officials committed to implement parts of the action plan. The following observations about the PCSD are most relevant to the treadmill model:

(1) Whereas the early efforts had fairly impressive participation by the private sector, this was short-lived. For example, by 1999 the Metropolitan and

Rural Strategies Task Force had no active private sector participation, despite being the task force charged with deal with urban and rural forms of sustainable economic development. Numerous participants commented to us that private sector representatives were initially active because they feared that the Vice President would push for a series of ecologically-motivated policies, as articulated in his book (Gore, 1992). When it became clear the PCSD would not have broad support within the administration to make sweeping changes, the private sector saw no need to continue its participation. In other words, when the threat disappeared, so did the private sector. The other side of this observation is our conclusion that the environmental movement's hope for meaningful reform from the PCSD was dependent upon the private sector's involvement. Ultimately, movement participants had no power to ensure that either the private sector or the state would participate in good faith and implement any final recommendations.

(2) The PCSD was part of Vice President Gore's *reinventing government* initiative. One early idea was to re-focus major federal policy around ecologically-sound production. There was some discussion of the possibility that the U.S.DA's Extension Service would become a sustainable development entity. Those early efforts to emancipate the environment within federal agencies met with fierce and consistent opposition. Their efforts were stymied and many of the key players moved on to other jobs.

(3) Two types of actions *have* been carried out. First, some of the action items have been implemented. However, they are primarily federal programs that required no private sector support. They are also issues that have broad political appeal. For example, "smart growth" has become a popular initiative. Following the logic of the treadmill, we note that smart growth is a weak environmental project. It has broad support from urban mayors who want reinvestment, suburban communities that want to contain congestion, and private sector actors that want the federal government to pay for their urban infrastructure needs. It is basically a gift from the federal government to powerful urban actors, who are concerned about economic and political needs.

Second, there is an coalition of federal extensions working together in a Sustainable Development Extension Service (SDEN). They are currently working on a series of innovative projects in Burlington, Vermont. However, the initial goal of revised SDEN has been reduced to a minuscule effort that exists alongside the more traditional massive extension service. Thus, even where there are innovative efforts they usually exist alongside identical programs pushing non-sustainable forms of production. One participant from a major federal agency involved in natural resource protection commented at a meeting:

"*You* take for granted that there is support for sustainable development. *I* have to go back and be able to make a strong case for these ideas. There is tremendous opposition. People are not going to just act because it seems like a good idea to protect the environment. There are a lot of other constituencies out there."

(4) Finally, we note that the term "sustainable development" has been dropped by the Vice President in the campaign in favor of the concept of *livability*. A group of major foundations had agreed in the summer of 1999 to help move forward some of the actions proposed in the last PCSD report. The initiative is called the *Livability Campaign*. The proposed Rural Sustainable Development Network is now called the *Rural Livability Project*. Our informants within the federal agencies commented that, the Administration felt that there was considerable hostility towards anything environmental (from the Republican congress especially), while there was insufficient support from any constituency powerful enough to get legislation passed or to get the Vice President elected. Hence a strong environmental agenda would most likely become an election obstacle, but was not likely to become a source of campaign strength. Thus, projects were reframed around "quality of life" issues, in hopes of attracting suburban constituencies, who are perceived to be substantially more powerful than environmentalists.

We believe that cases like the PCSD and U.S. recycling practices challenge two of the major tenets of ecological modernization theory: that the environment has been emancipated from the economic sphere, and that the environmental movement is a major political force. Neither of these claims holds up in the current U.S. administration, as environmental policy-making has continued to be written within an economic framework and where the participation of environmental organizations continues to be open to constant challenge. In a recent empirical assessment, Daynes states, "Even though it was clear that Bill Clinton was quite serious about the environment and quite unafraid to confront the most controversial issues, the 'politics of the moment' frequently interfered with the administration's environmental focus" (1999, p. 265). Daynes goes on to argue that the political opposition to anything that disrupts private sectors actors and their agendas has been too great for the administration to combat, especially in the aftermath of 1994 mid-term elections. He concludes that "the roles most commonly used (by the President to push for environmental reforms) were the roles that are traditionally the weakest" (1999, p. 300).

We find that the treadmill model has much more explanatory power with regard to the above dynamics. Specifically, the treadmill is premised on the argument that the major motives behind environmental policy-making are economic, and that the environmental movement – which, like all social movements, is driven by use values – is competing in a fierce struggle against powerful actors in biased political and social arenas to get competing agendas acknowledged.

THE "ONLY" PERSPECTIVE OF THE TREADMILL, VERSUS THE "FULLY" PERSPECTIVE OF ECOLOGICAL MODERNIZATION

In a 1994 book (Schnaiberg & Gould), we outlined an evaluation problem that is inherently political, and one that will perhaps help us understand the differences between the treadmill and ecological modernization theories in viewing the modern "environmental state." Briefly put, our argument was that there are two ways of evaluating any change in state (or firm) actions. One uses the *past* as a guide, and sees any positive change as "fully" moving from a negative past to a *more*-positive present. The other sees "only" a limited amount of change, comparing the present status to a *future* goal to be desired.

From the latter perspective, the state has actively or passively permitted the treadmill to achieve its current practices, which are inherently *un*sustainable on both ecological and social dimensions. Unsustainability is an outcome of this current economic and political arrangement (Schnaiberg, 1980, 1982, 1986a, 1994; Schnaiberg & Gould, 1994; Gould, Weinberg & Schnaiberg, 1993; Weinberg, 1995; Weinberg & Gould, 1993; Gould, Schnaiberg & Weinberg, 1996; Pellow, 1994). In terms of the criterion for "the environmental state" outlined above, it is clear that we have "only" moved in very small increments towards this goal, of making economic considerations on a parity with ecological protection.

Conversely, from the standpoint of some ecological modernization theorists, firms (under pressures or encouragements from their states and NGOs) have moved "fully" beyond their earlier dismissal of ecological costs of their profitable activities. The firms now take **some** ecological factors into some account in **some** of their planning and activities. Moreover, since the state has, over the past 25 years, incorporated **some** consideration of ecological outcomes for **some** economic policies, there has been "fully" some movement away from a strictly *economic synthesis* of the societal-environmental dialectic (Schnaiberg, 1980, Schnaiberg & Gould, 1994).

Tacitly or explicitly, some of these arguments by ecological modernization theorists seem to suggest that, if this ecological modernization is permitted to continue, we will achieve some ideal sustainable end-state. But, they argue, this will occur through processes of supra-industrialization, not through processes of de-industrialization (as might be shared by some theorists of the treadmill such as us). And states should encourage these forms of super-industrialization, to delink natural resources form economic development.

We will close with some difficulties we observe with projecting this end-state from the evidence accumulating from ecological modernization analyses.

CONCLUSION: WHY THE TREADMILL SEES ECOLOGICAL MODERNIZATION AS ONLY A SMALL CHANGE IN THE ECONOMIC STATE

Our analysis of the role of the state within the treadmill stresses the typical practices of economic organizations, their autonomy relative to the state, and their regulation by the state. Governments have (until the recent growth spurt) been increasingly restricted by policies promulgated by coalitions driven by reproducing the treadmill. As a result, ever more profitable corporations are now "generously" endowing local governments, schools and universities, and public broadcasting with "public support" ranging from motor vehicles to environmental curriculum. And also as a result, government regulation is increasingly curtailed around many environmental policies.

For example, Weinberg (1994) presented findings about how weakly the Illinois government supported citizen access to toxic substance data that the state collected under the Community Right to Know provisions of the Superfund Amendments and Reauthorization Act of 1986. Attending the session was a sociologist who worked for the Illinois Environmental Protection Agency – who affirmed Weinberg's findings. Moreover, he noted that, although the agency was mandated to receive these corporate toxic waste inventory statements, there were no personnel assigned to do anything to help communities get access to and understand these technical documents. Since firms understood this *de facto* **un**regulated situation, they were under few constraints in preparing these documents, and relatively few constraints in handling their toxic waste by-products. Thus, Kirsch finds in his work in Massachusetts that "establishing the State Department of Environmental Quality Engineering had the opposite effect of its creators' intentions. Instead of providing an umbrella that could monitor industrial effects on the environment, the agency tied up complaints regarding potential hazards. . . . There was no direct monitoring of the environment" (1998, pp. 108–109).

Why do our treadmill analyses seem to differ so broadly from those of ecological modernists? Part of the answer is a methodological one – the differences lie in: (1) sampling approaches, and (2) projections for future change. We will touch on these next.

Sampling Differences

The tendency for EM theorists is to sample "best practice" industries. This makes sense given the research orientation, which is to look for change and try to theorize the processes and significance. However, it makes it hard to distinguish between an "epidemic of reports" and a "report of an epidemic" of EM transformations. We experienced a similar example of purported innovations in community energy policies while serving on a National Research Council panel (Stern & Aronson, 1984). The panel was initially informed about "hundreds of communities" that had innovated to reduce energy use after the "oil crises" of the 1970s. Later, we discovered that there had only been two such communities – Davis, California, and Seattle, Washington – but that their "success" generated *hundreds* of media and scientific reports. Ironically, even for these two communities, there had been little evaluation of how these changes affected social distributional features of the cities.

This gives us further pause when we consider that EM may actually be a substitute for governmental attention to *other* dimensions of sustainable development – e.g. corporate innovations may have been paid for by regressive taxes on employees and/or communities in which the companies are embedded. Numerous public sector and private sector conferences are organized and task forces convened to extol the increased "greening" of production. But such developments are more cost-effective than capital-intensive changes of production technologies, and still cheaper than maintaining both social equity and environmental protection, as sustainable development practices are intended to do. Our experiences with the President's Council for Sustainable Development affirm this. While the participants were actively engaged in seeking sustainable development, the Council itself was a political shadow play, designed in part to boost the visibility of the Vice-President and presidential candidate Albert Gore – and it is now defunct.

Furthermore, the units being sampled may be inappropriate for the broader inferences of ecological modernization. For example, the apparent "decoupling" of economic development from energy consumption and other natural resource inputs may be misleading. The relocation of ever more industrial production abroad under globalization, while retaining profits in industrial countries, may separate ecological and economic outcomes of firms as **geographic networks** of production.

Moreover, firms may be increasingly outsourcing much of the negative aspects of production. Firms may have different roles within **commodity chains**, in which material transformations are tracked from initial ecological resources to final products and wastes. Thus, for example, recycling programs in cities are actually the outcomes of decisions made by container producers, consumer product manufacturers, and their trade associations.

Projections of Future Changes – The Negative

In some ways, EM examines the "cutting edge" of changes in corporate structure. It assumes that these changes will eventually diffuse into other corporate entities and actions. But instead, EM cases may simply represent a "creaming" of a program of ecological incorporation into production practices. This concept arose in projecting early rates of success in public programs. Initially, many innovative public programs have a high and positive selection rate. But this means that the early period has "creamed" or culled from the potential population of adopters. The remainder of the population has been negatively selected, to eschew the program. Thus, the early adoption rates will not be sustained by later groups encountering the program. Indeed, it is not yet clear whether enough time has elapsed so that EM cases have had a time series of evaluations, to examine whether early changes in the same firms had been institutionalized, in changing market conditions. Our recycling study was carried out in that arena of change, precisely because at least a decade had elapsed since communities had been incorporating recycling practices. Thus we could see whether these changes, even if once **attained**, could be **sustained**. And indeed, we found that many were not sustained even for a decade (Weinberg, Pellow & Schnaiberg, 2000).

Projections of Future Changes – The Positive

Even where we find change, we believe the treadmill to be a more persuasive model of the political economy of environmental problems and protection. Firms continue to push for higher profit margins to the neglect of both social equity and ecological concerns. Those firms that do make ecological improvements fall into one or more of the following categories: (1) firms were forced by regulation or social movement action to make improvements; (2) they made improvements only when their economic bottom line would be secure; or (3) they achieved the *appearance* of improvements through "creative accounting" or misreporting. Ecological modernization theorists tend to view such "improvements" as evidence that environmentalists are a powerful 'third force' in negotiating these changes (Mol, 2002), and as part of a trajectory toward an end state of sustainability. We challenge both of these claims. We find that economic criteria remain at the *foundation* of decision making processes. Further, the state also shares this orientation, despite its own political interests, and often cedes a great deal of power to private sector actors. Thus, we believe that political economy models in general, and the Treadmill in particular, continue to have strong explanatory power with their starting assumptions on conflict and politics, and the general dynamics of capitalism.

NOTES

1. Schnaiberg's earliest work (1973) delved into the components of the "environmental movement." He identified four different forms of environmental groups: cosmetologists, meliorists, reformers, and radicals. Each of the groups perceived the causes of environmental problems in quite different ways. The groups also differed in their views of the severity of environmental problems Thus, they offered quite different remedies for *environmental protection*.

2. There is an emerging case study literature on this topic, as it played itself out in the United States in the 1970s and 1980s. Thus, Dudley (1994) documents how Chrysler closed its Kenosha plant, even when workers had the highest productivity rate of any facility, so that jobs could be transferred to higher technology facilities that required fewer workers. Wellin's (1997) study was a particularly informative ethnography of a food manufacturer undergoing automation. Workers shared their special knowledge of intricate production processes with management, with a promise that they would share in the increased profits associated with rising productivity. At the end of this cycle, a small share of workers did indeed gain new positions in the control of operations, but the bulk of workers found themselves in more deskilled positions, with a net loss of status (see also Besser, 1996; Kirsch, 1998).

3. This was clearly true under Reagan and Bush, who had a Council on Competitiveness to ensure that no policy would negatively impact economic opportunities (Daynes, 1999). Under Clinton, many environmentalists assumed this would change. The Council was abolished by Executive Order. However, economic criteria have continued to dominate policy decesions. Even the Council on Environmental Quality (CEQ), which was suppose to be one of the main vechiles to role back the Reagan assault has "continue(d) to decline and its role in policy making is minimal at best" (Soden & Steel, 1999, p. 332).

4. Two of the authors (Weinberg and Pellow) were active in the PCSD, serving as Task Force members. Additionally, Weinberg helped prepare papers, meetings, and reports. The information in this paper derives from their experiences with the PCSD.

REFERENCES

Beeghley, L. (1996). *The Structure of Social Stratification in the United States* (2nd ed.). Boston: Allyn & Bacon.

Bluestone, B., & Bluestone, I. (1994). *Negotiating the Future: a Labor Perspective on American Business*. New York: Basic Books.

Daynes, B. (1999). Bill Clinton: The environmental presidency. In: D. Soden (Ed.), *The Environmental Presidency*. Albany, NY: SUNY Press.

Dudley, K. M. (1994). *The End of the Line. Lost Jobs, New Lives in Post-industrial America*. Chicago: University of Chicago Press.

Edwards, R. (1979). *Contested Terrain: The Transformation of the Workplace in the Twentieth Century*. New York: Basic Books.

Erikson, K. (1994). *A New Species of Trouble*. New York: W. W. Norton.

Gordon, D. (1996). *Fat and Mean: The Corporate Squeeze of Working Americans and the Myth of Managerial "Downsizing"*. New York: The Free Press.

Gore, A. (1992). *Earth in the Balance*. Boston: Houghton Mifflin.

Gould, K. (1991). The sweet smell of money: Economic dependence and local environmental political mobilization. *Society and Natural Resources*, *4*, 133–150.

Gould, K. (1992). Putting the (w)r.a.p.s on public participation: Remedial action planning and working-class power in the Great Lakes. *Sociological Practice Review 3*(3), 133–139.

Gould, K. (1993). Pollution and perception: social visiability and local environmental mobilization. *Qualitative Sociology*, *16*(2), 157–178.

Gould, K., Weinberg, A. S., & Schnaiberg, A. (1995). Natural resource use in a transnational treadmill: International agreements, national citizenship practices, and sustainable development. *Humboldt Journal of Social Relations*, *21*, 61–93.

Gould, K., Weinberg, A., & Schnaiberg, A. (1993). Legitimating impotence: Pyrrhic victories of the environmental movement. *Qualitative Sociology*, *16*, 207–246.

Gould, K., Schnaiberg, A., & Weinberg, A. (1996). *Local Environmental Struggles: Citizen Activism in the Treadmill of Production*. New York: Cambridge University Press.

Harrison, B. (1994). *Lean and Mean: The Changing Landscape of Corporate Power in the Age of Flexibility*. New York: Basic Books.

Kirsch, M. (1998). *In the Wake of the Giant: Multinational Restructuring and Uneven Development in a New England Community*. Albany, NY: SUNY Press.

Longworth, R. (1998). *Global Squeeze: The Coming Crisis for First-world Nations*. Chicago: Contemporary Books.

Mol, A. P. J. (1995). *The Refinement of Production: Ecological Modernisation Theory and the Chemical Industry*. Utrecht: van Arkel.

Mol, A. P. J. (2002). *Ecological modernisation and the environmental state* (this volume).

Pellow, D. (1994). Environmental justice and popular epidemiology: Symbolic politics, hidden transcripts. Paper Presented at the Annual meetings of the American Sociological Association. Los Angeles, CA. August.

Pellow, D. (1998). Bodies on the line: Environmental inequalities and hazardous work in the U.S. recycling industry. *Race, Gender & Class*, *6*, 124–151.

Pellow, D. (1999). Framing emerging environmental movement tactics: mobilizing consensus, demobilizing conflict. *Sociological Forum*, *14*, 659–683.

Pellow, D. (2000). Putting the ecological modernisation thesis to the test: Accounting for recycling's promises and performance. *Environmental Politics*, forthcoming.

Pellow, D., Schnaiberg, A., & Weinberg, A. S. (1995). Pragmatic corporate cultures: Insights from a recycling enterprise. *Green Management International*, *12*, 95–110.

President's Council on Sustainable Development (1994). *Education for Sustainability*. Washington, D.C.: United States Government Printing Office.

President's Council on Sustainable Development (1999). *Towards a Sustainable America: Advancing Prosperity, Opportunity, and a Healthy Environment for the 21st Century*. Washington, D.C.: United States Government Printing Office.

Reich, R. (1991). *The Work of Nations: Preparing Ourselves for 21st Century Capitalism*. New York: Knopf.

Rifkin, J. (1995). *The End of Work: The Decline of the Global Labor Force and the Dawn of the Post-market Era*. New York: G. P. Putnam's Sons.

Rubin, B. A. (1996). *Shifts in the Social Contract: Understanding Change in American Society.* Thousand Oaks, CA: Pine Forge Press.

Schnaiberg, A. (1980). *The Environment: From Surplus to Scarcity.* New York: Oxford University Press.

Schnaiberg, A. (1982). Did you ever meet a payroll? Contradictions in the structure of the appropriate technology movement. *Humboldt Journal of Social Relations, 9*, 38–62.

Schnaiberg, A. (1994). The political economy of environmental problems and policies: Consciousmness, conflict, and control capacity. In: L. Freese (Ed.), *Advances in Human Ecology* (Vol. 3, pp. 23–64). Greenwich, CT: JAI Press.

Schnaiberg, A., & Gould, K.. (2000 [1994]). *Environment and Society: The Enduring Conflict.* West Caldwell, New Jersey: Blackburn Press.

Schnaiberg, A., Weinberg, A. S., & Pellow, D. N. (1998). Politizando la rueda de produccion: Los programmas de reciclaje de residuos solidas en Estados Unidos. [Politicizing the treadmill of production: Reshaping social outcomes of efficient recycling.] *Revista Internacional de Sociología*, 19–20 (January-August), 181–222.

Soden, D., & Steel, B. (1999). Evaluating the environmental presidency. In: D. Soden (Ed.), *The Environmental Presidency.* Albany, NY: SUNY Press.

Spaargaren, G., & Mol, A. P. J. (1992). Sociology, environment, and modernity: Ecological modernisation as a theory of social change. *Society and Natural Resources, 5*(4), 323–344.

Stern, P., & Aronson, E. (Eds) (1984). *Energy Use: The Human Dimension.* New York: W. H. Freeman.

Weinberg, A. (1997a). Local organizing for environmental conflict: Explaining differences between cases of participation and non-participation. *Organization and Environment, 10*(2), 194–216.

Weinberg, A. (1997b). Power and public policy: Community right-to-know and the empowerment of people, places, and producers. *Humanity and Society, 21*, 240–257.

Weinberg, A. (1998). Distinguishing among green businesses: Growth, green and anomie. *Society and Natural Resources, 11*, 241–250.

Weinberg, A. (1994). Citizenship and natural resources: From rights in theory to rights in practice. Paper presented at the annual meetings of the American Sociological Association. Los Angeles, CA. August.

Weinberg, A., & Gould, K. (1993). Public participation in environmental regulatory conflicts: treading through the possibilities and pitfalls. *Law and Policy, 15*, 139–167.

Weinberg, A., Schnaiberg, A., & Pellow, D. (1996). Sustainable development as a sociologically defensible concept: From foxes and rovers to citizens. In: L. Freese (Ed.), *Advances in Human Ecology* (Vol. 5, pp. 261–302). Greenwich, CT: JAI Press.

Weinberg, A., Schnaiberg, A., & Gould, K. A. (1995). Recycling: Conserving resources or accelerating the treadmill of production? In: L. Freese (Ed.), *Advances in Human Ecology* (Vol. 4, pp. 173–205). Greenwich, CT: JAI Press.

ECOLOGICAL MODERNIZATION AND THE ENVIRONMENTAL STATE

Arthur P. J. Mol and Gert Spaargaren

INTRODUCTION

Most environmental sociologists have been heavily influenced by what can be labeled neo-Marxist analyses of environmental disruptions and decay. More than any of the other classical traditions in sociological thought (cf. Humprey & Buttel, 1982; Buttel, 2000a), it is especially the Marxian theoretical framework that has inspired many of us in explaining empirical cases of continuing environmental disruption by enterprises in a capitalist (world)economy, of unequal distributions of environmental and other costs in situations of environmental pollution and extraction, of powerless governmental agencies trying in vain to regulate major economic actors, and of citizens or environmental action groups contesting the powers that be.

In the rich literature that in one way or the other heavily relies on neo-Marxist ideas (ranging from certain branches of eco-feminist studies, via World-System Theory and some studies from an explicit Third World perspective, to certain branches of political sciences), Allan Schnaiberg's (1980) volume *The Environment. From surplus to scarcity* is still one of the most comprehensive studies that show the value of such a perspective in analyzing

The Environmental State Under Pressure, Volume 10, pages 33–52.

ISBN: 0-7623-0854-0

and understanding the social dynamics of environmental pollution and (failing) control. His notions of the Treadmill of Production, of additions and withdrawals, widely resonate in environmental sociology. Several more recent contributions in the neo-Marxist tradition – among which those by James O'Connor and the Journal *CNS*, those of the British neo-Marxists such as Peter Dickens and Ted Benton, the work of Martin O'Connor, and the work of the group around Allan Schnaiberg – have of course elaborated and refined Schnaiberg's initial analysis, both profiting from accumulated knowledge, analyses and insight and taking the changes in the social practices and institutional developments of the last 20 years into account. Nevertheless we will refer to these common neo-Marxist ideas as the Treadmill of Production perspective, giving some central stage to Schnaiberg's work.[1]

More recently and perhaps less well-founded on one classical sociological stream of thought (cf. Buttel, 2000b), the Ecological Modernization perspective has been developed against the background of especially some West-European countries. From the mid 1980s onward several lines of sociological and political science analyses on environmental disruption and reforms came together in a more or less coherent set of ideas. And as several contributors to both the Treadmill of Production perspective and the Ecological Modernization Theory have indicated there exist some major discrepancies between the two schools of thought, which partly reflect differences in environmental sociology across the Atlantic Ocean. In a similar way as Cohen's (2000a) volume has tried to explore the commonalties and differences in European and American risk studies, this article – together with some of the other articles in this volume – seeks to illuminate some of the differences and commonalties between the two theoretical perspectives in environmental sociology. This becomes of course even more relevant in a globalizing world with a globalizing science, in which local interpretation schemes will increasingly be questioned by dominant alternatives in other parts of the world. In making such a comparison, we will give special emphasis – but not limit ourselves – to the role of the state and politics in bringing about (or failing to bring about) environmental reforms, as well as the changes in state and political 'interventions' for the environment. We will start with pointing at some similarities of the two perspectives, vis-à-vis other theoretical traditions in environmental sociology. The third section will concentrate on some of the main differences, centered around the issue of continuity and change. The fourth section will focus on the position of the environmental state and environmental politics in both frameworks, while the closing section will look at some common challenges that lie ahead.

ToP AND EMT: NEGLECTED EPISTEMOLOGICAL COMMONALTIES

Irrespective of major controversies between EMT and ToP which will be explored below, it is important to notice some of the commonalties between both frameworks, especially vis-à-vis other more or less dominant theories in environmental sociology.[2] Besides the fact that both perspectives are founded on sociological insights and theories and take environment – society interactions as their core object of reflection, we want to point out three more specific parallels that are often neglected in comparing these frameworks.

Central objects in both the Treadmill of Production and in Ecological Modernization Theory are processes of production and consumption and the environmental disturbances that go along with these basically economic activities. The organization of production and consumption, and the material flows (the additions and withdrawals) that 'mediate' between society and the natural environment following production and consumption, are taken as a kind of definition of the environment. Both perspectives analyze how social dynamics, actors, institutional arrangements and processes structure in a specific way the additions and withdrawals in production and consumption processes.

That means, secondly, that both perspectives deviate to a major extent from stronger constructivist approaches that define environmental problems only in terms of social constructions and storylines. Neo-Marxist and Ecological Modernization theorists easily converge and agree in their criticism against strong social constructivism, without neglecting the social dimensions that are always involved in defining environmental problems. Both perspectives seem to agree on the fact that environmental problems do have a 'real' existence. "They belong to the type of problems which needs to be analyzed and understood not only as social constructs but also in terms of the language of the natural and biological sciences. If we ignore this fact, we would end up were we started in environmental sociology, namely with the HEP-NEP distinction, with postmodern constructivist environmental sociology as the latest variant of exemptionalist thinking." (Mol & Spaargaren, 2000). This comes very close to, for instance, O'Connor's (1998, p. 135ff) account of subjective and objective dimensions of the environmental crisis.

More in general, both perspectives can clearly be put into – different branches of – the modernist project, taking firm stance against all kind of post-modern analyses of environmental problems and solutions. In looking for alternative (organizational) structures that better meet the 'standards' of sustainability, the focus of both perspectives remains on the core clusters of modernity: science and technology, the industrial organization, the capitalist mode of production, and the state system. The two perspectives make different assessment of the contribution of the institutional clusters to environmental disruptions, and they propose (or analyze) each their own transformations of these clusters, but do not move beyond the project of modernity.

CONTINUITY AND CHANGE

Ecological Modernization Theory was originally developed to understand the changes that started to take place in the institutions and social practices involved in environmental deterioration and reform, especially from about the mid eighties onward in Germany, the Netherlands and Denmark. And still the common denominator of all ecological modernization studies is that these modern institutions and practices can no longer be only analyzed in terms of their detrimental, all-pervasive influence on the environment, as was dominant in most of the sociological analyses in the 1970s and early 1980s (and not in the least in the neo-Marxist ones). Or, to put it differently, the ecological modernization perspective analyzes how environmental interests and considerations are starting to make a difference with respect to the organization of our modern society. Through all kind of mechanisms, interest groups, and social processes/dynamics environmental considerations are beginning to transform processes of production and consumption, and the institutions linked to that. To put it provocatively, where neo-Marxist ToP analyses focus on continuity in the way capitalist economies (with all their fast developments and changes) persist in setting the scene for failures in environmental reforms, Ecological Modernization Theory concentrates on the changes in environmental control practices and institutions and point at discontinuities and transformations in modern society's institutional order with respect to the environmental question. This is not to say that EMT claims that the current institutional order is inherently sustainable or will develop more or less automatically into an environmentally sound production and consumption system. But it does mean that EMT identifies both actualities and further possibilities to transform the current institutional order into one that takes environmental considerations and interests increasingly into account. We will explain and further elaborate on this core controversy between ToP and EMT by paying attention to: (i) the greening of capitalism, (ii) small versus big changes, and (iii) globalization as the new phase of global capitalism.

The Sustainability of Capitalism

The possibilities, actuality and desirability of a green capitalism, put first and rather provocatively on the agenda of Ecological Modernization Theory by Joseph Huber, have resulted in an extensive debate. Scholars as diverse as Allan Schnaiberg (1980), David Goldblatt (1996) and James O'Connor (1998) have all, using different concepts, attacked the possibilities of an ecological sound capitalism. James O'Connor's second contradiction of capitalism, Schnaiberg's treadmill of capitalist production and Goldblatt's criticisms of Giddens' limitation to the industrial dimension of modernity in understanding the environmental crisis, all refer to the important role capitalism plays in environmental deterioration. Neglecting capitalism and failing to attack the fundaments of the capitalist world order will result in superficial and cosmetic environmental reforms that are unable to resolve the ecological crisis in any fundamental way. Moreover, some theorists argue that such measures will rather strengthen the capitalist mode of production as it makes capitalism less in need of a green critique (cf. Dryzek, 1995) and will promote and facilitate the continuation of established socio-economic practices that are to the benefit of those in power (Blühdorn, 2000).

Ecological Modernization Theory deviates from this view and to understand the fundamental background of the differences between the two perspectives Giddens' idea of the four clusters of modernity is helpful (Fig. 1). Giddens analyses our contemporary society as a modern industrial capitalist society, which exists as nation-state in a world military order. In analyzing environmental issues Treadmill of Production theorists now interpret the capitalist dimension as the all determining power of our society, completely subsuming the other institutional clusters. Ecological Modernization Theory does not give capitalism this pride of place. If anything, they see the industrial dimension of modernity as the key institutional cluster via which environmental issues should be understood, be it however in close interrelatedness with the three other institutional clusters. To be more specific EMT's position towards capitalism has changed throughout the various phases of its history (cf. Mol & Sonnenfeld, 2000). While initially the contribution of capitalism to the 'expansion of the limits' was celebrated by Ecological Modernization Theory and was even claimed to be a *condition sine qua non* by some (e.g. Huber, 1985; see Wehling, 1992 for a more elaborated analysis of this era), more recently a balanced position regarding capitalism is presented. It is not that capitalism is considered to be an essential precondition for environmentally sound production and consumption (as neo-liberal scholars still want us to believe), nor that capitalism

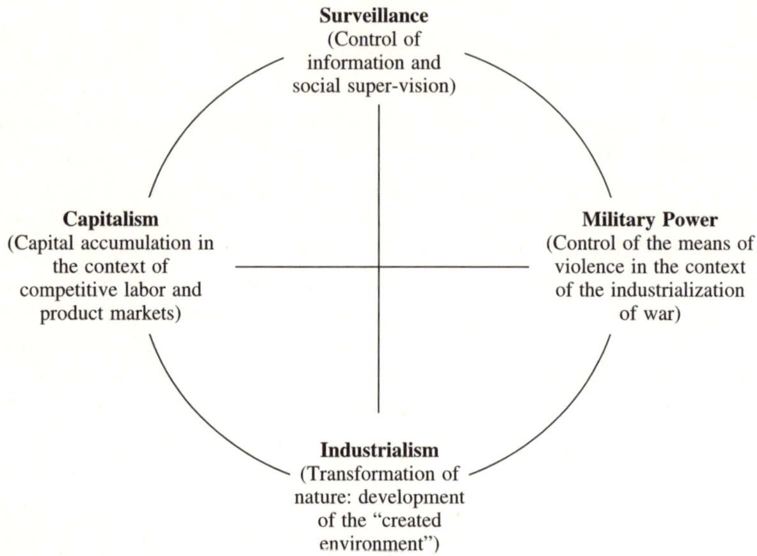

Fig. 1. The Institutional Dimensions of Modernity (Giddens, 1990).

is believed to play no role at all in environmental deterioration. But rather EMT claims that: (i) capitalism is changing constantly and one of the main triggers are environmental concerns and interests, (ii) significant environmental improvements in production and consumption are possible under different 'relations of production', and (iii) all major, fundamental alternatives to the present economic order have proved unfeasible according to various (economic, environmental and social) criteria. This does of course not mean that capitalist production is sustainable, or that one can no longer analyze the detrimental environmental consequences of a capitalist organization of production. That can be and is still done, and remains valuable. But it does affect the political consequences of and core value given to such analyses.

Consequently, mainstream ecological modernization theorists interpret capitalism neither as an essential precondition for, nor as the key obstruction to, stringent or radical environmental reform. They rather focus on redirecting and transforming 'free market capitalism' in such a way that it less and less obstructs, and increasingly contributes to, the preservation of society's sustenance base in a fundamental/structural way. While it can be argued – as some commentators do, but certainly not those in the ToP tradition – that this debate should be considered as rather abstract and outdated, especially since the 'end of history', it shows at the same time continuing relevance regarding two sets of controversies: (i) it is connected with discussions about presumed shortcomings of Ecological Modernization Theory in analyzing conflicts of interest in environmental reforms, and (ii) more concrete or down-to-earth controversies in contemporary environmental politics and policies are to some extent inspired by the earlier (and to some extent continuing) debate on capitalism. We will turn to both related sets of issues respectively.

With respect to the first point, conflictual models of social change that dominate neo-Marxist theories have inspired some authors to emphasize Ecological Modernization Theory's presumed undertheorized notions of power (Leroy, 1996; Schnaiberg et al., 2002), lack of attention to social contexts and ethical issues (Blowers, 1997), neglect of emancipatory concerns (Blühdorn, 2000), and even an absence of human agency (Wehling, 1992; Smidt, 1996). According to these and other scholars, Ecological Modernization Theory analyses environmental reforms primarily via Schumpeterian, evolutionary models that result almost automatically in the greening of production and consumption, without paying sufficient attention to severe struggles between interests (groups) and to normative, ethical or moral reflections and debates (cf. Sarkar, 1990; Leroy & Van Tatenhove, 2000; Blowers, 1997, p. 854). In reviewing these debates, we want to make two remarks. First, these observations are particularly relevant for the first generation studies in Ecological Modernization Theory conducted in the 1980s (cf. Mol & Sonnenfeld, 2000). There is indeed considerable merit in neo-Marxist analyses of environmental conflicts and Ecological Modernization Theory can profit – and has already to some extent, we would argue – from that in refining its analyses of social change. Secondly, these observations seem less appropriate as far as they focus on and respond to the more recent formulations of Ecological Modernization Theory, which emphasize the decreasing *fundamental* conflicts about environmental reform programs in industrialized countries in the late 1980s and 1990s. This EMT-observation that environmental interests become increasingly 'salonfähig' (cf. Mol, 2000) is, however, not pre-given. It is constantly (re)produced by struggles and clashes between diverging interests, changing ideologies, and historical transformations in other social arenas, as ecological modernization theorists have stressed in theoretical elaborations (cf. Spaargaren & Mol, 1991, 1992) and detailed case-studies (cf. Hajer, 1995; Mol, 1995; Rinkevicius, 2000).

With respect to the second point we should stress that the fundamental debate regarding capitalism also echoes to some extent more 'down-to-earth' debates, for instance regarding the discussions on market versus state involvement in environmental policy (with subjects as diverse as privatization, the adequacy of distinct regulatory or policy instruments/strategies, state failure versus market failure, deregulation, the modernization of state governance, etc.) and the distributional consequences of environmental problems and reforms. With respect to the first group of topics it can be concluded that these seem either no longer to be that controversial, as is shown by the growing consensus on the discussions on market based instruments versus command-and-control strategies, the increasing role of non-state actors in environmental policy and the new governance styles that seem to replace the old hierarchic state models (cf. Weale, 1992; Sarinen, 2001; Mol, Lauber & Liefferink, 2000; Hogenboom et al., 2000; Mol, Spaargaren & Frouws, 1998; Leroy & Van Tatenhove, 2000). Or these controversies stand less and less in a one-to-one relationship to neo-Marxist criticism of capitalism, as the debates on privatization and deregulation seem to exemplify. Neo-Marxist scholars have recently especially proved the ongoing relevance of their models in forcefully putting on the agenda the unequal distribution of both environmental problems and the social consequences of environmental policies (cf. Schnaiberg et al., 1986; Schnaiberg & Gould, 1994; Gould et al., 1996; Pellow et al., 2000). It is in these studies that the ToP perspective has still much to offer to other traditions in environmental sociology, among which EMT.

'Small' Change Versus 'Big' Change

In their analyses of Ecological Modernization perspectives, neo-Marxists have condemned the former set of ideas for: (i) focusing only on 'small' changes, on minor adaptations of the current institutional order, on taking the environmental window-dressing of the powers that be for actual environmental reforms and improvements, and failing to get at the fundamental "roots of the environmental crisis" (Pepper, 1984); and (ii) limiting its focus to environmental changes and thus leaving non-environmental consequences of the treadmill of production – and of the environmental reform programs attacking the consequences of the treadmill – unchallenged.[3] In contrast, ToP perspectives then look at major (non)transformations that actually happen and that are not limited to environmental dimensions but also include other distributional effects.[4]

In entering into this controversy a distinction should be made between the nature of the changes that are subject of both frameworks. Both ToP and EMT contain analytical as well as normative or even prescriptive dimensions; that is: they both analyze contemporary processes of social continuity and change and contribute to normative, political trajectories of transformation that should take place in order to turn the tide of structural environmental destruction. In most ToP studies there exists a major gap between the quite advanced and detailed theoretical analyses of the immanent destructive character of the treadmill of capitalist production on the one side, and the concrete trajectories for more beneficial social change that are build upon these analyses on the other. In analysing from a neo-Marxist position the roots of environmentalism and the environmental crisis David Pepper (1984) does not manage to put forward a feasible programme of social change that captures these fundamental roots. He ends up with environmental education as the main strategy. Equally, O'Connor latest book (1998) gives evidence of a detailed and refined neo-Marxist analysis of the destructive pattern of the capitalist world economy, and rather 'meagre' and utopian strategies for environmental reform that follow from that. It seems to us that the development of strategies for change within the ToP perspective: (i) have not been improved and refined in a similar way as its analysis of environmental disruption; (ii) are founded only marginally on existing patterns of social transformation and have thus a high 'utopian' character. In contrast, within EMT there is a closer line between the analyses of existing changes-in-the-making in the main institutions and social practices, and the designing of 'realist-utopian' (cf. Giddens, 1990) trajectories for environmental reform for the coming future.

In addition, in focusing on transformations EMT concentrates rather on environmental radicality than on 'social radicality'. That is, in analyzing existing patterns of change in-the-making EMT confines its assessments of these changes primarily to the contributions to environmental reforms, and not in first instance to the magnitude of these changes regarding all kinds of other criteria. 'Small' changes in terms of deviation from the existing institutions and practices *can* include big environmental improvements, as well as 'big' changes in terms of radical or fundamental reorganizations of the economic relations of production *can* have limited environmental benefits (as we know from former communist Eastern Europe). EMT is first and foremost an environmental social theory, analyzing the environmental origins and environmental consequences of social change. It does not deny that all kind of other social criteria (distributional effects, gender issues, etc.) are essential in proposing and evaluating social changes, but these are separate, relatively independent criteria and cannot be put under one common denominator with environmental criteria. In principle, ecological modernization theorists may very well come to the conclusion that green capitalism (in whatever form) is possible from an environmental point of view but that the social consequences would be so dramatic that it is very unlikely and undesirable to move into this trajectory. In that sense, EMT is a more focused – others would say more restricted – theoretical framework than the ToP perspective. ToP seems to be primarily interested in changes in terms of transforming the capitalist or treadmill character of production and consumption. Its one-to-one relation between the 'relations of production' and environmental disruption makes that changes only count as real if they undermine the treadmill, which is consistent with ToP's all-embracing notion of capitalism. In contrast, EMT's notion of growing autonomy of the ecological sphere contradicts such an automatic coupling of the economic sphere (or 'relations of production') and the environmental sphere.

Furthermore, the analysis of change in the two perspectives differs in terms of what might be called 'absolute' (ToP) versus 'relative' (EMT). In criticizing EMT on their rather naïve ideas on environmental improvements, ToP claims that all – or the very large majority – of production and consumption practices are still governed by treadmill logics, and hardly ever ecological, environmental or sustainability criteria dominate in organizing and designing production and consumption. But, according to us, this is not so much what ecological modernization theorists will or should deny. The latter would agree that treadmill (which they would rather call: economic) criteria and interests still play a dominant role in production and consumption, and that they will probably always remain at least as important as – among others – ecological criteria (cf. Mol, 1995, pp. 28–34). But the innovation is that ecological interests and criteria are slowly but steadily catching up with economic ones. Compared to some decades ago they can no longer be ignored and increasingly make a difference in organizing and designing production and consumption. This innovation does not mean that: (i) economic or treadmill logics (have) become subsumed, nor that (ii) economic production and consumption (has) become completely sustainable (whatever that may mean). In that sense EMT rather looks at relative (but significant) changes into more environmentally sound directions, in contrast to the 'absolute' sustainability of ToP.

Finally, there is a major difference between the two perspectives in assessing the environmental changes that have been set into motion from the late 1980s onwards: window-dressing versus structural changes in institutions and social practices. It goes without saying that empirical examples of both positions can easily be found. Although we have no reason at all to doubt the critical evaluation by Pellow et al. (2000) of the Blue Bag recycling program (which can be easily contrasted with the successful German DSD recycling system), we think they take more than one bridge to far to reject EMT – and celebrate ToP – on the basis of such a case study. Similar, we would not reject ToP on the basis of Mol's (1995) chemical industry study – or any of the other empirical analyses we have carried out – but it does prove, according to us, that something more is at stake in these examples than only ToP. We think we are moving into more fertile ground when Pellow *cum suis* suggest that the European context might for several reasons be more receptive for ecological modernization trajectories, while the USA context can still best be analyzed with a ToP framework. We will come back to that below. But still we would claim that also for the American context an assessment of the major environmental changes primarily in terms of window-dressing seems to bypass the differences that exist between the current period of institutionalization of the environment – regardless of all the shortcomings and limited successes – and that of the 1970s. Or, to quote Castells (1997, p. 336): "After all, if nothing is new under the sun, why bother to try to investigate, think, write, and read about it?"

Globalization and Ecological Reform

A last significant distinction between ToP and EMT positions is related to globalization. In short the position of ToP runs as follows: even if there is in some European nation-states an environmental reform taking place beyond simple public relations and window-dressing as EMT claims, than this process can only be identified at the detriment of other states in the world-economy. It is exactly in an era of globalization with global capital as the main driving force and determinant of global structures and interaction patterns that ToP proves the powerful analytical perspective to understand processes of environmental disruption and (failing) protection beyond the level of one nation-state.

Globalization is often closely associated with the dynamics of capitalism, especially – but not only – in studies focusing on the economic dimensions of globalization. The internal dynamics of the capitalist mode of production is then believed to explain to a large extent the emergence, form and dynamics of globalization (or whatever term is preferred). While traditionally (neo-)Marxist analyses started from the notion of the internal contradiction of capital, resulting in the end in the dissolvement of capitalism, most contemporary globalization scholars that have an economic focus diverge from such deterministic positions in acknowledging the flexibility of capitalism in overcoming these internal contradictions. For instance, in an excellent study Hoogvelt (1996, p. 132) concludes that:

> . . . capitalism, in stead of destroying itself in consequence of internal contradictions which are its inherent and systemic properties, time and again proves able to overcome the self-inflicted crisis by complete transformation. Total renewal is what makes possible the reproduction of capitalism, involving not only production technology and the organization of economic life but also the complex of institutions and norms which ensure that individual agents and social groups behave according to the overarching principles of economic life.

Nevertheless it may be that, as some put forward, globalization will not only be the final triumph over capitalism's internal economic contradictions but also the beginning of the end of the global capitalist economic order. And here we approach the environmental dynamics of globalization processes, as this line seems dominant among, for instance, a number of neo-Marxist environmental sociologists – among which Ted Benton, Peter Dickens and James O'Connor – who have combined the aggressive expansion of the capitalist economy around the globe with the ongoing and intensifying (global) environmental crisis in formulating the 'second contradiction of capitalism' argument. According to them the inherent economic growth and expansion within the global capitalist economy is confronted with environmental boundaries that in the end will turn the tide of a global capitalist economic order and change it beyond recognition. Hobsbawm (1994) seems to come to a similar conclusion on the environmental crisis in the last chapter of his study on the 'Age of Extremes'.

But in the neo-Marxist school-of-thought in environmental sociology there also exists confusion with respect to this environmental dimension of global capitalism. While James O'Connor (1998, p. 235) concludes that "a systematic answer to the question 'is an ecologically sustainable capitalism possible?' is, 'Not unless and until capital changes its face in ways that would make it unrecognizable to bankers, money managers, venture capitalists, and CEOs looking at themselves in the mirror today' ", Peter Dickens (1998, p. 191) comes with a more balanced assessment: "(. . .) according to this second contradiction argument, 'revenges' by nature on society will continue to be wreaked by capitalism. Several related questions remain, however. First, will capitalism be able to restructure itself once more, this time in the form of what has been called 'ecological modernization'?" And although Leff (1995) initially rejects from a neo-Marxist perspective attempts to simply incorporate environmental concerns into global capitalist development through means such as internalization of externalities and other key strategies of ecological modernization, he finally reaches the conclusion that an environmentally sound development is not "totally incompatible with capitalist production" (*ibid*, p. 126). It is not only the neo-Marxists who show ambivalences regarding a simple relation (or incompatibility) between a global capitalist world order and continuing environmental quality. A still small but increasing number of (environmental) sociologists, economists and political scientists emphasizes the relevance of globalization for environmental reforms and vice versa: the relevance of environmental decay, environmental perceptions and environmental reforms for the emergence, outlook and assessment of globalization. We still believe that with respect to globalization (and indeed maybe even more than with respect to national developments, as Schnaiberg et al. claim) ToP has much to offer, and make us understand how the dynamics of a global capitalist world-order undermine environmental improvements. But we do, however, not see how we can understand from a ToP perspective, for instance:

- major advancements in global environmental regime formation;
- those – more than individual and anecdotal – cases where global investments parallel environmental improvements;
- the absence of any substantial empirical proof of the pollution haven hypotheses;
- the environmental (side)agreements that go together with economic integration processes in the EU and NAFTA.

Ecological modernization ideas might help us here, as they can make us understand why in some – or an increasing number of – cases environmental considerations do make a difference in the organization of the global world and why this differs from some decade(s) or so ago (Mol, 2001).

THE ENVIRONMENTAL STATE

With respect to the position of the state or governmental agencies, there seem to be some common point of departure between the two perspectives, although the final analysis and evaluation of the state and political 'interventions' in the (capitalist) accumulation process in turning the latter's devastating environmental consequences diverge.

The evaluation of the environmental state by the early ecological modernization theorists in the 1980s converges to a major extent with neo-Marxist analyses. Authors such as Martin Jänicke (1986) and Joseph Huber (1982) have analyzed in detail the failure of the environmental state in bringing about any significant or fundamental environmental improvement.[5] For various reasons the environmental state was unable to carry out significant preventive environmental policies that would change economic processes of production and consumption at the core: at the investment decisions, at the design of new products, at the valuation of the third factor of production (nature). According to Jänicke (1986), there existed a structural affinity between capital and the bureaucratic state that made that both had an interest in curative environmental programs that would not threaten conventional capital accumulation. His analysis comes very close to and even draws strongly on neo-Marxist insights on the position and dependencies of the 'capitalist state' vis-à-vis capital (cf. on O'Connor's (1973) work on the Fiscal crisis and Habermas' (1973) work on Legitimation crisis). If we are well informed this basically still is the central theoretical position of most scholars in the ToP perspective regarding the environmental state.

Within EMT this rather critical analysis of the failure of the environmental state in the 1970s and 1980s has developed into two positions, both having analytical (in terms of developments that can be analyzed) as well as normative (designing a desirable trajectory of change) dimensions. The first position, of which Joseph Huber used to be a representative, can be characterized by a move away from the environmental state and environmental politics, towards the market and high-technological (or: super-industrial) developments that interdependently contribute to more, and more efficient, environmental improvements. Deregulation, privatization, and decentralization in environmental policy are then interpreted as potentially beneficial for a more efficient environmental reform, in contrast to a bureaucratic environmental Leviathan that frustrates all innovative power. This position can now be identified especially among more neo-liberal market-ideologies, and hardly among the core of contemporary ecological modernization theorists. There is considerable merit in neo-Marxist critiques attacking this neo-liberal position, as long as they are aware that this position hardly belongs to the contemporary core of eco-modernist thinking and theorizing (cf. Mol & Sonnenfeld, 2000). The second position can be identified around ideas of political modernization[6] and environmental sub-politics[7] and has become dominant in EM thinking from the early 1990s onward. Although in principle the position of the state has not altered fundamentally vis-à-vis capital, several more or less simultaneous developments make a more refined analysis of the environmental state necessary. Without going too much into detail, one should at least think of:

- following the fall of the Berlin wall, a fundamentally different 'institutional design' or type of state-market relation is no longer perceived as feasible, desirable or likely;
- growing globalization, among others, has both increased the complexity and difficulties for states to organize, plan and steer social and economic developments within their territory, and resulted in other (sub- and supra-national) actors entering the political stage;
- The centripetal movement of environmental ideas and interests in social developments has increased the pressure on the state to act and intervene on behalf of these environmental considerations.

While there remains agreement between ToP and EMT that there are still clear restrictions for the nation-state to intervene in the capitalist economy (or in the Treadmill of Production), EMT analyzes and concludes: (i) that the essence of these restrictions are related to the organization of our economy and that the (perceived) social and other costs for a fundamental change in state-market relations are too high, making a fundamental alternative unlikely; (ii) that these fundamental restrictions do not mean that significant improvements in the environmental performance of the state are impossible (e.g. by moving from a curative to a preventive strategy); (iii) that various transformations are taking place in the way nation-states and their conventional political institutions deal with the environmental crisis and with environmental conflicts and requests by environmentalists; and (iv) that a variety of new actors and institutions (e.g. environmental NGOs, sub-national governments, supranational organizations, private and market actors) appear on the (political) stage of environmental reform who partly take over traditional tasks of the conventional political institutions of the nation-states.

The innovations and transformations the environmental state is currently engaged in differ with respect to form and intensity from country to country, depending on among others the prevailing policy culture or style, the economic regimes, the (tradition in) state-market relations, the national systems of innovation, and the environmental pressure by NGOs. These transformations should, of course, by no means be interpreted as an evolutionary process of increasing improvement in the environmental state's performance. Constant battles are fought over these innovations and transformations both inside and outside the state (and it is of course here that ToP or neo-Marxist state theories can shed light). Incidentally these political modernizations or environmental sub-politics will in the end turn out to be a major loss for environmental reform. But we would claim that in all developed economies some commonalties can be seen in:

- innovations in environmental regulation that – generally speaking – increasingly respond to the changing social circumstances and increasingly perform better than the state regulatory strategies of the 1970s and 1980s;
- the emergence of new actors that take up tasks of conventional political institutions.

While ToP seems either to deny these transformations or interpret them as of no real improvement (or even a deterioration) of the environmental state's performance, EMT put its finger on the relevance of these transformations, both for understanding what is happening and for constructing future strategies of environmental reform involving the environmental state. It should be stressed again that neither the analyzed changes, nor the current performance of the environmental state are celebrated as undisputed improvements. But we do think that only via analyzing contemporary transformations feasible new strategies and institutions can be designed, which better protect the environment. And in that sense a significant part of the current 'political modernization' transformations are believed to be steps in the right directions, contributing to more preventive environmental policies (together with various other ecological modernization developments).

THEORETICAL AND EMPIRICAL CHALLENGES AHEAD

Above we have tried not so much to show the adequacy of EMT over ToP, but rather to point out differences and to explain the logic of the two positions in terms of internal coherence and historical background. In this final section – as a kind of conclusion – we want to point out some academic routes to explore these variations further, not only in terms of contradictory options for explaining social reality but by means of a kind of 'common' future challenge.

The differences between the two schools of thought in environmental sociology are rooted in fundamental dissimilarities on a number of strongly interconnected conceptualizations, making both schools-of-thought internally consistent to a large extent. A number of these fundamental distinctions have been elaborated above. In contrast to some 20 years ago, however, currently a focused theoretical debate – with exchange of arguments and attempts to understand the logic, internal coherence and scope of both frameworks – between two such opposing traditions in (environmental) sociology seems very well possible. The debate between these two frameworks does not remain restricted to the environmental social theories, but relates to the role of sociology as a discipline. To some extent this is related to the different social and academic contexts in which both theories emerged and prevail. Remarkably enough, however, while in general European sociology – and perhaps also environmental sociology – is often perceived as being more theoretical vis-à-vis the more empirical North American sociological traditions, European based Ecological Modernization Theory is more related to environmental reform practices than the American Treadmill-of-Production perspective. We think there is some value in further elaborating on the contextual differences and backgrounds between the ToP or other neo-Marxist perspectives on the one hand and EMT on the other. Ecological modernization theorists have made a plea for elaborating regional variations of ecological modernization theory, giving more credits to the regional specifics in terms of state-market relations, policy culture/style (Mol, 1999), "national character" (Cohen, 2000b), traditions in environmental protests and movements, national systems of innovation, accumulation regimes and the like (cf. Mol, 2001). In a similar way, a more European neo-Marxist ToP analysis might contribute to mutual understanding, be it that such elaboration will never bridge the gap between the two schools.

A second line – after filtering the misunderstandings and simple one-liners in both frameworks – might be to carry out comparative, theoretical-informed empirical research using both frameworks in two settings. Waste prevention and recycling in Western Europe and the USA might be an interesting case study, seeing the claims made by Pellow et al. (2000) on the U.S. and to a major extent contradictory experiences in Germany and the Netherlands. The European Union has stimulated comparative environmental research tremendously, but cross-Atlantic comparative research seems rather limited. Again, one should not expect that empirical research will verify or falsify either of the frameworks. But such research can illuminate the strong and weak points, and provide more profound insights in the contextual specificity of each perspective. In addition, such research might show us that some of the differences between the two perspectives are not mutual exclusive, as they are not related to the fundamental core. And that opens opportunities to enrich one framework by incorporating elements of the other. For instance, ToP insights in the relevance of distributional effects and social struggle have played a secondary, subsumed, role up till now within the EMT school-of-thought. Some of the ToP work done in this respect can be fruitfully included in EMT and given its own place (cf. some first attempts: Mol & Spaargaren, 2000).

Finally, some of the commonalties outlined in section two above provide of course ground for common explorations. Of these commonaltics, we think it is especially the common understanding of how to deal with the 'material' dimensions of social relations that deserves attention. Both sociological perspectives take a balanced position between 'strong' social constructivism and post-modernism on the one side, and socio-biologists and neo-Malthusianists on the other. Both the sub-discipline of environmental sociology and general and theoretical sociology can profit from such a balanced and refined sociological account of the relevance of the material dimensions in understanding social life.

NOTES

1. It goes without saying that there have also been – and still are – considerable internal debates between various branches of neo-Marxist environmental thought, as for instance the discussions in the journal *Capitalism, Nature, Socialism* prove.

2. It has been especially David Sonnenfeld who has invited us to look at the commonalties between ToP and EMT.

3. This has nothing to do with the sampling differences between EMT and ToP, as suggested by Schnaiberg et al. (2000). This seems to us an incorrect methodological claim that can not be sustained, giving the increasing number of EMT empirical studies.

4. Some contributions extent their analyses to gender issues, animal rights, indigenous people, and other categories of social conflict.

5. Two lines of clarification were put forward to understand the 'logic' of state failure. The first line of argument relied heavily on neo-Marxist and critical theory by claiming that the possibilities of the state in capitalist society to regulate the negative side effects of economic processes were limited. This specific position of the 'capitalist state' would eventually result in severe problems of legitimacy and effectiveness, especially in times of economic decline. The second line of argument followed a more historical perspective. While the national state is still held accountable for solving most of the social and environmental misuses within its territory, the powers of the nation-state to actually do so are undermined and to some extent wither away due to what Giddens (1990) analyses as "the intensification of worldwide social relations which link distant localities in such a way that local happenings are shaped by events occurring many miles away and vice versa." Global economic, political and cultural processes contribute both to the (perception of) failure of the nation-state to act effectively in protecting its territory from environmental deterioration and to difficulties in legitimizing its actions. This is all the more true for those environmental problems that have a strong supra-national dimension, either because pollutants cross borders or because the problems have close interrelations with supra-national economic processes.

6. Political modernization not only entails shifts from reactive/curative to a proactive/preventive environmental policies, from sectoral to integrated policies and from add-on technologies to preventive process integrated technological changes, it also includes less hierarchic policy styles, an increased involvement of polluters in designing and implementing environmental measures, a decentralization of environmental policy-making, a privatization of some traditional government tasks and an introduction of market mechanisms and self-regulation. These 'new politics of pollution' (Weale, 1992) or new environmental arrangements usually entails a redefinition of state – market relations and a new position of the central state in designing, implementing and enforcing environmental reforms vis-à-vis decentral state authorities and private parties.

7. The emergence of environmental 'subpolitics' (Beck, 1994) gives evidence to the idea that in a number of cases the core political institutions of parliament, bureaucracy and political parties are no longer considered adequate to deal with environmental risks, and alternative political processes and arrangements outside these core domains are explored, developed and used. At an earlier occasion we have for the Netherlands identified at least four categories of environmental subpolitics (Hogenboom, Mol & Spaargaren, 2000).

REFERENCES

Beck, U. (1994). The reinvention of politics: towards a theory of reflexive modernization. In: U. Beck, A. Giddens & S. Lash (Eds), *Reflexive Modernization. Politics, Tradition and Aesthetics in the Modern Social Order* (pp. 1–55). Polity Press, Cambridge.

Blowers, A. (1997). Environmental Policy: Ecological Modernization and the Risk Society? *Urban Studies*, *34*(5–6), 845–871.

Blühdorn, I. (2000). Ecological Modernization and Post-Ecologist Politics. In: G. Spaargaren, A. P. J. Mol & F. Buttel (Eds), *Environment and Global Modernity*. London: Sage.

Buttel, F. (2000a). Classical theory and contemporary environmental sociology: some reflections on the antecedents and prospects for reflexive modernization theories in the study of environment and society. In: G. Spaargaren, A. P. J. Mol & F. Buttel (Eds), *Environment and Global Modernity*. London: Sage.

Buttel, F. (2000b). Ecological Modernization as Social Theory. *Geoforum, 31*(4), 57–65.

Castells, M. (1997). *End of Millenium. Volume III of The Information Age: Economy, Society and Culture*. Malden/Oxford: Blackwell.

Cohen, M. (Ed.) (2000a). *Risk in the Modern Age. Social Theory, Science and Environmental Decision-Making*. Basingstoke: MacMillan.

Cohen, M. (2000b). Ecological Modernisation, Environmental Knowledge and National Character; A preliminary Analysis of the Netherlands. *Environmental Politics, 9*(1) 77–105.

Dickens, P. (1998). Beyond Sociology: Marxism and the environment. In: M. Redclift & G. Woodgate (Eds), *The International Handbook of Environmental Sociology* (pp. 179–192). Cheltenham/Northampton (Mass): Edward Elgar.

Dryzek, J. S. (1995). Environmental Compliance, Justice and Democracy. In: R. Eckersley (Ed.), *Markets, the State and the Environment. Towards Integration* (pp. 294–308). MacMillan: Houndsmill.

Giddens, A. (1990). *The Consequences of Modernity*, Cambridge: Polity Press.

Goldblatt, D. (1996). *Social Theory and the Environment*, Cambridge: Polity.

Gould, K. A., Schnaiberg, A., & Weinberg, A. S. (1996). *Local Environmental Struggles: Citizen Activism in the Treadmill of Production*. Cambridge: Cambridge University Press.

Habermas, J. (1973). *Legitimationsprobleme im Spätkapitalismus*. Frankfurt: Suhrkamp Verlag.

Hajer, M. A. (1995). *The Politics of Environmental Discourse. Ecological Modernization and the Policy Process*. Oxford: Clarendon Press.

Hobsbawm, E. (1994). *Age of Extremes. The Short Twentieth Century, 1914–1991*. London: Michael Joseph.

Hogenboom, J., Mol, A. P. J., & Spaargaren, G. (2000). Dealing with environmental risk in reflexive modernity. In: M. Cohen (Ed.), *Risk in the Modern Age. Social Theory, Science and Environmental Decision-making*. Basingstoke: MacMillan.

Hoogvelt, A. (1997). *Globalization and the Postcolonial World. The New Political Economy of Development*. Houdsmills and London: MacMillan Press.

Huber, J. (1982). *Die verlorene Unschuld der Ökologie. Neue Technologien und superindustrielle Entwicklung*. Frankfurt: Fisher.

Huber, J. (1985). *Die Regenbogengesellschaft. Ökologie und Sozialpolitik*. Frankfurt am Main: Fisher Verlag.

Humprey, C. R., & Buttel, F. H. (1982). *Environment, Energy and Society*. Belmont, CA: Wadworth.

Jänicke, M. (1986). *Staatsversagen. Die Ohnmacht der Politik in die Industriegesellschaft*. München: Piper.

Leff, E. (1995). *Green Production: Toward an Environmental Rationality*. New York: Guilford Press.

Leroy, P. (1996). Nieuwe stappen in de Milieusociologie? *Tijdschrift voor Sociologie, 15*(2), 67ff.

Leroy, P., & van Tatenhove, J. (2000). New policy arrangements in environmental politics: the relevance of political and ecological modernization. In: G. Spaargaren, A. P. J. Mol & F. Buttel (Eds), *Environment and Global Modernity*. London: Sage.

Mol, A. P. J. (1995). *The Refinement of Production. Ecological Modernization Theory and the Chemical Industry*. Utrecht: Jan van Arkel/international books.

Mol, A. P. J. (1999). Ecological modernization and the environmental transition of Europe. Between national variations and common denominators. *Environmental Policy and Planning, 1*(3), 167–181.

Mol, A. P. J. (2000). The environmental movement in an era of ecological modernization. *Geoforum, 31(4)*, 45–56.

Mol, A. P. J. (2001). *Globalisation and Environmental Reform. An Inquiry into the Ecological Modernisation of the Global Economy*. Cambridge (Mass): MIT (forthcoming).

Mol, A. P. J., Lauber, V., & Liefferink, J. D. (Ed.) (2000). *Joint Environmental Policy-making. New Interactive Approaches in the European Union and selected Member States*. Oxford: OUP.

Mol, A. P. J., & Sonnenfeld, D. S. (2000). Ecological modernization around the world: an introduction. *Environmental Politics*, *9*(1), 3–15.

Mol, A. P. J., & Spaargaren, G. (2000). Ecological Modernization Theory in debate: a review. *Environmental Politics*, *9*(1), 17–49.

Mol, A. P. J., Spaargaren, G., & Frouws, J. (1998). Milieurisico's als nieuw sociaal probleem'. In: K. Schuyt (Ed.), *Het sociaal tekort. Veertien sociale problemen in Nederland* (pp. 229–243). Amsterdam: de Balie.

O'Connor, J. (1973). *The Fiscal Crisis of the State*. New York: St. Martin's Press.

O'Connor, J. (1998). *Natural Causes. Essays in Ecological Marxism*. New York and London: Guilford.

Pellow, D. N., Weinberg, A. S., & Schnaiberg, A. (2000). Putting Ecological Modernization to the Test: Accounting for Recycling's Promises and Performance. *Environmental Politics*, *9*(1), 109–137.

Pepper, D. (1984), *The Roots of modern Environmentalism*, London etc.: Croom Helm.

Rinckevicius, L. (2000). The ideology of ecological modernization in 'double-risk societies: A case study of Lithuanian environmental policy. In: G. Spaargaren, A. P. J. Mol & F. Buttel (Eds), *Environment and Global Modernity*. London: Sage.

Sairinen, R. (2001). *Governing Capacity of Environmental Policy in Finland. An assessment of making the EIA-law and CO2-tax*. Helsinki: University of Technology (dissertation).

Sarkar, S. (1990). Accommodating Industrialism: a Third World View of the West German Ecological Movement. *The Ecologist*, *20*(4), 147–152.

Schnaiberg, A. (1980). *The Environment. From Surplus to Scarcity*. Oxford/New York: Oxford University Press.

Schnaiberg, A., Watts, N., & Zimmermann, K. (Ed.) (1986). *Distributional Conflicts in Environmental-Resource Policy*. Aldershot: Gower.

Schnaiberg, A., & Gould, K. (1994). *Environment and Society: The Enduring Conflict*. New York: St. Martin's Press.

Schnaiberg, A., Weinberg, A., & Pellow, D. (2002). *The Treadmill of Production and the Environmental State* (this Volume).

Smidt, K. (1996). Over beschaving en milieu. *Amsterdams Sociologisch Tijdschrift*, *23*(1), 60–81.

Sonnenfeld, D. (1999). *Social movements and ecological modernization: the transformation of Pulp and Paper Manufacturing*. Paper prepared for the ASA conference, August 1999, Chicago, Illinois.

Spaargaren, G., & Mol, A. P. J. (1991). Ecologie, technologie en sociale verandering. Naar een ecologisch meer rationele vorm van productie en consumptie. In: A. P. J. Mol, G. Spaargaren & A. Klapwijk (Eds), *Technologie en Milieubeheer. Tussen sanering en ecologische modernisering* (pp. 185–207). Den Haag: SDU.

Spaargaren, G., & Mol, A. P. J. (1992). Sociology, environment and modernity. Ecological modernization as a theory of social change. *Society and Natural Resources*, *5*, 323–344.

Weale, A. (1992). *The New Politics of Pollution*. Manchester: Manchester University Press.

Wehling, P. (1992). *Die Moderne als Sozialmythos. Zur Kritik sozialwissenschaftlicher modernisierungstheorien*. Frankfurt/New York: Campus.

FROM THE TREADMILL OF PRODUCTION TO ECOLOGICAL MODERNIZATION? APPLYING A HABERMASIAN FRAMEWORK TO SOCIETY-ENVIRONMENT RELATIONSHIPS

Dana R. Fisher

INTRODUCTION

Recent years have seen a growing debate among the scholars who study society-environment relationships. Since the 1970s, there has been an increasing attention to societies' effects on the natural environment, with sociologists beginning to think in new ways about these relationships. Many of the best-known scholars in the field have looked at the ways that societies have been destroying the environment, referring to the potential for "overshooting" global carrying capacity (see, e.g. Catton, 1980; Dunlap & Van Liere, 1978, 1984), the emergence of a "second contradiction of capitalism" (see, e.g. Foster, 1992, 2000; O'Connor, 1988, 1991), or the problems of a "treadmill of production" (see e.g. Schnaiberg, 1980; Schnaiberg & Gould, 1994; Gould

The Environmental State Under Pressure, Volume 10, pages 53–64.

ISBN: 0-7623-0854-0

et al., 1996). Despite their many differences, all of these perspectives have pointed to environmental problems as being a consequence or correlate of capitalist accumulation. More recently, however, the theory of ecological modernization has pointed to a distinctly different set of conclusions, seeing environmental concerns as becoming internalized in modern institutions, particularly in the developed world (see e.g. Buttel, 2000a, b, 2001; Christoff, 1996; Cohen, 2000; Fisher & Freudenburg, 2001; Hajer, 1995; Huber, 1985; Mol, 1995, 1997, 1999, 2000a, b, 2001; Mol & Sonnefeld, 2000; Mol & Spaargaren, 2000; Spaargaren, 1997, 2000; Spaargaren & Mol, 1992; Spaargaren & van Vliet, 2000).

Although these older and newer approaches yield distinctly different results – one seeing technological development as being a correlate of environmental destruction, while the other looks at environmental improvements as being economically and politically feasible – it is possible that the differences are not the product of one set of approaches being right and one being wrong. Instead, this paper presents an interpretation of the significant differences between these two basic approaches in terms of a still broader theoretical argument, involving what Habermas describes as the different types of "crisis tendencies" in his work on the *Legitimation Crisis* (1975; see also Habermas, 1970, 1984; McCarthy, 1978). As will be noted in the pages that follow, the differences between the older and newer approaches to understanding relationships between society and the environment parallel the changes that Habermas sees as being among the implications of capitalism's shift from a liberal to an advanced stage. This paper applies these broader theoretical characteristics of the differences in the distinct stages of capitalism, as outlined by Habermas, to understand the debate that is taking place in environmental sociology today.

LIBERAL CAPITALISM VERSUS ADVANCED CAPITALISM

Particularly in his work during the 1970s, Habermas devoted a good deal of attention to the crisis tendencies of capitalism. Although this paper is not the place for a detailed introduction to his work (for that, see Habermas, 1970, 1975; McCarthy, 1978), the key argument that takes central stage in this work has to do with what Habermas characterized as a transformation from liberal to advanced capitalism. Within this transformation, the central, fundamental problems or crises tendencies in society were seen as shifting from the economic sphere to the political and socio-cultural spheres. Although Habermas does not focus on the actual transition from liberal to advanced capitalism, his analysis of the specific characteristics of each stage is very useful for understanding both the social dynamics of economic growth and the social ramifications of such growth. Through his analysis, it is possible to glean useful insights into societies that he describes as being at different stages of capitalist development as well as the perspectives of the scholars who study such societies.

In his description of the liberal capitalist state, Habermas identifies the principle of organization as the relationship between wage labor and capital (1975, p. 20). In his words, economic exchange is the "dominant steering medium" in liberal capitalist societies (1975, p. 21). The particular role of the liberal capitalist state is to "secure the prerequisites for the continued existence of the mode of production and – as a supplement to the market mechanism – to satisfy the needs of the accumulation process controlled by the market" (1975, p. 55). In other words, the state secures the general conditions of production. In this stage of capitalism, when a crisis occurs, it is economic in nature; it is both economically driven and must be addressed economically.

Habermas argues that with a transition from the liberal capitalist to the advanced capitalist state, a change in the relationship between two of the main actors within society takes place. In McCarthy's concise summary (1978, p. 363), Habermas's view is that the economy "no longer has the degree of autonomy" that it previously had. The crisis tendencies in the advanced capitalist state "are no longer located immediately in the economic sphere but in the socio-cultural sphere" (McCarthy, 1978, p. 358). In Habermas' own words, "The continuing tendency toward disturbance of capitalist growth can be administratively processed and transferred, by stages, through the political and into the socio-cultural system" (1975, p. 40). When society changes from liberal capitalism to advanced capitalism, in other words, the origins of social crisis shift away from the economic sphere and the potential problems themselves shift from economic crises to legitimation, rationality, and motivation crises. Within these crises, the problems and resolutions of advanced capitalist societies are no longer only stemming from and resolved by economic means. Table 1 presents Habermas's interpretation of the relationship between different sectors of society and the types of crises that may ensue.

Habermas also analyzes the roles of different sectors of society in responding to such crises. In the advanced capitalist system, he identifies the economic, administrative, and what he calls legitimation systems – or what many sociologists call the market, the state, and democratic institutions that engage civil society and the public sphere – as all playing a part in maintaining legitimacy and control over society (for a full discussion of these systems, see Habermas,

Table 1. Crisis Tendencies and their Origins.

Type of Crisis	Point of Origin
Economic Crisis	Economic System
Legitimation Crisis and Rationality Crisis	Political System
Motivation Crisis	Socio-Cultural System

(Adapted from Habermas 1975, p. 45).

1975, pp. 35–36). Even in advanced capitalist states, however, Habermas does not see a particularly active role for the citizen. Rather, he notes that "the citizenry, in the midst of an objectively political society, enjoy the status of passive citizens with only the right to withhold acclamation" (1975, p. 37). Both in this older work and in his work on the public sphere (1998, 1992; see also Calhoun, 1992), Habermas notes a structural depoliticization of the public sphere and civil society (see also McCarthy, 1978). In his more recent work, the author further develops his understanding of civil society and the role that it can play in advanced capitalist regimes. Although he does not see citizens directly engaging with other social actors in contemporary advanced capitalist states, Habermas identifies the participation of an engaged civil society as one of the main ways that "public, unrestricted discussion, free from domination" will take place thereby leading to what he might view as true democracy (1970, p. 118).

Habermas describes the emergence of civil society in advanced capitalism as having been "differentiated out of the political-economic system" (1975, p. 21). In his more recent work, Habermas further explicates his understanding of the development of civil society. "With the conceptual move from the horizontal association of consociates who reciprocally accord rights to one another to the vertical organization of citizens within the state, the practice of self-determination is institutionalized in a number of ways" (Habermas, 1998, p. 135). In particular, he sees citizens in advanced capitalist regimes as becoming actors within the social system, rather than outside of the institutional framework of society.

One particular type of problem that Habermas addresses – be it only marginally – is that of the disturbances to the ecological balance. He mentions two important ecological limitations: finite resources and the capacity to absorb production's by-products – considerations that closely parallel the topics that are addressed in much of the literature on environmental sociology. In his own words, the "ecological balance designates an absolute limit to growth" (Habermas, 1975, p. 41).

Although not explicitly stated or compared, the differences that are outlined by Habermas in his discussion of the differences between liberal and advanced capitalism are reflected in the arguments of two competing theories in environmental sociology. By looking at the underlying assumptions regarding the social system in each theory, the aim of this paper is to point out how these assumptions are consistent with Habermas's conception of the different stages of capitalism.

ENVIRONMENTAL PROBLEMS ORIGINATING FROM THE ECONOMIC SPHERE

In some ways, the view presented by Habermas about what he calls the "ecological balance" is similar to the expectations that are evident in much of the work in environmental sociology over the past several decades. As noted by Humphrey and Buttel (1982), the explosion in interest in environmental sociology in the 1970s and 1980s was, in part, a response to the societal debates about the limits to growth. Over the past quarter of a century, in fact, the work of many of the main figures in environmental sociology has often involved a concern about the degree to which society's consistent growth appears to have come at the expense of the natural environment (see, for example, Catton, 1980; Dunlap & Van Liere, 1978, 1984; Foster, 1992; O'Connor, 1991; Schnaiberg & Gould, 1994). In essence, these theories have noted that, as societies have grown economically, their overall impact on the environment has increased; environmental destruction has thus been identified as a relatively straightforward result of capitalist accumulation. This presentation of environmental problems mirrors that of Habermas who states that "Capitalist societies cannot follow imperatives of growth limitation without abandoning their principle of organization . . . The development of productive forces, cannot, however, be uncoupled from the production of *exchange values* without violating the logic of the system (emphasis in original, 1975, pp. 42–43).

Although there are similarities between Habermas and these environmental sociologists' understanding of environmental problems, their perceptions of the steering media of society are very different. Habermas identifies a decreasing autonomy of the market and the increasing influence of political and sociocultural spheres within advanced capitalism. In contrast, one of the more predominant theories that spells out connections between environmental destruction and economic prosperity, the treadmill of production, focuses most of its attention on the economic sphere. This theory emphasizes that economic growth would increase the societal need to confront scarcity – and hence to confront as well a breakdown of the apparent victory over scarcity that had previously done so much to bring legitimacy and a relative social peace to capitalistic systems (cf. Habermas, 1975; Block, 1987). In some of the earliest writings on the theory, Schnaiberg (1980) devoted increased attention to the dynamics behind the societal speed-up, holding in essence that producers have a need for increasing profits, which they attempt to achieve by means of ever-increasing production. This system results in ever-increasing impacts on the natural environment, and hence a simultaneous hastening of the coming of an industrial crisis – a set of factors that Schnaiberg aptly termed "the treadmill of production." It is defined as an expanding process of production and accumulation in which consumption increases "at ever faster rates to offset the substitution of capital for labor in the production process" while natural resources are consumed in the search for growing prosperity (Schnaiberg, 1980, p. 229).

In the more recent work that emphasizes what they call "the enduring conflict" between the environment and the economy, Schnaiberg and Gould (1994) state that, ultimately, environmental destruction will become the limiting factor in economic growth. The environmental destruction that they see as being a necessary component of economic growth, in other words, will eventually lead to such an erosion of the natural resource base that future economic growth becomes impossible. Although Schnaiberg and his colleagues refer to the potential of social movements to break the treadmill of production in their more recent work, thus far, they see "the driving logic and contradictions of modern industrial production" as constraining "the ability of the environmental movement to protect ecosystems" (Gould et al., 1996, p. 1). In other words, although the authors look outside the market for ways to break the treadmill, they see the economy as determining the efficacy of other social spheres. As the authors point out, there is an "increasing domination of transnational treadmill market actors over national institutions of the nation-state, and its society (including both its population and its labor force)" (Gould et al., 1996, p. 8). With economic globalization, international actors from the economic sphere hold even more power over social actors in the political and socio-cultural spheres of a country.

Like Habermas's presentation of liberal capitalism, scholars of the treadmill of production see economic exchange as the "dominant steering medium in society" (Habermas, 1975, p. 21). In other words, they consider environmental degradation to be the product of an unregulated liberal economic system in which the material sustenance base for economic activities is being consumed and the production process itself befouls the environment. Rather than the steering medium being state-led policies or civil society interventions into capitalistic processes, the economic treadmill of production drives social change.

Although the expectations of Schnaiberg and his colleagues echo Habermas's descriptions of liberal capitalism, that is not to say that they have frozen their perspective in an earlier era. Rather, the authors have followed an alternative trajectory of explaining the developments of capitalism by focusing their more recent work on issues emerging from neo-liberal trade practices and economic globalization. Within this newer work, the underlying expectations of the treadmill of production continue to hold, although they are somewhat adjusted: until the treadmill is slowed, environmental degradation will continue to increase.

Even though they include references to other variables in their discussions, these scholars inevitably trace ecological crises back to inherent characteristics of capitalist accumulation and the economic system. In essence, the only way to resolve the environmental crises that result from capitalism is to stop capitalist accumulation itself. Although the scholars of the treadmill of production are not focusing on an earlier form of capitalism, they look at the same phenomenon described by Habermas when he talks about economic crises stemming from the liberal stage of capitalism. In Habermas's own words, "the liberal-capitalist state takes action . . . in order to secure the prerequisites for the continued existence of the mode of production and – as a supplement to the market mechanism – to satisfy the needs of the accumulation process controlled by the market" (1975, p. 55).

ENVIRONMENTAL PROBLEMS WITHIN THE ADMINISTRATIVE, SOCIO-CULTURAL, AND ECONOMIC SPHERES

In contrast to the focus on the economic sphere that can be seen within the aforementioned literature in environmental sociology, some of the more recent theories of the relationship between society and the natural environment tend to share Habermas's views of advanced capitalism, in that they see the economy as no longer independently driving society (see e.g. Beck, 1987; Beck et al., 1994; Buttel, 2000a, b; Christoff, 1996; Cohen, 2000; Fisher & Freudenburg, 2001; Hajer, 1995; Huber, 1985; Leroy & van Tatenhove, 2000; Mol, 1995, 1997, 1999, 2000a, b; 2001; Mol & Sonnefeld, 2000; Mol & Spaargaren, 2000; Spaargaren, 1997, 2000; Spaargaren & Mol, 1992; Spaargaren & van Vliet, 2000). The positions put forth by these scholars involve social actors from the state and civil society as driving social change. In other words, these views are very similar to McCarthy's concise summary mentioned earlier in this paper: the economy "no longer has the degree of autonomy" that it once had in liberal capitalist regimes (1978, p. 363). Some might even say, in fact, that some of this newer research in environmental sociology is consistent with the institutionalization of the new ecological paradigm that Dunlap and Van Liere describe (1978, 1984), in that it concludes that environmental concerns have been folded into the social structures of the developed world.

Perhaps the clearest elucidation of the importance of social actors outside of the economic sphere is put forth within the growing literature on ecological modernization. In fact, scholars working from the ecological modernization perspective include a number of other socio-cultural variables, along with economic variables, in their understanding of the relationship between society and the natural environment, and the ecological crises and solutions that emerge. It is important to note that scholars of this theory do not discredit the role that the economic sphere plays in environmental crisis and environmental solutions. In the words of Spaargaren and Mol (1992, p. 334), "Ecological modernization stands for a major transformation, and ecological switch of the industrialization process into a direction that takes into account maintaining the sustenance base." Although ecological modernizationists pay attention to the economic sphere, in contrast to the expectations of the treadmill of production, it is not expected to be the solitary driver of social change. When the theory was first presented in the English language by Spaargaren and Mol (1992, p. 334), in fact, it was described as a theory of social change that incorporates both the economic sphere as well as the two other – political and socio-cultural – spheres to overcome the "environmental crisis without leaving the path of modernization."

In contrast to those theories that continue to look at the economic sphere as the sole origin of social crisis, ecological modernization includes other socio-cultural variables. Similar to Habermas, who saw technology and science as playing an important role in advanced capitalism (1970), ecological modernization theorists looks to the "diffusion of new technologies that are more intelligent than the older ones and that benefit the environment" as the center of ecological modernization (Spaargaren & Mol, 1992, p. 335). In other words, the focal point of ecological modernization is the dimension of industrialism that involves an intersection between the economic and socio-cultural spheres. Perhaps Buttel best summarizes the role of technology and industrialization in ecological modernization as compared to social actors from other social spheres:

> Ecological modernization theorists are basically of the view that as much as environmental problems in the past have been caused by an industrially driven process of expanded production and consumption, the solution to environmental problems cannot be found in

> radical movements that seek to restore the lower levels of output and consumption that prevailed years ago, or in centralized command-and-control regulation. Rather, in the ecological modernization perspective, the solution to environmental problems caused by industrialization requires more industrialization – or "superindstrialization" – albeit industrial development of a far different sort that that which prevailed during most of the twentieth century (Buttel, 2001, p. 18).

Although ecological modernization scholars might not all agree about Buttel's focus on "superindustrialization," most tend to agree that the theory of ecological modernization includes an expectation that technology and science will interact with the market sector to solve environmental problems instead of making them worse. Beyond the focus on the economic and socio-cultural spheres, ecological modernization includes expectations about the role of the administrative or political sphere in addressing environmental issues. In a later work by Mol (1997, p. 140), he discusses all three social spheres: "ecological modernization is, above all, a concept dealing with the institutions of modern technology, (market) economy and state intervention." Consistent with Habermas's emphasis on the role of the political sphere in advanced capitalism, implicit to the theory of ecological modernization is a role for the political sphere in solving environmental problems.

In the collaborations between the economic, political and the socio-cultural spheres mentioned above, proponents of ecological modernization identify the formation of new coalitions of actors in advanced capitalist societies. Mol and Sonnenfeld (2000, pp. 6–7), for example, suggest that ecological modernization involves changes in the traditional roles of actors, specifically including "More opportunities for non-state actors to assume traditional administrative, regulatory, managerial, corporate, and mediating functions of the nation-state." Included in these "non-state actors" are economic and civil society actors. In Mol's recent work on social movements, he discusses the role of environmental social movement organizations: "Environmental organizations are engaged in constant dynamic processes of coalition building with rapidly changing opponents and partners, with the aim of maximizing and safeguarding environmental gains" (Mol, 2000a, p. 49). In other words, environmental organizations are not the driving force behind environmental change, but they do play a role in the process. This interpretation of the role of civil society actors is similar to Habermas's understanding of a "vertical organization of citizens within the state" (Habermas, 1998, p. 135). In sum, the ecological modernization literature presents civil society and science and technological actors from the socio-cultural sphere, along with social actors from the political and economic spheres playing a role in what Habermas would call the crisis tendencies of advanced capitalism.

Table 2. The Leading Spheres in Theories of Society/Environment Relationships.

Theory	Leading Sphere
Treadmill of Production	Economic Sphere
Ecological Modernization	Economic, Administrative, and Socio-Cultural Spheres

CONCLUDING REMARKS

The application of a Habermasian framework to society/environment relationships can have a variety of uses, but perhaps the greatest usefulness comes if such a framework is used more as a starting point than as a destination. On the one hand, it gives us the ability to place the debate that is taking place in the field of environmental sociology in a broader framework of social theory. On the other hand, it may be that the distinctive differences between the theories discussed above point to overall weaknesses in the theories themselves. Perhaps they are too focused on society – environment relationships to capture the full complexity and historic development as a background against which this changing relationship should be placed. Either way, using the work of Habermas to highlight the basic assumptions behind these theories of environmental sociology pushes us forward in understanding better the driving forces behind the theories. Table 2 presents a summary of the leading spheres for each of the theories that have been discussed in this paper.

Once again, it is important to note that this focus on Habermas's descriptions of different stages of capitalism is not meant to suggest that the treadmill of production is out-of-date and only applies to liberal capitalist societies. With their recent work on transnational actors, in fact, Gould et al. (1996) discuss one of the significant contributors to contemporary global environmental problems (similar to what Mol (2001) does from a ecological modernization perspective). Rather, this analysis is meant to highlight the underlying differences between the treadmill of production and ecological modernization: their focus on different steering media and the implications of such foci that has been clearly outlined in the broader theoretical work by Jürgen Habermas.

ACKNOWLEDGMENTS

The author would like to thank Professor William R. Freudenbrug and an anonymous reviewer for comments on an earlier version of this paper.

REFERENCES

Beck, U. (1987). The Anthropological Shock: Chernobyl and the Contours of the Risk Society. *Berkeley Journal of Sociology, 32.*

Beck, U., Giddens, A., & Lash, S. (1994). *Reflexive Modernization: Politics, Tradition and Aesthetics in the Modern Social Order.* Stanford: Stanford University Press.

Block, F. (1987). *Revising State Theory: Essays in Politics and Postindustrialism.* Philadelphia: Temple Univ. Press.

Buttel, F. H. (2001). Environmental Sociology and the Explanation of Environmental Reform. Paper presented at the Kyoto Environmental Sociology Conference. Kyoto: October.

Buttel, F. H. (2000a). Ecological Modernization as Social Theory. *GeoForum, 31*, 57–65.

Buttel, F. H. (2000b). Classical Theory and Contemporary Environmental Sociology. In: G. Spaargaren, A. P. J. Mol & F. H Buttel (Eds), *Environment and Global Modernity* (pp. 17–40). London: Sage Studies in International Sociology.

Calhoun, C. (Ed.) (1992). *Habermas in the Public Sphere.* Cambridge, MA: MIT Press.

Catton, W. R., Jr. (1980). *Overshoot: The Ecological Basis of Revolutionary Change.* Urbana: Univ. of Illinois Press.

Christoff, P. (1996). Ecological Modernisation, Ecological Modernities. *Environmental Politics, 5*, 476–500.

Cohen, M. J. (2000). Ecological Modernisation, Environmental Knowledge and National Character: A Preliminary Analysis of the Netherlands. *Environmental Politics, 9*(1), 77–105.

Dunlap, R. E., & Van Liere, K. D. (1984). Commitment to the Dominant Social Paradigm and Concern for Environmental Quality. *Social Science Quarterly, 65*, 1013–1028.

Dunlap, R. E., & Van Liere, K. D. (1978). The 'New Environmental Paradigm. *Journal of Environmental Education, 9*(Summer), 10–19.

Fisher, D. R., & Freudenburg, W. R. (2001). Ecological Modernization and Its Critics: Assessing the Past and Looking Toward the Future. *Society and Natural Resources, 14*, 701–709.

Foster, J. B. (2000). *Marx's Ecology: Materialism and Nature.* New York: Monthly Review Press.

Foster, J. B. (1992). The Absolute General Law of Environmental Degradation Under Capitalism. *Capitalism, Nature, Socialism, 2*(3, Sept.), 77–82.

Gould, K. A., Weinberg, A. S., & Schnaiberg, A. (1996). *Local Environmental Struggles: Citizen Activism in the Treadmill of Production.* New York: Cambridge University Press.

Habermas, J. (1970). *Towards a Rational Society.* Boston: Beacon.

Habermas, J. (1975). *The Legitimation Crisis.* Boston Beacon Press.

Habermas, J. (1984). *The Theory of Communicative Action.* Boston: Beacon Press.

Habermas, J. (1998). *Between Facts and Norms.* Cambridge: MIT Press.

Hajer, M. A. (1995). *The Politics of Environmental Discourse: Ecological Modernization and the Policy Process.* Oxford: Clarendon Press.

Huber, J. (1985). *Die Regenbogengesellschaft. Ökologie und Sozialpolitik.* Frankfurt am Main: Fisher Verlag.

Huber, J. (1991). *Unternehmen Umwelt. Weichenstellungen für eine ökologische Marktwirtschart.* Frankfurt am Maim: Fisher.

Humphrey, C. R., & Buttel, F. H. (1982). *Environment, Energy and Society.* Belmont, CA: Wadsworth.

Leroy, P., & van Tatenhove, J. (2000). Political Modernization Theory and Environmental Politics. In: G. Spaargaren, A. P. J. Mol & F. H. Buttel (Eds), *Environment and Global Modernity* (pp. 187–208). London: Sage Studies in International Sociology.

McCarthy, T. (1978). *The Social Theory of Jürgen Habermas*. Cambridge: MIT Press.

Mol, A. P. J. (2001). *Globalization and Environmental Reform. The ecological modernization of the global economy*, Cambridge (Mass): MIT.

Mol, A. P. J. (2000a). The Environmental movement in an Era of Ecological Modernization. *GeoForum, 31*, 45–56.

Mol, A. P. J. (2000b). Globalization and Environment: between apocalypse-blindness and ecological modernization. In: G. Spaargaren, A. P. J. Mol & F. H. Buttel (Eds), *Environment and Global Modernity* (pp. 121–150). London: Sage Studies in International Sociology.

Mol, A. P. J. (1999). Ecological Modernization and the Environmental Transformation of Europe: Between National Variations and Common Denominators. *Journal of Environmental Policy & Planning, 1*, 167–181.

Mol, A. P. J. (1997). Ecological Modernization: industrial transformations and environmental reform. In: M. Redclift & G. Woodgate (Eds), *The International Handbook of Environmental Sociology* (pp. 138–149). London: Edward Elgar.

Mol, A. P. J. (1995). *The Refinement of Production*. Utrect: Van Arkel.

Mol, A. P. J., & Sonnenfeld, D. A. (Eds) (2000). *Ecological Modernisation Around the World: Perspectives and Critical Debates*. Essex: Frank Cass & Co. Ltd.

Mol, A. P. J., & Spaargaren, G. (1993). Environment, Modernity and the Risk Society: The Apocalyptic Horizon of Environmental Reform. *International Sociology, 8*(1993), 431–459.

Mol, A. P. J., & Spaargaren, G. (2000). Ecological Modernization Theory in debate: a review. *Environmental Politics, 9*(1), 17–49.

O'Connor, J. R. (1988). Capitalism, Nature, Socialism: A Theoretical Introduction. *Capitalism, Nature, Socialism, 1*(1, Fall), 11–38.

O'Connor, J. (1991). On the Two Contradictions of Capitalism. *Capitalism, Nature, Socialism*, 2(3, Oct.), 107–109.

Schnaiberg, A. (1980). *The Environment: From Surplus to Scarcity*. New York: Oxford University Press.

Schnaiberg, A., & Gould, K. (1994). *Environment and Society: The Enduring Conflict*. New York: St. Martin's Press.

Spaargaren, G. (2000). Ecological Modernization Theory and the Changing Discourse on Environment and Modernity. In: G. Spaargaren A. P. J. Mol & F. H. Buttel (Eds), *Environment and Global Modernity* (pp. 41–72). London: Sage Studies in International Sociology.

Spaargaren, G. (1997). *The Ecological Modernization of Production and Consumption: Essays in Environmental Sociology*. Wageningen, Netherlands: Wageningen University.

Spaargaren, G., & Mol, A. P. J. (1992). Sociology, Environment, and Modernity: Ecological Modernization as a Theory of Social Change. *Society and Natural Resources, 5*, 323–344.

Spaargaren, G., & van Vliet, B. (2000). Lifestyles, Consumption and the Environment: The Ecological Modernisation of Domestic Consumption. In: A. P. J. Mol & D. A. Sonnenfeld (Eds), *Ecological Modernisation Around the World: Perspectives and Critical Debates* (pp. 50–76). Essex: Frank Cass & Co. Ltd.

PART II:

THE ENVIRONMENTAL STATE IN NORTH-AMERICA AND EUROPE

STATE POLICIES TO IMPROVE AIR QUALITY

Allan Mazur and Eric W. Welch

INTRODUCTION

Health risk from air pollutants is well recognized, as is the need to reduce pollutant emissions through governmental regulation (EPA, 1997). State governments carry the main burden of implementing federal anti-pollution laws (Davies & Mazurek, 1997). The Clean Air Act (CAA), for example, requires the Environmental Protection Agency (EPA) to issue national standards for air quality, but the EPA then delegates responsibility for control to each state that demonstrates its ability to administer the program. States may impose stricter standards than are required by the EPA. Generally it is state pollution-control agencies that negotiate and issue permits allowing the sources of pollution to operate, and it is mainly state (and local) agencies that enforce these permits and monitor pollution levels. With increasing competence of state environmental administrators, decreasing federal funding, and sentiment favoring decentralization, importance of state-level pollution administration has been growing (Rosenbaum, 1997).

There are large differences among the states in pollution controls, reflecting differences in need, resources and political will (Lowry, 1992; Lester, 1994, 1995). Smog-plagued California has the nation's strongest air quality program; West Virginia, Arkansas and South Dakota are among the lax states (Ridley, 1987; Hall & Kerr, 1991).

The Environmental State Under Pressure, Volume 10, pages 67–84.

ISBN: 0-7623-0854-0

Whether or not states' administrative efforts have directly improved air quality remains in doubt, despite excellent pioneering research efforts (Ringquist, 1993a, b). It is difficult to measure the stringency of controls. Often monitoring data are inadequate to assess improvements in pollution (so we focus our attention on air quality, where monitoring is better than in other media). When improvement does occur, it is unclear whether it should be attributed to state policy or to other characteristics of the state that correlate with policy. Here we address these problems, asking if states with apparently the most stringent air regulation effect the greatest improvement in air quality.

MODEL

We presume that a state's change (reduction or increase) in emissions of a pollutant from Time 1 to Time 2 is a function of its emissions at Time 1, of background characteristics of the state, and of efforts by the state's air quality agency to reduce emissions (Fig. 1).

Lacking a mature theory that would specify the explanatory variables in this model, we have adopted Lowry's (1992) suggestion that the most remediation is likely to occur in states with the most severe initial (Time 1) pollution. The sources of pollution are also relevant. SO_2 is produced mostly from the generation of electricity, secondarily from other industrial processes; the same sources account for nearly half of NO_X emissions (EPA, 1997). Therefore it is pertinent to consider the amount of electricity production and manufacturing in a state. Researchers have included such background variables as the utility and manufacturing components of gross state product, number of employees in polluting industries, or fossil fuel consumption as indicators of industrialization in a state (Lowry, 1992; Ringquist, 1993a, b; Lombard, 1993). Reductions in highly polluting economic activities, or adoption of more cost-effective

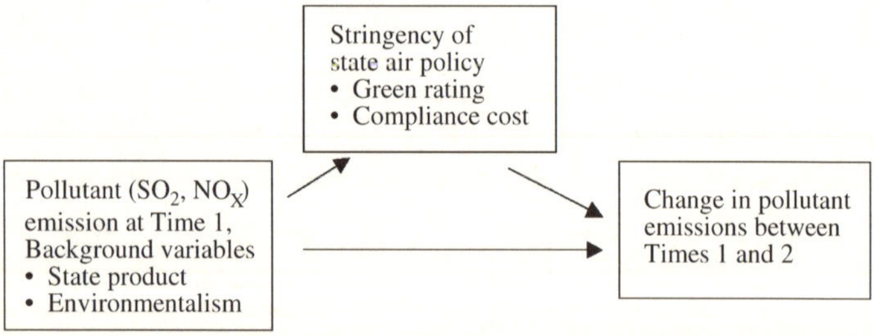

Fig. 1. Modeling the Effects of Air Quality Regulation.

(therefore less polluting) technologies, may reduce air emissions independently of state regulatory efforts.

Apart from industrial activity, researchers agree that a state's citizenry – its wealth, political views, or environmental ideology – provides more or less public support for pollution control. Attempts have been made to measure this public support by such background indicators as personal income, membership in environmental organizations, voter turnout, and political liberalism (Lowry, 1992; Ringquist, 1993a, b).

Our model suggests that these background variables – Time 1 pollution, industrial activity, public culture – influence the stringency of a state's air quality regulation, which in turn affects the degree of emissions reduction. Thus, background variables may have an *indirect* causal effect on reductions. In addition, these background variables are expected to have a *direct* effect on reductions, apart from regulatory agency actions. For example, it may be easier or more cost effective to reduce emissions in a highly polluted state than in a relatively clean one. Some industrial activities are more conducive to cleanup than others. Citizen pressure for clean air may be expressed through complaints to industry, public expectations, elected local officials, or the willingness of an affluent population to pay additional costs of pollution control, rather than directly through state air regulation. Also, the executives of a polluting industry likely have personal views that reflect the culture in which they live, making industrial leaders from environmentally conscious states more amenable to cooperative efforts at pollution reduction, even when they are not required by state regulation.

A more fully specified model is obviously desirable, however theory is insufficient to go further with confidence; detailed calculation of effects, based on indefensible specifications, is not productive. However, the model is adequate to raise the possibility that observed correlations between regulatory stringency and emission reductions are spurious. States with pro-environmental background characteristics tend to have stringent air regulations; they may also have steep reductions in pollution, not because of their stringent regulations but as a direct result of their pro-environmental background factors. If so, one would observe a spurious correlation between stringency and emission reduction, giving the false impression that regulatory stringency was responsible for the steep pollution reductions when in fact the background factors deserved the credit. The well known test for spuriousness is to statistically control on background factors. If the correlation between stringency and emission reduction greatly diminishes in strength, then the relationship is spurious. If stringency truly causes emission reduction, this relationship will maintain its strength despite statistical controls.

VARIABLES

Numerous characteristics of states, e.g. gross state product, increase with population size. As a result, such characteristics are spuriously correlated simply because they tend to have high values in populous states and low values in less populated states. Calculating state characteristics on a per capita basis does not fully address this problem because often per capita measures still correlate with population, if to a lessor degree; furthermore, some variables have little meaning as per capita measures.

State characteristics used as independent variables in this analysis are correlated, partly the result of their mutual dependence on population. Some analysts would handle this by including population as a control variable in a regression, however when population introduces high collinearity, as here, this produces severe ambiguities into the interpretation of coefficients. Following Tukey (1977), we prefer another tactic to control on population. We subtract from our variables common variance due to population, in essence creating an idealized nation comprising states each with the same number of people. We then examine substantive relationships among population-free residuals. (Partial correlation follows the same logic.) At the end of our analysis, we release this control on population to examine the robustness of our conclusions.

To remove effects of population, we regress each variable on state population (actually, log population, to reduce skew produced by a few very large states); if the population coefficient is significant, then residuals from the regression are substituted for the variable's original values, thus removing the population effect. Distributions of variables are checked for symmetry, and appropriate transformations applied as needed.

Some readers may regard the use of significance tests problematic since the 50 states are not a random sample of some larger population; indeed, if the states are the entire population then the only relevant statistics are population parameters. We subscribe to the conventional view that the state-level data in hand may be conceptualized as a representative sample from a larger universe of state-level policy outcomes. In any case, our use of significance tests is justified as a non-arbitrary criterion for judging a relationship as worthy of substantive attention.

Change in Emissions between Times 1 and 2

The CAA gives priority for reduction to six "criteria" air pollutants: carbon monoxide, nitrogen dioxide, ground-level ozone, sulfur dioxide (SO_2), particulates, and lead. Most criteria air pollutant emission levels have declined since

1970, the beginning of CAA regulations, even though vehicle miles traveled and gross domestic product increased (EPA, 1997). The lead problem has been greatly reduced because of the federal ban on leaded gasoline.

We examine the criteria pollutants mostly emitted by large industrial and electric generation facilities, which are the focus of control by state air quality agencies: nitrogen oxides (NO_X) and SO_2. NO_X emissions have remained roughly constant since 1970; SO_2, after declining from 1970, remained fairly constant from the mid-1980s to the mid-1990s (EPA, 1997). The EPA has continually improved its methodology and data base for the estimation of pollutant emissions, most recently in 1997 (EPA, 1997, Chapter 6). As a result, there are no consistent data series running from the 1970s into the 1990s. To evaluate the most recent changes in SO_2 and NO_X emissions, from 1986 through 1996, we use state-level emissions (in thousands of short tons of pollutant), as estimated by EPA's newest method. [Data for 1996 appear in EPA (1997, Table 2–3); EPA's Office of Air Quality Planning and Standards supplied data for other years]. For earlier changes, from 1973 to 1987, we use *changes* in pollutant emissions as reported by Ringquist (1993).

There can be considerable fluctuations from year to year in a state's emissions. An extreme example is Alaska, with SO_2 emissions for most of the years from 1986 through 1996 reported by the EPA as 2 to 4 thousand short tons, but SO_2 rose to 9 thousand tons in 1990 (the result of forest fires), and to 24 thousand tons in 1993. To remove such erratic fluctuations, Ringquist (1993 a, b) averaged state-level emissions over the periods 1973–1975 (Time 1) and 1985–1987 (Time 2). He then subtracted average emission during the former period from the latter period to obtain emission change over 1973–1987. The most populous states, with the highest emission levels, tend to show the largest changes. We have adjusted Ringquist's measure, removing this population effect, and denote it *Change 1973–1987*.

We use a different, preferable measure of emission changes for the period from 1986 (Time 1) to 1996 (Time 2). For each pollutant in each state, we fit a regression line through the graph of emissions by year, taking the standardized regression coefficient (beta) as a measure of changing emissions over the period 1986–1996. (Unstandardized coefficients are biased, showing the most polluting states with the largest year-to-year changes in pollution.) We remove the effect of population size and denote this measure *βChange 1986–1996*. Our beta measure produces generally more significant correlations than Ringquist's difference measure, leading us to judge it superior. [Note: There are other reasons why *Change 1973–1987* is not strictly comparable to *βChange 1986–1996*. Ringquist's emission levels are based on an early EPA methodology, subsequently improved, and his nitrogen emissions are limited to

NO_2 rather than all NO_X. Ringquist's difference measure of SO_2 change, calculated for the period 1986–1996, correlates $r = 0.56$ with *SO_2 βChange 1986–1996*; his measure of NO_X change correlates $r = 0.67$ with *NOx βChange 1986–1996* (both $p < 0.0001$).]

Stringency of State Regulatory Policy

It is difficult to measure the stringency of a state's air regulatory policies, which may refer to tough standards, omnipresent monitoring, aggressive enforcement, or other actions. The states differ considerably in the severity of air pollution as a problem, they may regulate air emissions differently (as long as they are consistent with federal requirements), and state air quality agencies differ in the seriousness with which they enforce antipollution regulations that are on the books. Therefore we consider alternate measures of the stringency of state policy.

Government Expenditures

Following Lester (1994, 1995), we first measure the strength of a state's anti-pollution efforts by the amount of government money it spends on air quality control, taking fiscal year 1991 as representative (Brown & Marshall, 1993; see Ridley, 1987 and Hall & Kerr, 1991 for expenditures in other years). On average, about one third of state air expenditures are contributed by the federal government. In general, state and federal expenditures increase with population size. Our variables *Total state expenditure* and *Federal contribution* are adjusted to remove population effects.

Environmentalist Ratings

Following Ringquist (1993), we adopt ratings by environmental organizations of the stringency of each state's regulatory policies. The group Renew America in 1987 rated the strength of state air programs on a scale of one to ten (best) based on legislative authority for programs, scope of established programs, funding, extent of monitoring, research activity, enforcement, and indications of progress (Ridley, 1987, pp. 8, 32). Features of the rating give an overall advantage to states with larger populations, an effect that we removed from our variable *Renew rating*.

Another environmental organization, the Institute for Southern Studies, scored the states according to the percentage of 50 environmental policies they had adopted, including measures affecting recycling, landfills, toxic waste, water quality, agriculture, energy and transit, and pollution (Hall & Kerr, 1991). Often called the Green index, this rating includes four policies concerning air quality, causing a slight overlap with *Renew rating*. While the Green index does not focus on air quality, it has the advantage of being a purer measure of environmental policy, independent of expenditures or degree of pollution. Green index values correlate with population size, an effect we have removed to obtain the corrected variable *Green rating*.

Compliance Cost

Levinson (1997) proposes a new economic measure for the stringency of state environmental regulation. The Census Bureau's Pollution Abatement Costs and Expenditures survey asks manufacturers to complete questionnaires about their pollution abatement costs, providing data of unknown validity. Levinson statistically equates the industrial mix of all states. His method is to first calculate the nationwide pollution abatement cost for each major industry, then to calculate each state's adjusted pollution abatement cost as a weighted average of the nationwide abatement costs for all of its industries. He then regards each state's industry-adjusted abatement cost, averaged over the years 1977–1992, as a measure of its regulatory stringency. Although Levinson's measure of state stringency may partly reflect non-regulatory costs, such as those based on differences in geography or climate, we adopt it as our variable *Compliance cost* after removing its correlation with state population size. The period over which Levinson has averaged, 1977–1992, approximates our period of concern.

Background Variables

Federal agencies report many state-level data, if not always on characteristics we wish to measure. Given the limited degrees of freedom in a 50-state data set, it is necessary to exclude potentially interesting background variables too numerous to use. For example, Ringquist (1993) found that states with the most professional legislatures (indicated by the number of days in the legislative session, number of bills introduced, compensation level of state legislators, etc) had the most stringent regulatory policy; however we found legislative professionalism to be strongly correlated with state population size, and therefore, since any effects of professionalism and population cannot be separated, we dropped professionalism as being redundant.

Time 1 Pollution

In order to average out year-to-year fluctuations in a state's emission levels, we follow Ringquist in calculating mean emissions over the period 1986–1991 for SO_2 (*Time 1* SO_2) and for NO_X (*Time 1* NO_X). Effects of population size are removed. *Time 1* SO_2 is used in models of SO_2 change, *Time 1* NO_X in models of NO_X change.

State Product

There is considerable redundancy among the many measures of a state's economic and industrial activity. We have chosen an overall indicator, gross state product, defined as the gross market value of the goods and services attributable to labor and property located in a state. We use values for 1989 (U.S. Census, 1992, Table 685), calling the variable *State product* after removing the population effect. *State product* is correlated with other indicators of industrialism, for example electricity production ($r = 0.65$, $p < 0.0001$), and inversely with coal use ($r = -0.36$, $p < 0.01$).

Environmentalism

Early researchers recognized that a critical element of state culture is the extent of public support for environmental issues, but they lacked adequate means to measure it. We create a new state-level measure, *Environmentalism*, by combining (with equal weights) membership in environmental organizations, the environmental voting record of the state's delegation to the U.S. Congress, and public opinion about environmental spending (Cronbach alpha for standardized variables = 0.77); as usual, the population effect is removed.

More specifically, for environmental organizations, we use total membership (per 1,000 population) in the Sierra Club, National Wildlife Federation, and Greenpeace USA (Hall & Kerr, 1991, p. 111). The League of Conservation Voters (1998; Hall & Kerr, 1991, p. 125) yearly rates members of the U.S. Congress on about 15 bills selected for having clear pro-environmental and anti-environmental positions. Each state's environmental record in the U.S. Congress is here calculated as the average pro-environmental vote for all its members of the House and Senate over the years 1970 to 1990. (Since these are federal legislators, their votes have no direct impact on state-to-state variation in regulatory stringency.) Public opinion is based on the General Social Survey, which has asked national samples nearly every year since 1973 if the country is spending too much money, too little, or about the right amount on "improving and protecting the environment" (Davis & Smith, 1996). Merging answers from over 23,000 respondents with a separate file giving respondents' state of residence, we obtained adequate state-level samples (Mazur & Welch, 1998). Alaska and Hawaii are excluded from this survey, so *Environmentalism* is available for only 48 states.

Environmentalism is correlated with other relevant indicators of state culture, including vote for Ronald Reagan in the 1984 presidential election ($r = -0.45$, $p < 0.001$), and average personal income ($r = 0.78$, $p < 0.001$). Therefore we use it as our single indicator of citizen characteristics.

Unfortunately, a time-series analysis is precluded because the public opinion component of *Environmentalism* is aggregated over the period 1973–1996 in order to obtain a sufficient number of respondents in each state. Also, state-level membership in environmental organizations is not easily obtainable for each year. Additionally, the considerable noise in yearly values for pollutant emissions, noted above, diminishes our prospects for systematically explaining year-to-year variation. Therefore we rely on cross-sectional models to explain state-to-state variation.

RESULTS

Are States Consistent over Time in Pollution Reductions?

Table 1 is a correlation matrix of changes in each pollutant (SO_2 and NO_X) in each time period (1973–1987 and 1986–1996). For neither pollutant is there a significant correlation between *Change 1973–1987* and *βChange 1986–1996.* Thus, states are not consistent across time periods in their emission reductions. On the other hand, *within each time period* there is a significant correlation between SO_2 change and NO_X change, indicating that pollutants go up and down together.

Table 1. Correlations Among Changes in Pollutant Emissions During Two Time Periods.

	SO_2 ßChange 1986–1996	NO_2 Change 1973–1987	NOx ßChange 1986–1996
SO_2 Change 1973–1987	0.04	0.58***	0.01
SO_2 ßChange 1986–1996		0.11	0.33*
NO_2 Change 1973–1987			0.07

*** $p < 0.001$; ** $p < 0.01$; * $p < 0.05$.

Are Diverse Measures of State Stringency Consistent and Valid?

We have measured the stringency of state regulatory policies in three ways: by expenditures for air quality (*Total state expenditure*, and *Federal contribution*), by environmentalist ratings of the stringency of control policies (*Renew* and *Green ratings*), and by the *compliance cost* to meet the state's regulatory demands – all adjusted for population size. Do these measures identify the same states as being more or less stringent? If all, or nearly all, measures cluster together, we gain confidence that they have "convergent validity" (Pettigrew, 1996), tapping the same underlying dimension of regulatory stringency.

Table 2 (top) is a correlation matrix among the five measures. The two measures of government expenditure are highly correlated, and both are moderately correlated to *Green rating* (but not to *Renew rating*). *Renew rating* and *Green rating* are moderately correlated. *Compliance cost* stands by itself, showing no relationship to environmentalist ratings or to government expenditures. Thus, we must abandon any hope that these measures tap a common dimension of regulatory stringency.

The "criterion validity" of these measures may be assessed by asking which ones, if any, actually relate to decreases in pollutant emissions, the reasoning being that the most valid indicator of stringency is the one that best predicts its presumed effect (Pettigrew, 1996). Table 2 (bottom) shows correlations between the measures of regulatory stringency and changes in pollutant emissions in both time periods. A negative correlation indicates that stringency is associated with a reduction in pollution. *Green rating* shows the most significantly negative correlations; it consistently outperforms *Renew index* as a predictor of emissions reductions. *Compliance cost* is significantly related to SO_2 changes in both periods but not to NO_X changes. Correlation between expenditures and emissions changes, while usually negative, never reach significance.

Since *Green rating* and *Compliance cost* (both adjusted for population) are the measures of regulatory stringency that best yield significant relationships with emissions changes, and they are independent, we use both in the following analysis.

The Full Model

We implement the model in Fig. 1 with independent variables representing stringency of state air policy (*Green rating* and *Compliance cost*), Time 1 pollution (SO_2 or NO_X), and background indicators of state economic activity (*State product*) and citizen culture (*Environmentalism*). Although population effects have been removed from all these variables to minimize collinearity,

Table 2. Correlation Among Measures of State Regulatory Stringency (Top), and Correlation Between Regulatory Stringency and Changes in Emissions (Bottom).

	Total state expenditure	Federal contribution	Renew rating	Green rating	Compliance cost
Federal Contribution	0.78***				
Renew Rating	0.17	0.10			
Green Rating	0.29*	0.29*	0.42**		
Compliance Cost	–0.07	–0.08	–0.21	–0.19	
SO_2 Change 1973–1987	–0.01	–0.08	–0.35**	–0.46***	–0.33*
SO_2 ßChange 1986–1996	–0.04	–0.20	0.11	0.00	–0.32*
NO_2 Change 1973–1987	–0.04	–0.08	–0.29*	–0.56***	0.03
NO_X ßChange 1986–1996	–0.14	–0.26	–0.06	–0.29*	–0.06

*** $p < 0.001$; ** $p < 0.01$; * $p < 0.05$.

there is still considerable correlation among them (Table 3). The high association between *Environmentalism* and *Green rating* ($r = 0.80$) suggests that in other theoretical contexts these might be conceptualized as two faces of a single construct (Mazur & Welch, 1998). Its relevance in this context is that *Environmentalism* may explain the relationship between *Green rating* and emission reduction, rendering it spurious.

Collinearity among independent variables raises problems of interpretation, even with moderate correlation like the $r = 0.58$ between *State product* and

Table 3. Correlation Among Independent Variables.

	Time 1 NO_X	State product	Environmentalism	Green rating	Compliance cost
Time 1 SO_2	0.32*	–0.41**	–0.22	–0.38**	0.13
Time 1 NO_X		0.03	–0.39**	–0.38**	0.22
State Product			0.58***	0.37**	–0.34**
Environmentalism				0.80***	–0.25
Green rating					–0.19

*** $p < 0.001$; ** $p < 0.01$; * $p < 0.05$.

Environmentalism (Gordon, 1968). If their shared variance explains variation in the dependent variable, there is no way to properly apportion explanatory effects between them; the regression coefficients of correlated independent variables cannot be interpreted at face value.

We will test for a spurious relationship between stringency and emission reduction, first for SO_2, then for NO_X. Table 4 contains standardized coefficients (betas) and explained variances ($R^2_{adjusted}$) for six regression equations. *SO_2 βChange 1986–1996* is the dependent variable in Eqs. 1 to 3; *NO_X βChange 1986–1996* is the dependent variable in Eqs. 4 to 6. $R^2_{adjusted}$ ranges over the six models from moderate (0.24) to low (0.03), indicating that most of the variation in pollutant emissions is unexplained either by regulatory stringency or background variables. Of course, explained variance would be higher if the controls on population were released, but we regard this as an improvement without substance.

The first step in evaluating the model for SO_2 is to regress *SO_2 βChange 1986–1996* on our two measures of regulatory stringency (*Green rating* and *Compliance cost*) and the initial emission level (*Time 1 SO_2*). The betas in Eq. 1 show *Compliance cost*, but not *Green rating*, to be related significantly and negatively to *SO_2 βChange 1986–1996*. These results, consistent with those in Table 2, show the greatest reductions in SO_2 to be in states with the highest *Compliance cost*; *Green rating* is irrelevant.

In Eq. 2, *SO_2 βChange 1986–1996* is regressed on our two background variables (*State product* and *Environmentalism*) and *Time 1 SO_2*. *Time 1 SO_2* is the sole variable with a significant effect, and this model explains little of the change in SO_2, its R^2 – adjusted for the number of independent variables – only 0.03.

Table 4. Standardized Regression Coefficients (Betas) for Six Equations of Pollution Change During the Period 1986–1996.

Equation:	(1)	(2)	(3)	(4)	(5)	(6)
Dep. var:	SO_2 βchange 1986–1996	SO_2 βchange 1986–1996	SO_2 βchange 1986–1996	NO_X βchange 1986–1996	NO_X βchange 1986–1996	NO_X βchange 1986–1996
Time 1 SO_2	–0.27	–0.32*	–0.35*	–	–	–
Time 1 NO_X	–	–	–	–0.09	–0.10	–0.03
State Product	–	–0.34	–0.27	–	–0.27	–0.34*
Environmentalism	–	–0.07	–0.06	–	–0.32	–0.38
Green Rating	–0.17	–	–0.05	–0.34*	–	0.10
Compliance cost	–0.31*	–	–0.38**	–0.11	–	0.26
$R^2_{adjusted}$	0.11*	0.03	0.13*	0.05	0.21**	0.24**

** $p < 0.01$; * $p < 0.05$.

Equation 3, the full model, allows us to evaluate the effect of *Compliance cost* on emission reduction while controlling all other independent variables. Here the beta for *Compliance cost* is stronger and more significant than in the first equation; the only other variable that has explanatory power is *Time 1* SO_2. Other background variables add practically nothing; the $R^2 = 0.13$ of the full model is barely higher than the $R^2 = 0.11$ of Eq. 1.

We obtain a different picture when we repeat these steps for the NO_X model. Equation 4 shows that *Green rating*, but not *Compliance cost*, is significantly and negatively related to NO_X *ßChange 1986–1996*. Equation 5 has considerably more explanatory power than Eq. 4 ($R^2 = 0.21$ versus $R^2 = 0.05$), however none of its betas reach significance. [Note: This seeming inconsistency is explained by the high correlation between *State product* and *Environmentalism*, which "splits" their shared explanatory effect between them. If either is entered alone into the equation, it has a significant beta].

Finally, the full model in Eq. 6 shows the effect of each variable with all others controlled. The result, a disappointment for policy makers, is that regulatory stringency, whether measured by the *Green rating* or *Compliance cost*, has no significant effect on NO_X reduction that is independent of the background variables.

If background variables – especially *Environmentalism* – eliminate the ostensibly felicitous effect of *Green rating* on pollutant reductions over

Table 5. Standardized Regression Coefficients (Betas) for Six Models of Pollution Change During the Period 1973–1987

Model:	(1)	(2)	(3)	(4)	(5)	(6)
Dep. var:	SO_2 change 1973–1987	SO_2 change 1973–1987	SO_2 change 1973–1987	NO_2 change 1973–1987	NO_2 change 1973–1987	NO_2 change 1973–1987
GSP	–	0.37*	0.23	–	0.31*	0.29*
Environmentalism	–	–0.66***	–0.51*	–	–0.78***	–0.61**
Green rating	–0.54***	–	–0.22	–0.58***	–	–0.20
Compliance cost	–0.43***	–	–0.42***	–0.08	–	–0.04
$R^2_{adjusted}$	0.36***	0.26***	0.41***	0.29***	0.40***	0.39***

*** $p < 0.001$; ** $p < 0.01$; * $p < 0.05$.

the period 1986–1996, might they also do so for 1973–1987? We pursue this question by applying the model (less T1 pollutant levels, which we lack) to this earlier period. Standardized coefficients for the relevant regression equations appear in Table 5, where the dependent variables are *SO_2 Change 1973–1987* in Eqs. 1 to 3, and *NO_2 Change 1973–1987* in Eqs. 4 to 6.

The results of Eqs. 1 to 3, in abbreviate form, show that after controlling on background factors, *Compliance cost*, but not *Green rating*, has a significant and negative effect on *SO_2 Change 1973–1987*. Equations 4 to 6 show that after controlling on background factors, neither measure of regulatory stringency has a significant effect on *NO_2 Change 1973–1987*. Thus, these overall conclusions are essentially the same for both time periods, although there are for unknown reasons considerably higher significance levels and explained variances in Table 5 than Table 4.

Population

Population effects were removed from all variables in the analysis, as if making the states statistically equal in size. As a final step, empirical conclusions were re-examined with these population controls removed. Some zero-order correlations changed greatly. An extreme example is the correlation between *Time 1 SO_2* and *State product*, its population-corrected value reported in Table 3 as $r = –0.41$, now becoming $r = +0.55$. Despite these changes, *Compliance cost* remains a significant predictor of SO_2 change, with background variables controlled, but not of NO_X change. *Green rating* still has insignificant effects on both pollutants. Thus, our basic findings are robust.

DISCUSSION

The various states are faced with pollution problems that are physically different, and they take diverse approaches to control that are sometimes pursued with vigor but sometimes not, making it hard to gauge their regulatory efforts. We find, after comparing several quantitative measures of state regulatory stringency – government expenditures, environmentalist ratings, compliance cost – that these do not tap a common dimension.

Beside lacking convergent validity, most measures of regulatory stringency lack criterion validity too. Government expenditures for air quality do not correlate with changes in emissions. Environmentalist ratings, especially the Green index, do have significant zero-order correlation with some emission reductions, but these become insignificant when background variables are controlled. Only *Compliance cost* robustly correlates with emission change, despite statistical controls, but only for SO_2 reductions, not for NO_X.

Yet *Compliance cost* is a problematic measure of regulation, based not on overt actions by state government, but on dollars spent by manufacturers for pollution abatement – both operating and capital costs. Levenson (1997) describes these compliance costs (after statistical adjustment to give each state an equivalent industry mix) as an "index of state environmental regulatory stringency." His premise is that abatement costs to industry are primarily due to regulatory demands of the state, and that state-to-state variation in these costs (after adjusting for industry mix) reflects variation in regulatory demands. But abatement costs may vary from state to state if for no other reason than differing physical conditions. For example, coal is cheaply availability in some states, hydro power in others; also, local climate affects the need for ozone control. Thus, compliance costs conflate state differences in physical conditions with state differences in regulatory stringency. Levenson (personal communication) responds that if local geographical differences make pollution abatement an important policy objective, then those will be reflected in costs via regulations (in the same way that local tastes will be); it doesn't matter if the source of the relative stringency differences is local tastes or local climates. To resolve this debate, we need a better understanding of the motivations behind corporate spending for pollution abatement. Is spending essentially driven by state regulatory demands, or are non-regulatory factors important too?

In any case, our results barely sustain Ringquist's (1993a, b) optimistic conclusion that stringent state regulation pays off in reduced pollution emissions. Indeed, controlling on public *Environmentalism*, a variable not available to Ringquist, renders insignificant those correlations that supported his conclusion. The most we can say for the power of regulation is that *Compliance cost* – a dubious conceptualization of regulatory stringency – predicts reductions of SO_2 (but not of NO_X).

Our background variables sometimes explain as much or more change in emissions than does regulatory stringency. For SO_2, but not NO_X, we find support for the common assumption that Time 1 pollution level predicts subsequent changes in emissions: higher initial SO_2 meant greater subsequent reductions in SO_2. The combination of gross state product and *Environmentalism* is especially potent in explaining changes in NO_X emissions. Despite interpretive problems caused by the high correlation between these variables, it is clear that *Environmentalism*, the tendency of a state's citizens to support environmental issues, strongly predicted pollutant reductions in the period 1973–1987, less so in the later period.

What are the policy implications of this analysis? Our failure to find a correlation between government expenditures and emission reductions should not be seen as a green light to reduce expenditures. One can hardly doubt that government regulation requires funding. We do wonder, however, if states optimally use these funds.

Our most important and disturbing finding is that, overall, regulatory stringency does not predict pollution reduction (excepting the problematic effect of *Compliance cost* on SO_2). In interpreting this result, we emphasize its limitations. First of all, it does *not* mean that air regulation accomplishes no good. Clearly, environmental regulation at the federal level has reduced air pollution overall (EPA, 1997). At issue is whether state-to-state variation in the stringency of regulation produces an observable effect on emissions in each state, and on this point we are pessimistic. Our failure to find a robust relationship may simply reflect the difficulty of measuring regulatory stringency. The fact remains, however, that those states which most observers *think* are the most stringent have little more success in reducing emissions than states with reputations for relaxed regulation, after background variables are controlled.

We suggest that a state's background factors, especially its level of *Environmentalism*, can lead to reduced emissions by some mechanism other than the stringency of the state's regulatory enforcement. Possibly the citizens and non-governmental institutions of highly environmental states place direct pressure on polluters, effecting reductions apart from the mediation of regulatory agencies. Possibly executives of polluting corporations who reside in these states are themselves relatively concerned with air quality and therefore amenable to emission reductions without being forced into them, or perhaps they see pollution reduction simply as good for their public image, as good business. Legal enforcement aside, it is more socially unacceptable to run a blatantly polluting facility in an environmentally conscious state like California or Maine than in states whose citizens show little concern, like Utah or Mississippi (Mazur & Welch, 1998). We advocate a double-barreled approach to pollution reduction, based not only on stronger government enforcement but on stronger citizen pressure too.

One might argue that *Environmentalism* and regulatory stringency are not really separate variables, that regulation is the instrument through which the state affects pollution, so together they make a single package. Analogously, one might argue that a weapon is the instrument with which a murderer affects his victim; therefore the presence of killers and the availability of weapons ought not be regarded as separate variables in explaining murder rates, that they operate as a package. In this conceptualization, it is pointless to explain away the association between killers and murder by controlling on the availability of weapons. This is an issue that cannot be settled with correlational data. Its resolution would require a grand social experiment, comparing reductions in pollution (or murder) in states with and without stringent regulation (weapons). For conceptual discussions of these explanatory issues, see Barron and Kenny (1986) or Pettigrew (1996).

In any case, we see that changes in NO_X emissions are explained differently than changes in SO_2 emissions, suggesting that the two pollutants require different strategies for reduction. In retrospect this is not surprising. Nearly all SO_2 comes from large stationary industrial sources, mostly electric generation plants. It is fairly easy to control a few large and salient polluters, who may even control themselves under cooperative inducements. NO_X, in contrast, comes from more dispersed sources; about a third is produced by vehicles. These source differences may explain the relatively successful reduction of SO_2 since 1970, while NO_X emissions have not changed much. Although we have not analyzed CO_2 emissions, their origination from numerous dispersed sources suggests that, like NO_X, they will be harder to reduce than SO_2.

REFERENCES

Baron, R., & Kenny, D. (1986). The Moderator-mediator Variable Distinction in Social Psychology Research. *Journal of Personality and Social Psychology*, *51*, 1173–1182.

Brown, R., & Marshall, K. (1993). *Resource Guide to State Environmental Management* (3rd ed.). Lexington KY: Council of State Governments.

Davies, J., & Mazurek, J. (1997). *Regulating Pollution*. Washington, D.C.: Resources for the Future.

Davis, J., & Smith, T. (1996). *General Social Surveys, 1972–1996*: Cumulative Codebook. Chicago: National Opinion Research Center.

EPA (1997). *National Air Pollutant Emission Trends, 1900–1996*. EPA-454/R-97-011. Research Triangle Park NC: EPA.

Gordon, R. (1968). Issues in Multiple Regression. *American Journal of Sociology*, *73*, 592–616.

Hall, B., & Kerr, M. (1991). *1991–1992 Green Index*. Washington, D.C.: Island Press.

Lester, J. (1994). A New Federalism? Environmental Policy in the States. In: N. Vig & M. Kraft (Eds), *Environmental Policy in the 1990s* (pp. 51–68). Washington, D.C.: Congressional Quarterly Press.

Lester, J. (1995). Federalism and State Environmental Policy. In: J. Lester (Ed.), *Environmental Politics & Policy* (2nd ed.) (pp. 39–60). Durham NC: Duke University Press.

Levinson, A. (1997). *An Industry-Adjusted Index of State Environmental Regulatory Stringency*. Economics Department. University of Wisconsin-Madison.

Lombard, E. (1993). Determinants of State Air-Quality Management: A Comparative Analysis. *American Review of Public Administration*, *23*, 57–73.

Lowry, W. (1992). *The Dimensions of Federalism: State Governments and Pollution Control Policies*. Durham NC: Duke University Press.

Mazur, A., & Welch, E. (1998). *The Geography of American Environmentalism*. Syracuse University.

Pettigrew, T. (1966). *How to Think Like a Social Scientist*. New York: HarperCollins.

Ridley, S. (1987). *The State of the States 1987*. Washington, D.C.: Fund for Renewable Energy and the Environment.

Ringquist, E. (1993a). *Environmental Protection at the State Level*. London: M. E. Sharpe.

Ringquist, E. (1993b). Does Regulation Matter?: Evaluating the Effects of State Air Pollution Control Programs. *Journal of Politics*, *55*, 1022–1045.

Rosenbaum, W. (1997). The EPA at Risk: Conflicts over Institutional Reform. In: N. Vig & M. Kraft (Eds), *Environmental Policy in the 1990s* (3rd ed.) (pp. 143–167). Washington, D.C.: CQ Press.

Tukey, J. (1977). *Exploratory Data Analysis*. Reading, MA: Addison-Wesley.

U.S. Bureau of the Census (1992). *Statistical Abstract of the United States: 1992*. Washington, D.C.

ENVIRONMENTAL GOVERNMENTALITY AS A BASIS FOR REGULATORY REFORM: THE ADAPTATION OF NEW POLICY INSTRUMENTS IN FINLAND

Rauno Sairinen

REGULATORY REFORM AND THE SHIFT TOWARDS NEW POLICY INSTRUMENTS

The limitations and regulatory failures of the traditional command and control approach have sparked a search for a *second generation* of instruments, which promises greater flexibility, efficiency, effectiveness and legitimacy. Leveque (1996a) has noted that there is a general *regulatory reform* taking place in environmental policy-making. The change in the choice of policy instruments is a world-wide trend. Since the beginning of the nineties, the number of eco-taxes, tradeable permits and voluntary approaches has been increasing in industrialized countries. This development means that the features of emerging environmental state are continuously in transition.

The regulatory reform has been especially drastic inside the European Union. The broadening of the set of policy instruments has been one of the key orientations of the new EU approach, as defined in the fifth action program

The article is based on the dissertation of the author (Sairinen, 2000).

The Environmental State Under Pressure, Volume 10, pages 85–103.

ISBN: 0-7623-0854-0

'*Towards Sustainability*' (COM, 1993). Another key orientation of the new EU approach is the dialogue and consultation with the concerned parties. Nowadays, most member states endorse the use of stakeholder consultation in the development of new environmental regulation (Leveque, 1996a). According to an analysis by Kooiman et al. *(Modern Governance*, 1993), new ways of interaction between government and society in terms of governance and governing exist. Governing is not considered an activity restricted to governments and ministries, but as more or less continuous process of interaction between social actors, groups and forces and public or semi public organizations, institutions and authorities.

The regulatory reform has experimented with an impressive range of new public policy tools, which can be classified as '*economic*', '*co-regulation*' and '*planning*' instruments. In addition, the private sector has itself developed so-called '*self-regulation*' instruments (Leveque, 1996b; Glasbergen, 1998; Mol, Lauber & Liefferink, 2000). The economic instruments include several types of environmental taxes and charges, tradeable pollution permit systems and government subsidies for environmental improvement. New planning instruments for environmental improvement include different types of activities that may involve, for instance, urban compaction, energy demand management and environmental impact assessment. Co-regulation (joint policy-making) is a category that covers cases where the interactive relationships between public authorities and firms are especially pervasive and close. It consists of voluntary agreements, ecolabels and conflict resolution models. Self-regulation corresponds to the increasing number of so-called self-initiatives and responsible care programs.

THE GOVERNING MENTALITIES BEHIND THE REGULATORY REFORM

The emergence of the new environmental policy instruments has often been associated with the ideas of '*free-market environmentalism*' and the more general deregulative policies (Eckersley, 1995; Collier, 1998). Supporters of these ideas favor the reduction of pollution into an optimal level – defined as the amount of reduction which consumers are willing to pay for once the full social costs of negative externalities are reflected in market prices. The idea is that policy instruments should inhibit the 'market efficient behavior' of economic actors as little as possible.

On the other hand, the regulatory reform has been linked to the strategy of ecological modernization (Mol, Lauber & Liefferink, 2000; Liefferink & Mol,

1998). In its different modes, the ecological modernization theory has stressed the increasing importance of economic and market dynamics in ecological reform and the role of innovators, entrepreneurs and other economic agents as social carriers of ecological restructuring, in addition to state agencies and new social movements.

If regulatory reform is linked to these general societal trends, such as deregulation and ecological modernization, the whole question can be connected to the governing rationalities and mentalities. For example, it has been argued that in the era of ecological modernization, direct regulation is not always the best way to attain additional environmental benefits, at least in a cost-efficient way. These conditions justify the regulatory reform and also change the underlying mentalities of environmental governing. Using Foucault's concept, we may speak of changes in '*governmentality*'.

The changes in governmentality as well as the reactions, discourses and ethical judgements about these changes, produce continuous pressures to develop the governing systems and tools. The most obvious question is, how the emerging 'environmental state' and its policy actors can govern the complex and dynamic systems of different authorities, governing tools and new public/private relationships. In this context, the environmental state refers to the state institution which receives and also actively assumes more and more environmental duties and develops various administrative systems and new governing instruments for this purpose. To study this is to ask, in what direction the governing mentality of environmental policy is developing; what factors and forces influence this development; and what the effects of new policy initiatives in society are. From the governmentality perspective, regulatory reform is not only an issue that concerns new administrative 'tools' to be used in an instrumental fashion, but a question of new kinds of policy styles, rationalities, procedures and mentalities of policy-making.

What is Governmentality?

The term '*governmentality*' ('*gouvernementalite*') is a neologism Foucault presented and explored at the end of the 1970s (Foucault, 1991, 1984). There are two important aspects to governmentality in Foucault's writings (see also Darier, 1996). First, this concept is based on the European historical context. Secondly, it implies a novel definition of power that has profound implications for our understanding of contemporary political power and, in particular, public policy. Governmentality implied the establishment of complex social techniques and institutions to intensify the mechanism of control over the population in the name of what became known as the 'reason of state'.

When analysing the concept of governmentality, it should be noted that Foucault was mainly interested in long-term historical trends. He wrote about what he terms *"a history of governmentality"* (Foucault, 1991). For Foucault, governmentality describes a new form of deployment of political power that emerged in Europe in the sixteenth century and established a new world order based on states. In the context of an international system based on state interests and competition between states, it became imperative for each state to create conditions for ensuring its security and ultimately its survival. Among other things, this implied a greater control over its population for obvious military purposes, and an interventionist attitude to promote the economic well-being of the country to finance the state's efforts in guaranteeing its security (Foucault, 1991; Darier, 1996). It also led to the state's increasing concern with the biological well-being of the population, including disease control and prevention, adequate food and water supply, sanitary dwellings, education and so on. The new pastoral techniques meant that the 'shepherd' (the church and now the state) 'took care' of the well-being of the population, while guiding them by instilling in each individual the techniques of self-control. In Foucault's writings, the emancipatory project of the Enlightenment is exemplified by such theories as the 'sovereignty' of the people, which legitimised power only by referring to the willingness of its subjects to obey.

The term governmentality sought to draw attention to a certain way of thinking and acting embodied in all such attempts to know and govern the wealth, health and happiness of the population (Rose & Miller, 1992, pp. 174–175). Foucault argued that, since the eighteenth century, this way of reflecting upon power and seeking to render it operable had achieved pre-eminence over other forms of political power. It was linked to the proliferation of a whole range of apparatuses pertaining to government and a complex body of knowledges about government, the means of its exercise and the nature of those over whom it was to be exercised. For Foucault, governmentality is a fundamental feature of the modern state.

Most significantly, Foucault sees state authorities and policies as mobilising governmentality which tries to incorporate the economy and the population into the political practices of the state in order to be able to govern effectively in a rational and conscious manner (Foucault, 1991; Luke, 1995). Governmentality, then, applies techniques of instrumental rationality to the arts of everyday management exercised over the economy, the society and, in the context of this study, also the environment.

In order to study Canadian environmental politics, Darier (1996) has crystallised Foucault's idea of governmentality into a three-dimensional framework, where the central components are institutional centralisation, normalisation and the intensification of the effects of power and power/knowledge. These categories also represent the main power effects which modern state policies can have on private and societal lives.[1]

(1) The centralization of power around the government (army, education, governmental ministries, justice etc.). Here, we ask whether the centralization of institutions, procedures, strategies and policy activities around the state is increasing or decreasing. This component is what policy studies usually examine. Foucault's strong argument is that the long-term historical trend is characterized by governmental centralization that has as its target the population and the technical means of security.
(2) The intensification of the effects of power at the levels of the entire population, the economy and the individual. Traditional policy studies rest on the core assumption that there is a central locus of power that can be the state, a social class or an elite. This view rests on an assumption of a 'top-down' model of political power in which the exercise of power is mainly repressive. Policy decisions are made at the 'top' and the population (the 'bottom') merely obeys or disobeys orders. For Foucault, 'power produces': it produces reality, it produces domains of objects and rituals of truth (Foucault, 1991). This 'positive' or 'productive' side of modern power means that control, and self-control, of the population is considered achievable by the standardization of individual and collective conducts through the normalization of individual and collective subjectivity. The normalization of subjectivity gives individuals and groups an identity which in turn enables them to act in congruence with or to resist the objectives of the normalization process. In this sense, it can be claimed that 'modern society has no control center' (Beck, 1992) and that power can be conceptualized as a 'field of power' as was already stated earlier.
(3) The emergence of new forms of (scientific) knowledge useful for the implementation of centralization and/or intensification of power (power/knowledge). For Foucault – and for an increasing number of historians, philosophers and sociologists – knowledge can no longer be perceived as the objective and politically detached study of the reality of truth. On the contrary, the objects of scientific knowledge are intimately intertwined with existing power relations. This is what Foucault calls '*power/knowledge*' – ('*pouvoir/savoir*') a single word – to epitomize the inescapable links between 'power' and 'knowledge'. Although there are some differences, a similar concern with the power effects of knowledge claims is an important feature of the sociology of reflexivity formulated by Beck, Giddens and Lash (1994). In the theory of reflexive modernization, conflicting 'expert

> systems' and new problems concerning trust and security are seen to open up new political spaces and fields of power struggle. The notions of nowledge/power and expert systems generate a research interests where the object of study is the ways in which knowledge is used socially and politically rather than the question of whether knowledge is true or false.

The concept of governmentality offers a different perspective on political phenomena conventionally addressed in terms of the state and state intervention or regulation. But, it is also clear that governmentality is a concept that is very difficult to define explicitly. It is more an approach for understanding and interpreting the elements of power in the policy process than a clearly defined analytic concept. According to this logic, the priority is to answer questions about what it means to individuals, populations or organizations to be governed and be under governance, and how the modes of governance influence our lives, cultures, actor relations, etc. (Helen, 1995).

A THEORETICAL FRAMEWORK FOR ANALYZING REGULATORY REFORM

In policy science literature the choice and formation of policy instruments has been modeled by several authors. Linder and Peters (1989) have developed a model that integrates many of the various conceptions of instrument choice put forward in both economics and political science literatures. They list the following five factors as playing a critical role in shaping instrument choice (Table 1).

First, *the features of policy instruments* are important for selection purposes, because some instruments are more suited for a task at hand than others. Second, they argue that a nation's *policy style and political culture*, and the depth of its social cleavages, have a critical bearing on the choice of an instrument. Each nation has a peculiar national style, culture, and pattern of social conflicts, which predispose its decision-makers to choose a particular instrument. Third, they argue that the choice of an instrument is circumscribed by the *organizational culture* of the agencies concerned and by the nature of their links with clients and other agencies. Fourth, they argue that the *context of the problem situation* will also affect the choice of instruments.

For Linder and Peters, however, instrument choice is ultimately a matter of the decision-makers' subjective preferences, which is based on their professional background, institutional affiliation, and cognitive make-up. They define the situational context constraining choice and implant their professional and personal preferences on instrument choice.

Table 1. Model of Policy Instrument Choice (Linder & Peters, 1989).

(1) The features of policy instruments	
	Resource intensiveness (including administrative costs and operational simplicity).
	Targeting (including precision and selectivity).
	Political risk (including nature of support and opposition, public visibility and chances of failure).
	Constraints on state activity (including difficulties with coerciveness and ideological principles limiting government activity).
(2) The political culture and the nation's policy style	
	predispose decision-makers to choose a particular instrument.
(3) The organizational culture	
	The organizational culture of the concerned agencies and the nature of their links with clients and other agencies.
(4) The context of the problem situation	
	Its timing and the scope of actors.
(5) The decision-makers' subjective preferences	
	These are based on their professional background, institutional affiliation and cognitive makeup.

In Linder and Peters' model, there is a complex rationale for instrument choice emphasizing the characteristics of different instruments and the situational context in which the choice is made. However, the model has some major shortcoming. The main shortcoming lies in inadequate conceptualization of how the actor's preferences and mentalities are formed and realized. In addition, the institutional backgrounds need some further elaboration, so that the dynamics between different dimensions becomes clearer.

By combining the main features of Linder and Peters' model and the concept of governmentality, we can present the following theoretical framework for analyzing regulatory reform (see Fig. 1 for a schematic overview). The model does not provide a strict explanatory framework for the analysis of regulatory reform, because, although some causalities are obvious, I do not believe that any strong causal relationships between different influencing factors exist. Thus, the framework has the same heuristic intention as the approach of Linder and Peters.

Foucault's concept of governmentality brings up important approaches, which are not involved in Linder and Peters' model. It seems that, as a concept of policy analysis, governmentality refers to two different approaches: (1) the 'fixed' and structured approach of governance, and (2) the 'power effects' of policy activities and processes. The former refers to the mentality of governing in which the interpretation, general approach and the institutional framework to policy problems (here, policy instrument choice) are more or less fixed. This 'fixed' approach can contain institutional, politico-cultural and knowledge/

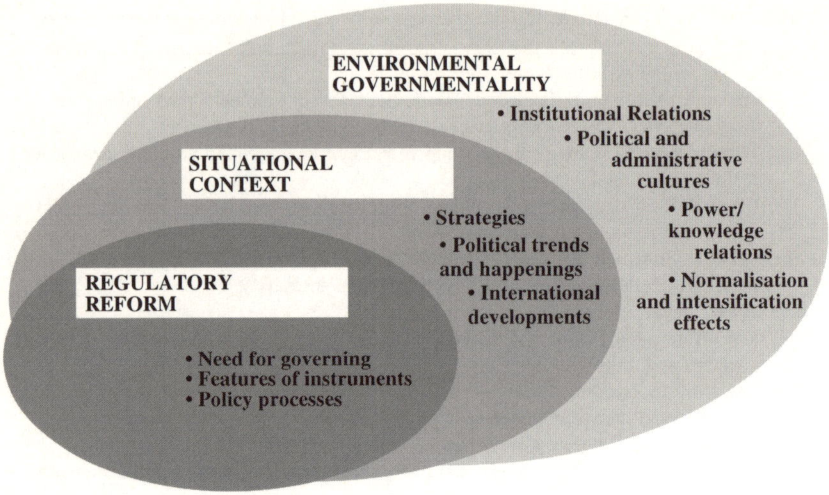

Fig. 1. The Framework for Analysing Regulatory Reform.

power aspects of the policy process. The governing actors always have a particular mentality for main policy issues such as welfare, foreign relations or quality of the environment (Rose & Miller, 1992, p. 189). The latter perspective concerns the power effects of policy choices for e.g. normalization and intensification processes and changes of the institutional actor-structure. These governmentality effects refer to the dynamics through which policy choices produce new routines in the societal life.

The theoretical framework introduces the concept of 'environmental governmentality' that refers to the general mentalities and power structures of environmental governance (see Darier, 1996; Luke, 1995). Here, Darier's three-dimensional typology of Foucault's governmentality provides a useful starting point. But it needs some reformulation. The centralization of power around the government is a macro-political trend, which can be analyzed in different ways during different time-periods. For example, the deregulative trend is a clear 'anti-trend' towards the centralization. After the crisis of welfare state institutions and the global trend of neoliberalism as a political rationality, the centralization thesis could be interpreted in a rather different manner (Collier, 1998; Barry, Osborne & Rose, 1996). Nevertheless, in this study the main need for reformulation is to make the dimension more analytic and less normative. Thus, the dimension can be named 'institutional actor-structure'.

In addition, Foucault's typology proves problematic when it comes to presenting the cultural perspective of the policy process. As a concept, governmentality is in some way close to policy culture, yet it is something different and more complex. Where policy culture provides an understanding of the cultural factors and actor relationships affecting the national policy process, the concept of governmentality tells a wider story about the whole mentality of governing, both about its content and structure. 'Centralisation', 'power/knowledge' and 'normalisation/intensification' are all explicitly connected to the different forms of power and, of course, to the 'productive' aspects of it. The cultural dimension of politics can be seen as an implicit content of Foucault's concept. But the main focus of Foucault's analysis is in the results of the policy process, not so much in its features. When applied to the analysis of policy processes, the cultural perspective should be explicit. This can be done by combining the concepts of 'political and administrative cultures' to the typology of governmentality.

Regulatory Reform in the Field of Environmental Policy

The starting point for environmental governing and for the adoption of new policy instruments is the need for governing. This need is based on 'problem pressure', meaning perceived or predicted environmental problems, or on problems in the existing systems of governance. But a problem is only a problem in terms of governing when it has been articulated as such. In this respect, governing needs are the results of the social and political processes of agenda-setting and problem definition. Of course, public opinion and interest groups can affect the 'problem pressure'.

New environmental policy instruments have their own characteristics, which concern the level of public-private interaction, the level of voluntariness, resource intensiveness, targeting and political risk. They intended to reduce the regulatory burden on firms; to provide positive incentives instead of negative ones (win-win option); to harness the market power of green consumerism; and to provide efficiency by using market-mechanisms and target-specific governing (Golub, 1998, pp. 6–8). Because little (domestic) information and experiences on how these new instruments really work in practice exist, decision-makers have to rely on beliefs, experts and foreign experiences (if there are any). New policy instruments are often promises of new problem-solving models and practices. Of the policy actors, some strongly believe in these promises while others are afraid of changes.

The features of the policy process in which the new policy instruments are chosen, designed and formulated, affect the final content of the instrument. In addition, situational factors (such as governmental coalition, the subjective preferences of policy actors, Parliament elections or unexpected political or economic crises) often have an influence both on the policy process and on the outcome.

The Societal Context of the Problem Situation

Existing environmental policy strategies and the general development of governing modes form an ideological background and motivation base for the adoption or prohibition of new environmental policy instruments. General societal conditions, events and policy developments provide possibilities or restraints for regulatory reform. Such background factors can be membership in the EU, deregulative trends in politics, the need for European harmonisation, general environmental values, changes in the economic trend etc. In addition, international trends and discourses play an important role in national developments. In the European context, the EU policy trends and strategies have a special influence, of course.

Environmental Governmentality

The features (and changes) of institutional actor structure define the level of (de)centralisation of environmental policy preparations and decision-making. This dimension concerns especially administrative structures, responsibilities and institutional relationships behind the regulatory reform. Political and administrative cultures and the national environmental policy style predispose decision-makers to choose a particular instrument. The administrative culture refers to the inner organisational and professional culture of the relevant public authorities and ministries and the nature of their links with clients and other agencies. This also involves the relationships with different fields of expertise. The knowledge-base of policy development and its connections to power relations. The role of scientific research and expertise in providing the conceptual framework employed in the contemporary definition of environmental problems and the content of policy making. Finally, environmental normalisation and intensification processes have two sides. On the one hand, we can ask how environmental governing and its changes create new environmentally-oriented routines both on the level of individuals and of organisations; how intensification and normalisation processes are implemented; and which governing tools and policy styles are most convenient for these purposes? On the other hand, we can ask how the new policy instrument fits into the existing governing systems and to what extent does it change the policy styles? In the context of regulatory reform, we can ask how 'normal' the new policy instrument is likely to become in the national governing system.

THE CASE OF ENVIRONMENTAL REGULATORY REFORM IN FINLAND

In this section three Finnish cases illustrate how the concept of environmental governmentality could be applied when analysing the regulatory reform in national policy context. The central point of attention is what kind of features the environmental governmentality has in Finland during the emerging regulatory reform. The analysis includes the following three case studies (Sairinen, 2000):

(1) The drafting of the EIA Act in 1982–1994. The Finnish EIA Act was enacted in 1994 as one of the latest countries in Europe. The drafting process was prolonged and very contradictory.
(2) The formation of the CO_2-tax policy in 1989–1996. In 1990, Finland was the first country in the world to introduce the carbon dioxide tax on fossil fuels. During the second policy phase (1991–1994), the carbon tax level was raised significantly and it also faced a structural change. During the third phase (1994–1996), the structure of the energy taxation was altered by decreasing the role of carbon taxes, but simltaneously the level of energy taxation was again increased. The increase was compensated for a part of the state's income tax relief. As a political solution, the result was the first sleight of hand towards the ecological tax reform.
(3) The usage of the voluntary agreements (1987–1999). VAs have been carried out in relation to four policy objectives: reducing the use of CFCs (1987–1988), reducing the amounts of packaging wastes (1995), promoting energy conservation (1992 & 1997) and remediation of contaminated soil (Soili-agreement in 1996). All together 17 agreements have been made.

In the Finnish context, these instruments represent the aspirations towards regulatory reform and the developments of 'preventive environmental policy' and 'ecological modernisation'. In Finland, the development of the EIA Act and the CO_2-taxation have been among the most important environmental policy questions in the early 1990s. The voluntary agreements have instead been quite marginal phenomenon, unlike in some other EU-countries. Because the cases represent different governing modes, they provide many-sided perspectives to the question of regulatory reform.

The Characteristics of the Institutional Actor Structure

In order to study institutional actor structures and the relationships between them, we need to analyse environmental policy actors, institutional settings and policy networks (or coalitions). Such an analysis describes the level of centralisation (or decentralisation) of decision-making and the role of environmental actors in politics. The type of networks which develop often depend on the groups involved, the interests of the various actors within the government, the nature of the policy, and the institutional arrangements that are available. The relationships between different actors depend also on the governing ideology: deregulative policies reduce the concentration of power in the hands of state authorities, and simultaneously increase the co-operation between public and private actors.

The general tendency to develop sustainability programmes, policies and tools has changed the relationships between policy sectors, and also administrative responsibilities. Although the environmental ministries have frequently had legitimacy to be active in several policy sectors, political practice is nevertheless full of disagreements about how environmental policy integration (and the new responsibilities) should be organised. Thus, because environmental policy integration is a growing tendency, it is important to analyse the changing role of environmental authorities and the power relations between different ministries. There are several ways of reorganising administrative relations: shared responsibilities between different administrative sectors; centralisation of decision-making and of the preparation of environmental administration; decentralisation of power to local and regional actors; and adding the environmental approach to the traditional sectoral power structure.

One basic feature of the new policy instruments is their tendency to decentralise environmental governing. As policy measures, they emphasise the ideas of shared responsibility, participation of stakeholders, subsidiarity and the market mechanism. These principles all have the effect of distributing influence and power from the state institutions to other policy actors.

In Finland, the role of the Ministry of the Environment in promoting regulatory reform has varied depending on the policy instrument in question. On the one hand it seems that the Ministry for the Environment (or part of it) was initially sceptical or critical towards the new instruments in question, but has gradually adopted a more supportive attitude. In the field of co-regulation, the sceptical attitude continued over a longer period. On the other hand, regulatory reform has clearly distributed environmental governing power to other ministries. For example, the formal preparatory mandate of environmental taxation belongs to the Ministry of Finance and voluntary agreements can be developed under different ministries.

All four agreements where the Ministry for the Environment was a signatory have mainly been based on ad hoc practices rather than on planned strategic decisions. The Ministry for the Environment has at all times been quite cautious about developing VAs. The energy conservation agreements were an exception in this respect: they acquired a significant role in the national energy programmes and the responsible official, the Ministry of Trade and Industry, was clearly in favour of the deregulative measures.

In the case of carbon taxation, the Ministry for the Environment was initially a significant policy actor and mediator. The adoption of shared-responsibility and consensual-problem-solving styles, where all the stakeholders participated in the policy process, moved the preparations forward. When criticism towards increasing energy taxes was growing, the Ministry for the Environment lost its role. As a result of several factors, a policy model evolved where the responsibility for the preparation of energy taxes was centralised to the Ministry of Finance backed by the Ministry of Trade and Industry. More than once, the Ministry for the Environment unsuccessfully tried to be admitted to the administrative working groups. The case indicates that the relationship between the three ministries seems to be vulnerable to conflict, because of their very different mentality in environmental tax policy.

Political and Administrative Culture

Political culture refers to the manners and styles of action in the policy process, especially in conflict situations. Each country has its own political culture, which affects public governing and the choice of policy instruments. The traditional distinction between policy cultures is based on corporatism and pluralism (Crepaz, 1995; Mol, Lauber & Liefferink, 2000). It is argued quite often that environmental performance has been less successful in pluralist countries such as the U.K. and USA than in the (small) corporatist states of Europe (Scruggs, 1998; Jänicke, 1997). Some writers have challenged the corporatist argument, however. For instance, Hukkinen (1995) has concluded that the corporatist system runs the risk of having policies that are too narrow-minded and short-sighted.

The question whether corporatism promotes or retards pollution is thus, as yet, undecided. What we can argue here, however, is that there is a need for a broader and more fine-grained analytical tool for investigating the impact of policy culture on environmental policy-making (Mol, Lauber & Liefferink, 2000). Thus, it is reasonable to employ other dimensions of policy style (Van Waarden, 1995). In the context of tregulatory reform, the typologies of consensual/adversial, legalistic/pragmatic and formal/informal policy styles seem to be relevant. It is evident that various features of policy styles are always closely connected to features of the institutional actor-structure. For example, administrative culture (such as legalism) is clearly linked to the administrative set-up.

Regulatory reform in Finland has been clearly influenced (restricted) by the national environmental policy cultures. Consequently, it has been quite difficult to alter the balance of the traditional regulatory system. The traditonal Finnish environmental policy style can be divided into two different kind of styles. On the one side, from the late 1970s, the (air and water) pollution policies have been based on a *consensual policy style* between different actors, ranging from industry to environmental NGOs. In these policy fields, the public governing mode has been based on legal state regulation, albeit in the form of negotiative problems-solving. At first, the content of emission control activities and regulations were negotiated between different actors, and thereafter the Government or permit authorities made their decision on the basis of those regulations. This policy style has also been called 'negotiated rule-making' in contrast to 'command-and-control regulation' (Mol, Lauber & Liefferink, 2000). Structural changes favourable to emission reduction and pollution-control investments that fit the timetables of major process retrofits constituted an effort to avoid additional costs. National 'neocorporatism' in the context of the Nordic welfare states is an obvious example of the development of a consensual style.

On the other side, nature conservation has been based on *adversial policy style*. The cultural importance of landownership and the strong role of the rural political parties and interest groups has given rise to much conflict over nature-conservation issues at the national policy level. Furthermore, environmental governing measures that concern landownership have recurrently been difficult to agree upon at the governmental level. Nearly all the various conservation programmes have a history of conflict. In these policy fields, policy actors have been divided into sharply confronting policy networks.

The environmental results of the Finnish consensual policy style have been quite effective in the areas of both air and water pollution. It can be argued that this success within the regulatory system to some extent prevented the more active development of new instruments. In Finland, the application of VAs has been slow in comparison to other small European neo-corporatist countries such as Denmark and the Netherlands. The consensual policy style has provided possibilities for informal actor relations inside the regulatory system, to the extent that industry has not been very interested in the voluntary approaches.

Similarly, the environmental administration was at first so satisfied with the systems of legal regulation that the concepts of EIA and environmental taxation had to wait some time before they were more readily accepted. Thus, it can be argued that administrative legalism has in some cases delayed the use of new policy instruments. Many influential officials in the ME were committed to the legalistic culture, and initially showed no interest in developing new measures. The new instruments all differ markedly from the classic model of regulation. It has been claimed that in this kind of regulatory reform, the Government refrains from using any instruments of formal power, i.e. from enacting legal norms. Instead, the authorities enter into questionable negotiations with the polluters or trust to the steering power of market prices. The Finnish environmental administrators were not familiar with these types of new governing mentalities.

The Knowledge Base of Policy Development and its Relationships to Power Relations

Scientific expertise has been fundamental in defining environmental problems and policy solutions (Rutherford, 1999). It is therefore necessary to consider the role of scientific research (especially of scientific ecology) and expertise in the formation of the conceptual framework employed in the contemporary definition of environmental problems. The basic assumption here is that the scientific knowledge-base and its main features have been important factors in the preparation of environmental policies and also in regulatory reforms. Thus, environmental scientists are in many ways participants in the policy processes. They often promote, consciously or by default, their own role through social and/or political processes.

The question of power/knowledge concerns not just the role of science and experts, but also the role of professions in environmental policy-making. A person's professional background has often a direct influence on the contents of policy. Jurists are in favour of legal regulation, economists prefer economic instruments, and planners want to develop impact assessment procedures (see also Glasbergen, 1998). Thus the professional structure of environmental administration has an influence on which governing modes the administration is in favour of. As environmental policy develops, the content of environmental professions becomes wider and dispersed among different expert fields. Thus, a continuous professionalisation and specialisation process takes place. The new environmental professions create new institutional cultures and pressures for regulatory changes (Järvelä, 1998).

The regulatory reform calls for new kinds of expert systems and knowledge base both among the polluters and the administrators. This has also been the case in Finland, but the attitude towards new needs in expertise has proven to be very different in the three cases examined. The content and usage of new expertise had a great influence on the Finnish EIA policy. Based on EIA activities, an *epistemic community* was created which, in turn, directly affected the policy process. At the end of the 1980s, several experimental projects were launched and training was organised. In just a few years, the environmental administration was educated to adopt the new "*EIA-way-of-thinking*". The Finnish EIA case shows that in order to gain social acceptance, especially among the relevant professionals, the new policy instruments also need experimental studies and information structures that create possibilities for a new way of thinking. Only after this kind of policy learning has taken place does the integration of the instrument into an existing system become possible.

In the case of carbon taxation, some problems in the knowledge base of the ME's personnel was revealed. In the past, the ME has not taken part in tax preparation and has neither strong nor extensive expertise in energy policy issues. The lack of expertise was mainly the result of the organisation's historical development. Environmental economy and energy policy are subjects that are only now being constructed as an environmental policy issue.

In Finland, VAs were implemented as ad hoc practices without much knowledge about the principles of voluntary approaches. After the first experiences, there was an increasing need for deeper understanding, but the ad hoc policy processes have not provided good opportunities for that. Another knowledge (information) problem was the question of developing effective monitoring systems. The public legitimacy of VAs is strongly dependent on the effectiveness of the instruments, the kinds of expert institutions that support the instruments, and how the benefits can be monitored reliably.

The Environmental Normalisation and Intensification Processes

In studying environmental intensification and normalisation, we must ask whether there are ongoing processes in the society in which we can find the 'positive' or 'productive' sides of modern power. In the case of environmental policy, we can argue that the strategies of sustainable development strive for the environmental mobilisation of the population. This means that the power effects of these policies are an attempt at normalising the population, as well as companies and public organisations, into disciplined environmental subjects. Thus, on the level of policy instruments, this dimension concerns the questions of how environmental governing and its changes create new environmentally-oriented routines, both on the individual and the organisational level; how the intensification and normalisation processes are implemented; and which governing tools and policy styles are the most suitable for these purposes.

All the new policy instruments are based on the idea of integrating environmental awareness into the normal activities of consumption, production, planning or politics. Thus, regulatory reform as a policy project aims at environmental policy integration, which in turn is expected to generate environmental normalisation and intensification processes. For example, the EIA contains the aim to develop a systematic and broad routine for assessing the impacts of different kinds of building, planning and policy projects. In Finland, the EIA law has been very successful with regard to this aim by introducing a comprehensive assessment procedure that also includes aspirations towards both social and strategic impact assessment, and wide participatory practices. On the other hand, in VAs, the polluters are willing to develop voluntarily environmental protection measures in certain areas of their activities. In all the Finnish VA cases, the clearest environmental benefit has been to promote the broader adoption of an environmental management culture within companies. The Finnish case of carbon tax illustrates how environmental taxation gradually became normalised for the state administration. Economic control was first established through committees. In this way, different ministries were expected to commit themselves to the issue. From 1994 to 1996, the carbon tax was disputed and reformulated, but the basic idea was accepted. In addition, the high taxation of labour (and the need for reducing income taxes) in Finland has provided a suitable ground for a discussion on a green tax reform containing a shift from labour taxation towards taxes on pollution and natural resources.

CONCLUSIONS

In this article, the regulatory reform has been analysed using the concept of 'environmental governmentality'. The developed theoretical framework was illustrated by the cases from Finland. It seems that the concept of governmentality provides a useful framework for understanding both the appeal of the environmental regulatory reform and the conditions under which it might occur. It is clear that the current regulatory reform in environmental policy is not just a technical change in policy tools, but implies and requires several types of societal changes.

The development of environmental policy strategies from the 1960s can be seen as a transition to a comprehensive policy plan that includes wider and deeper public policy intervention in personal and corporate lives. Modern environmental policies tend toward preventive approaches, sustainable development and ecological modernisation. Governments are using a variety of policy measures in order to intervene and change the behaviour of citizens, markets, companies and other organisations. According to Foucauldian concepts, an environmental normalisation process is in progress. In this respect, the 'environmental state' is similar to the welfare state of earlier years. Particularly in the era of environmental modernisation, the strengthening of environmental governmentality provides interesting and important perspectives for the further analysis at both the theoretical and the empirical level.

The challenge of the emerging 'environmental state' is to find better ways to make the population, companies and various administrations adopt new forms of environment-conscious conduct. In governmental policies, environmental intensification and normalisation also need new qualities at the environmental administration level. The environmental ministry cannot just dictate the contents of sustainable development to other policy sectors. In addition, although it seems that the institutional structure of environmental policy making has initially developed toward centralisation and the top-down governing style, recent approaches connected to ecological modernisation emphasise decentralisation. This means Europeanisation, on the one hand, and local and actor-based activities on the other. Simultaneously, policy cultures have been changing from contradictory to increasingly consensual styles. This has opened up new possibilities for self- and co-regulation.

On the other hand, the processes of regulatory reform are not at all only consensual. The political and administrative conflicts will be always there and the environmental administration has to keep its eyes open because of the threat of regulative capture. Thus, the interactive policy styles also require administrative strength and capacity for regulation.

NOTE

1. There exist also other interpretations of the governmentality concept which are not presented here (see Rose & Miller, 1992).

REFERENCES

Barry, A., Osborne, T., & Rose, N. (Ed.) (1996). *Foucault and Political Reason. Liberalism, Neo-Liberalism and Rationalities of Government*. London: University College London: UCL Press.

Beck, U. (1992). *Risk Society: Towards a New Modernity*. London: Sage.

Beck, U., Giddens, A., & Lash, S. (1994). *Reflexive Modernization, Politics, Tradition and Aesthetics in the Modern Social Order*. Cambridge: Polity Press.

Collier, U. (Ed.) (1998). *Deregulation in the European Union. Environmental Perspectives*. London: Routledge.

COM (= Commission of the European Communities) (1993). Towards Sustainability. *Fifth Environmental Action Programme*. OJC 138, 17 May, Luxembourg.

Crepaz, M. (1995). Explaining national variations of air pollution levels: political institutions and their impact on environmental policy-making. *Environmental Politics*, *4*(3), 391–414.

Darier, E. (1996). Environmental Governmentality: The Case of Canada's Green Plan. *Environmental Politics, 5*(4), Winter, 585–606.

Eckersley, R. (Ed.) (1995). *Markets, the State and the Environment: Towards Integration*. London: Macmillan.

Foucault, M. (1984). Space, Knowledge, and Power. In: P. Rabinow (Ed.), *The Foucault Reader* (pp. 239–256). New York: Pantheon Books.

Foucault, M. (1991). Governmentality. In: G. Burchell, C. Gordon & P. Miller (Eds), *The Foucault Effect. Studies in Governmentality* (pp. 87–104). London: Harvester Wheatsheaf.

Glasbergen, P. (1998). The Question of Environmental Governance. In: P. Glasbergen (Ed.), *Co-operative Environmental Governance* (pp. 1–20). Dordrecht: Kluwer Academic Publishers.

Helen, I. (1995). Michel Foucault'n valta-analytiikka. In: R. Heiskala (Ed.), *Sosiologisen Teorian Nykysuuntauksia* (pp. 270–315). Helsinki: Gaudeamus.

Howlett, M., & Ramesh, H. (1995). *Studying Public Policy: Policy Cycles and Policy Subsystems.* Oxford.: Oxford University Press

Hukkinen, J. (1995). Long-Term Environmental Policy under Corporatist Institutions. *European Environment, 5*(4), 98–105.

Jänicke, M. (1997). The Political System's Capacity for Environmental Policy. In: M. Jänicke & H. Weidner (Ed.), *National Environmental Policies* (pp. 1–24). Berlin: Springer Verlag.

Järvelä, M. (1998). Ekososiaalinen politiikka ja ympäristövaikuttajuuden professionalisoituminen. In: J. Mykkänen & I. Koskinen (Ed.), *Asiantuntemuksen Politiikka. Professiot ja Julkisvalta Suomessa* (pp. 153–165). Helsinki: Helsinki University Press.

Kooiman, J. (Ed) (1993). *Modern Governance. New Government – Society Interactions*. London: Sage.

Leveque, F. (1996a). The European Fabric of Environmental Regulations. In: F. Leveque (Ed.), *Environmental Policy in Europe* (pp. 9–30). Cheltenham, U.K.: Edward Elgar.

Leveque, F. (1996b). The Regulatory Game. In: F. Leveque (Ed.), *Environmental Policy in Europe* (pp. 31–52). Cheltenham, U.K.: Edward Elgar.

Liefferink, D., & Arthur, M. (1998). Voluntary Agreements as a Form of Deregulation? The Dutch Experience. In: U. Collier (Ed.), *Deregulation in the European Union. Environmental Perspectives* (pp. 181–197). London: Routledge.

Linder, S., & Peters, G. (1989). Instruments of government: Perception and contexts. *Journal of Public Policy, 9*(1), 35–58.

Luke, T. (1995). Sustainable Development as a Power/Knowledge System: the Problem of 'Governmentality'. In: F. Fischer & M. Black, *Greening Environmental Policy* (pp. 21–32). New York: St. Martin's Press.

Mol, A. P. J., Lauber, V., & Liefferink, J. D. (Ed.) (2000). *The Voluntary Approach to Environmental Policy*. Environmental Policy-making in Europe. Oxford: OUP.

Rose, N., & Miller, P. (1992). Political power beyond the State: problematics of government. *The British Journal of Sociology, 43*(2), 173–205.

Rutherford, P. (1999). Ecological Modernization and Environmental Risk. In: E. Darier (Ed.), *Discourses of the Environment*. (pp. 95–118).

Sairinen, R. (2000). Regulatory reform of Finnish environmental policy. Centre for Urban and Regional Studies. *Publications A 27*. University of Technology, Espoo.

Sairinen, R., & Outi T. (1999). Voluntary Agreements as an Environmental Policy Instrument in Finland. *European Environment, 9*(2), 67–74.

Scruggs, A. (1998). Institutions and Environmental Performance in 17 Western Democracies. *British Journal of Political Science*.

Van Waarden, F. (1995). Persistence of national policy styles: a study of their institutional foundations. In: Unger & van Waarden (Eds), *Teoksessa: Convergence or Diversity: Internationalization and Economic Policy Response* (pp. 333–372). Aldershot: Avebury.

THE EUROPEAN UNION AS A SUPRASTATE IN AGRI-ENVIRONMENTAL ISSUES: THE FINNISH PERSPECTIVE

Pekka Jokinen

INTRODUCTION

The development of the state of the world is increasingly discussed at a level beyond nation-states, which refers to the processes of economic, social and cultural globalisation. Nation states and localities form a part of the global economy and culture and, thus, of the multi-level social reality (e.g. Castells, 1996). The European Union can certainly be understood as a type of political entity responding to the assumed effects of globalisation. However, it has also been argued that international and supranational phenomena as foci of theoretical work and as research topics have been largely neglected by social scientists, mainly because they have committed themselves to the traditional state theory and to society-centred thinking (Ebbinghaus, 1998; Walby, 1999). It would thus follow that 'Europeanisation' has also largely been excluded from the field of social sciences. According to Walby (*ibid.*), however, the EU is to be considered a suprastate or a regulatory state whose legal interventions in markets have major effects on social relations. If the emphasis is laid on the EU regulatory framework, Europeanisation certainly appears as a serious challenge also for environmental social scientists: nowadays EU environmental regulation is an illustrative example of the supranational process, though it is

The Environmental State Under Pressure, Volume 10, pages 105–120.

ISBN: 0-7623-0854-0

well known that the original reasons for founding the European Community did not yet involve any consideration for environmental issues.

Environmental policies are produced by a continuing process of interactions between different spatial levels (e.g. Young, 1995). Transnationalisation of environmental regulation is also one of the key characteristics on grounds of which the ecological modernisation theorists have suggested that an important transition of the traditional role of the 'environmental nation-state' is imminent (Mol & Sonnenfeld, 2000). As van Tatenhove (1999) has put it, the institutionalisation of environmental policies has been increasingly influenced by the interaction between political modernisation and new environmental discourses. The challenges to environmental policy by 'reflexive' political modernisation include, among others, restructuring the networks and coalitions of actors at various spatial levels and crossing the horizontal boundaries of sector bureaucracy. It is obvious that the advancing globalisation of environmental issues further strengthens the transnational framework of environmental regulation.

This paper deals with the relationship between supranational regulation and national policy approach. The focus is on the case of agriculture and the environment in Finland. In the European Union there exists a particular model of supranational agri-environmental policy, which mainly acquired its current form in the Common Agricultural Policy reform in 1992. Since Finland became an EU member state in 1995, she began to adopt to this 'completed' supranational agri-environmental regulation. However, the national responses to the supranational regulation should not be understood as existing in a vacuum. Instead, agri-environmental policy solutions are highly political (Daugbjerg, 1999); thus, it is supposed that regulation might result in 'creating turbulence' in the national policy arena due to important historical, cultural and institutional factors. In other words, it is assumed that attention should also be paid to the national history of agri-environmental policy and to the traditional character of the national policy formation process.

First, a look is taken at the agri-environmental policy in the EU. Second, the traditionally strong position of agriculture and the Nordic welfare state tradition are discussed in order to clarify their relevance for the current agri-environmental regulation in Finland. Next, the focus shifts to the development of the dominant Finnish discourses on agriculture and the environment. During the first five years (1995–1999) of Finnish EU membership, two especially important agriculture/environment-related EU-based schemes have emerged. The first was related to agricultural pollution control and resulted in the building of the national agri-environmental programme. The second resulted in the national implementation of the European nature conservation network, 'Natura 2000'. In the light of these issues, I pose the question, what kind of effects has supranationalisation had on the agri-environmental policy in Finland and, further, how have the national policy traditions manifested themselves in the new agri-environmental management.

THE ESSENCE OF SUPRANATIONAL AGRI-ENVIRONMENTAL REGULATION IN THE EU

In EU policy structure, the position of the agri-environmental issue is inevitably linked to traditions and current modifications of the Common Agricultural Policy (CAP), which dates back to the beginning of the 1960s. The Community's agricultural policy in its early decades was characterised by purely productivist goals, but in the 1980s it was redirected at decreasing the chronic surplus production and massive budgetary costs. As regards agri-environmental regulation, it consists, however, of somewhat divergent socio-political elements involving both the 'agricultural and rural development angle' and the 'environmental policy and nature conservation angle'. This has put pressure on the existing narrow sector policy models and called for the 'integration' of policy issue areas. The relevance of the aim to integrate environmental considerations into other policy areas seems to be quite clear: if environmental factors are ignored in the formulation of policies regulating economic and social organisation, an 'environmentally and socially sustained development' cannot be achieved in the long term (Liberatore, 1997).

Environmental targets have, indeed, also been incorporated into the EU agricultural policy reforms in the 1990s, and the greening of agricultural policy discourse was highlighted in the 1992 CAP reform. One of the outcomes was a specific Regulation, which defined the possible agri-environmental support schemes and distinguished several subsidised environmental measures in member states (for detailed analyses on the Regulation, see e.g. Baldock & Lowe, 1996; Wilson et al., 1999). In line with the strengthening of the 'post-productivist' ethos, at the end of the 1990s, a demand for the further incorporation of environmental issues into the agricultural policy emerged. This is illustrated by the recently approved 'Agenda 2000' package, i.e. the framework for the EU agricultural policy until 2006 (European agriculture, overall, will continue to be a highly supra state-centred industry in the future, too). According to this, the reform aims to provide grounds for the European model of agriculture, which 'is based on healthy and pro-environmental production practices and capable of producing high-quality products that meet the requirements of society'.

In practice, however, the integration of policies has been at least as difficult for the EU as it has been for single states (Baker, 1997). There is still a rather strict sectorisation and detachment of environmental and agricultural policy goals, and, for instance, the EU's agri-environmental measures are only a very minor part of the total structure of the common agricultural policy, the consequences of which are, however, fundamental for the rural areas (Winter, 1996). It has been concluded that a particular reason for these difficulties is the EU's historical commitment to ensuring economic growth through traditional economic goals and objectives (Baker et al., 1997). This commitment has resulted in policy priorities overlooking environmental objectives. In other words, in past decades the EU has affected the environment more through its free-trade principles and intensification of agricultural practices than by its environmental measures (Yearley et al., 1994). Buller et al. (1995) have also noted that as a result of the regulatory style of EU environmental policy, the European environment is increasingly defined rather in 'normative', 'scientific' terms than in 'cultural' terms; especially in agri-environmental management this failure to respond to cultural values is one of the main reasons for policy failures. Overall, the critics have argued that several CAP reform measures have been promoted as 'environmental' whilst having in fact very limited environmental content (Winter, 2000). The entire present EU agricultural policy would, thus, be increasingly legitimated by the environmental rhetoric, instead of the earlier discursive priority given to food security.

In addition to the horizontal problems of European supranational agri-environmental policy, theoretical and practical issues on the vertical dimension of European agri-environmental regulation are important. Firstly, is it actually justified to make strong generalisations on the mode of European agri-environmental policy? In other words, can we assume that there is a certain EU level model of agri-environmental regulation, the main characters of which also hold true at the national level? And if there exists such a model, are we to suppose a (at least relatively) direct transmission of the principles of the general regulation model to the lower levels? Or, alternatively, are there some (or even many) 'intermediating mechanisms' between the various levels, which might ultimately lead to rather contingent agri-environmental regulation principles and practices in a member state's policy framework (e.g. Wilson et al., 1999)? Such mechanisms might refer, for instance, to national traditions in agricultural and environmental thinking or to national differences in the relative strength of the key agri-environmental policy actors. Secondly, in the examination of a national agri-environmental policy, a necessary theoretical question is also whether a strong or a weak impact as such of the supranational policy on a member state's policy formation and agri-environmental practices should be assumed (Winter, 2000).

Buller et al (1995) have distinguished two basic positions in studies on the relationship between the EU policies and national environmental policy-making. On the one hand, they have identified the approach inside which the processes of environmental policy are mainly taken as institutional and regulatory responses at the national level to (more or less) specific EU rules. It is supposed, of course, that there are important variations to be found in the ways supranational regulatory measures are interpreted and implemented by single states. On the other, studies have also conceptualised EU policy as an increasingly unified and coordinated action amongst nations responding to a common environmental challenge. Buller et al. (*ibid.*) suggest that agricultural pollution control in particular serves as an example of a policy of the latter type.

In principle, EU agri-environmental regulation is a part of the strongly harmonising common agricultural policy. It consists of issue-specific measures, which, however, seem to be quite loose from the practical viewpoint. For instance, the EU Regulation of 1992 has resulted in a remarkable variety of objectives and resources in national agri-environmental programmes (Brouwer & Lowe, 1998). This gives good reasons to suppose that regulation is, in practice, also strongly formulated on the basis of particular 'national interests', not only of supranational 'common challenges' (Niemi-Iilahti & Jokinen, 1999). Thus, the former of the approaches mentioned by Buller et al. (i.e. 'national responses to EU rules') seems to be more consistent with the state of affairs than does the latter (i.e. 'unified and coordinated responses to common environmental challenges'). The former approach, however, easily results in a tendency to understand policy-making as a purely rational 'top-down' process, where there is no room for policy re-formulations by the national policy networks (e.g. Wilson et al., 1999).

Basically, it can be presumed that neither of the regulation approaches discussed above is convincing enough and acceptable as an appropriate starting point for the supranational vs. national policy style examination. Namely, on the one hand, the European agri-environmental policy still lacks a strong and credible vision of 'sustainable agriculture' and it notably lacks binding specific rules (Cobb et al., 1999). On the other, however, it is hard to interpret the prevailing European agri-environmental policy model as a 'bottom up' type common policy in any ambitious sense. Fairly consistent with this, Billaud et al. (1997) have concluded that EU agri-environmental regulation indeed manifests itself through re-definitions of the social role and legitimacy of agriculture in various European countries – instead of being a purely 'European' approach and of creating a new social reality at the transnational level. Thus, according to this position, the EU schemes do not primarily have a homogenising effect on agriculture-related environmental policy but rather result in 'creating turbulence' in conflicts and discourses on agriculture and the environment.

TRADITIONS IN THE FINNISH POLICY APPROACH: PEASANT IDEOLOGY AND THE WELFARE THINKING

The last of the above-mentioned positions, proposed by Billaud et al. (*ibid.*), is preferred in this paper, since it allows the identification of contingency in the outcomes of supranational agri-environmental regulation due to historical, cultural and institutional factors in the national policy approaches. The importance of institutional and cultural traditions has been nicely illustrated, for instance, by Jamison and Baark (1999) in the case of Swedish and Danish science and technology policy in the environmental field. They found that especially in Sweden environmental policy issues have had difficulties in leaving their sectoral status and entering into broader discourses about industrial and economic development. To a large extent, this is explained by structural factors: the industrial corporations, built up in the late nineteenth century, have been based on the exploitation of natural resources (referring especially to the forest industry and mining); thus, it has been difficult to incorporate environmental concern into the basic forms of economic activity. From the environmental policy perspective, a historical parallel between the dominance of industrial corporations and agricultural industry is a potential. There has been a strong tradition of independent farmers and politically active rural areas in Finland. In particular, the land reforms in the 1920s and 1940s strengthened the structural base of 'peasant' ideology by decisively increasing the number of small farms. The ideology has manifested itself especially in a strong sense of independence and in a 'frame of self-determination' (Alanen, 1995; Konttinen, 1999; Katajamäki, 1999).

In addition to the tradition of independent farmers, attention has to be paid to the 'Nordic Model' of the welfare state in order to understand the Finnish state policy style and the response to supranational regulation. Generally speaking, the Nordic model refers to the type of social organisation adopted in the five Nordic countries; the Finnish welfare state began to develop markedly from the late 1950s on (e.g. Mjoset, 1992; Kosonen, 1993). In its modern form the core characteristics of an ideal-typed universalist welfare state include a high proportion of public services and public employment, redistribution by income transfers, and heavy taxation. Importantly, the basis of combining private capitalism and ideas of citizens' social equality and workers' rights has been characterised by strong domestic consensus and low level of social conflicts, and by high levels of organisation (e.g. labour and farmers). Though the ideal-typed description of the birth of the welfare state is usually connected with the living conditions of workers, agrarian interests had a pivotal role in the early development of the Scandinavian welfare state; correspondingly, 'the welfare rationality' has also contributed considerably to the living of farmers and, more generally, to that of rural inhabitants (Granberg, 1999; Rannikko, 1999).

According to Granberg (1995, 1999), 'a welfare state contains a visible core of social policy schemes and institutions, and a welfare rationality adopted in other domains of government policies'. This appears to be important, firstly, for the Nordic environmental policy tradition. For instance, Lundqvist (1999) notes that in the Nordic counties the efforts to integrate the environmental dimension into other policy sectors have not led to radical reorganisation of political institutions and practices. Rather, the approach has been reformistic, resembling thus the building strategy of the Nordic welfare state. Since the Nordic model of environmental policy is typically 'cooperative and consensual' and developed in a 'corporatist and rule-deferential' culture (Christiansen & Lundqvist, 1996), the current Nordic response to the ecological challenge has led to the adoption of a rather moderate version of ecological modernisation in the field of environmental policy (i.e. not of a 'super-environmentalism'). Secondly, the welfare rationality has dominated especially the development of the national agricultural policy (Granberg, 1999). Without going into detail, it can be said that the agricultural policy measures by the Finnish state until 1995, such as the regional price subsidies, income support for small farms, and the extent of public services, have explicitly served the idea of regional equality, whereas agricultural income policy has, in practice, equalised Finnish farmers' average incomes with those of industrial workers. The main principle has been (for instance, instead of equality of opportunity) the equality of results (*ibid.*). This is a conclusion of crucial importance: it means that until 1995 the equalising and re-distributive impact of Finnish agricultural policy has in practice been comparable with that of social policy.

THE FINNISH AGRICULTURE BEFORE 1995: POLICY AND DISCOURSES ON THE ENVIRONMENT

The modernisation of Finnish society, 'from a rural peasant society to an urban welfare society' (Granberg, 1995), has resulted in the somewhat late but then rapid transition of the industrial structure into a service-dominated society and also in the depopulation of rural areas. The role of farming has also gradually changed, and in pure national economic terms, the significance of agriculture nowadays seems to be very minor (a good percent of GDP), though agriculture still is certainly significant in numerous local economies. Oksa and Rannikko

(1996) are presumably correct in stating that it is not only the rural Finland but also its image which has undergone a thorough change in the very recent decades. Consistent with several authors (e.g. Marsden et al., 1993; Macnaghten & Urry, 1998), they have argued that there simply no longer exists any single, commonly held definition of the countryside, but rather there appear different definitions such as countryside as 'a place of production', 'a foundation of national identity', or as 'a landscape'. Most importantly, they have emphasised that the development of rural areas is a joint result of separate state policy processes applying those differing definitions.

As in other Western countries, the development of Finnish agriculture has been controlled by policy factors. Up to 1995 the state was the ultimate guarantee of the continuity of agriculture, though the policy had intentionally also advanced rationalisation, increased productivity and decreased the number of farms. These trends have even strengthened in the present context of the EU agricultural policy. However, one predominant feature of the industry has been preserved: Finnish agriculture is steadily based on family-farming, which had far-sightedly been supported by rural policy ideas stressing the farm as the basic unit for the vitality of the countryside. The agricultural policy community, which generally speaking refers to the close co-operation of agricultural administration and the farmers' interest organisation (Winter, 1996; Epstein, 1997), has defined rural areas in terms of production simply because agricultural policy has been the major mechanism of income redistribution.

As then regards the definition of agri-environmental problems, the 'agrarian' agri-environmental discourse, also engaged in by the agricultural policy community actors, has dominated the problem definition arena since the rise of Finnish agri-environmental issues, i.e. from the early 1970s (Jokinen, 2000). The core of this discourse on agriculture and the environment can be characterised by the basic idea that agri-environmental problems and their solutions must be adjusted to a broad context. This context has been concern for the social and economic position of farmers and the vitality of rural areas. Instead, as an expression of a weak 'counter-discourse', environmental state officials and environmentalists have tried to discuss agri-environmental issues in the context of environmental protection and nature conservation. However, this description is obviously somewhat rough. Given the several meanings attached to the countryside, it is justifiable to distinguish further two issues within the development of the Finnish policy discourse on agriculture and the environment (Jokinen, 1995, 1997). They are the rural stewardship issue and the farm pollution issue.

With respect to rural stewardship, until the 1970s farming was self-evidently considered an industry utilising natural resources in a sustainable way; thus, the stewardship of natural resources was seen as a 'natural task' for farmers. In the 1980s, this view seemed to disappear from the agri-environmental agenda to some extent. This was possibly due to the increasing discussion of agri-environmental problems but also to the effect of the new actor in policy, the Ministry of the Environment, whose relationship to the agricultural policy actors was relatively distant from the very beginning. In the early 1990s, however, the ideas of rural stewardship re-entered Finnish policies, but unlike in the 1970s, agricultural policy actors no longer defined the management of the countryside as a natural task of farmers but rather as active production of services, which the farmers should be paid for. This turn to a discourse on countryside-oriented environmental management 'serving the common good' was clearly linked to the foreseen membership of the EU and, thus, to the option of agri-environmental subsidies. This discursive shift seemed to be rather important since the conflict between agricultural land use and nature conservation had been profound in Finland (e.g. Sairinen, 2000).

The content and development of the agricultural pollution discourse, which in Finland has been connected especially to water quality issues, has somewhat differed from that of countryside management (Niemi-Iilahti & Jokinen, 1999; Jokinen, 2000). In the 1970s and early 1980s farming was primarily regarded as a non-polluting industry. In the late 1980s, however, along with the relatively uncontested science-based identification of agriculture-related water pollution, the conceptualisation of the farm pollution issue changed rather radically: it turned rapidly from a 'non-problem' to a challenge for different actors, including agricultural policy-makers. This change in agri-environmental problem framing was undoubtedly also supported by a more widespread change in Finnish environmental discussion: namely, in the late 1980s, the optimistic notion of 'sustainable development' penetrated different sectors of society, agriculture being no exception (e.g. Macnaghten & Urry, 1998). Thus, a discoursive re-orientation appeared: along with the general greening of Finnish society the agricultural policy-makers also adopted an environmental discourse in the early 1990s.

THE COMING OF SUPRANATIONAL REGULATION: TWO AGRI-ENVIRONMENTAL EXAMPLES

With Finnish EU membership, it became very clear that in *agricultural* policy area the 'supra-state' (i.e. the EU) had in practice taken the full competence to formulate binding policies: due to the CAP, the power of the national agricultural policy community diminished sharply. Thus, the Ministry of Agriculture and Forestry began to focus on the implementation of EU agricultural policy.

The farmers' union, again, began to adapt to the role of a traditional-type pressure group. However, primarily due to the rather loose EU rules, in *agri-environmental* policy the re-definition of EU policy objectives (and, thus, the discourse conflicts and struggle for power) remained on the national level. Overall, the 'dominant agri-environmental discourse' is undoubtedly becoming more heterogeneous: in addition to traditional nature conservation and agricultural pollution issues, it increasingly also consists of other issues, such as biodiversity and organic farming. It is, of course, very difficult to make clear distinctions between 'exogeneous' and 'endogeneous' factors, but the notion of biodiversity loss as an elementary part of the general discourse on the global environmental change especially seems also to have a marked effect on the national agri-environmental discourse.

During the first five years of Finnish EU membership, some new agri-environmental schemes have been introduced. As has been emphasised above, agri-environmental regulation includes differing policy elements. From the institutional perspective, it is characteristic of the present Finnish agri-environmental regulation that agricultural and environmental policy-makers have to co-operate more on farm pollution issues at the central agency level. Thus, at least superficially, the integration of sector policies has increased. The implementation of EU rules, however, has also raised tension between agricultural and environmental policy objectives (after the fairly consensual period from the late 1980s up to the middle of the 1990s). The turbulence in the national agri-environmental policy arena is briefly illustrated by the two most important agriculture/environment-related EU schemes. The one, the building of the national agri-environmental programme in the middle of the 1990s, was related to agri-environmental pollution control, and the other, the implementation of the European nature conservation network, to nature conservation.

CASE 1: THE POLICY RATIONALE OF THE FINNISH AGRI-ENVIRONMENTAL PROGRAMME

Very briefly, on the basis of the EU Regulation, every member state has to set up an agri-environmental subsidy system, the form and content of which, however, are not determined by the EU rule. Instead of obligatory activities, it makes financial support available for different agri-environmental measures (for details and comparisons see e.g. Baldock & Lowe, 1996; Curry & Stucki, 1997; Brouwer & Lowe, 1998; Miettinen, 1998; Wilson et al., 1999). The Finnish support programme, entitled the 'Finnish Agri-environmental Programme for the Years 1995–1999', has from the financial viewpoint been among the most extensive in the EU. When the main lines of this national programme were planned in the middle of the 1990s, there were two principal and contradicting basic options: whether to have as many farmers as possible involved in the subsidy scheme or to have as targeted and effective agri-environmental policy tools as possible under subsidisation. Indeed, a principal policy conflict on the essence of agri-environmental state support appeared, and agricultural policy-makers were more powerful than environmental policy players. Thus, the former option was preferred: the main part of the agri-environmental subsidies has been legitimised by the thinking that environmentally light measures with fairly good financial compensation will result in a large number of farmers joining the programme and in an improvement of the environmental awareness of farmers (MAF, 1996).

In general, Finland's entrance to the European market era stopped the major national re-distribution of agricultural income. Thus, the dominant 'welfare guarantee' for the rural Finland and the farmers is now seriously threatened – it might even be said that it has simply disappeared. Granberg (1999) has argued that nowadays welfare rationality is expressed only from the regional point of view, since the Finnish Government has prioritised the maximisation of EU income support for the 'northern' and the 'less favoured' areas. However, also the Finnish agri-environmental support, which has covered as much as 90% of the arable area, must necessarily be seen as essential income support and, thus, as typically serving the welfarist idea of equality of results between different agricultural regions and between different types of farms.

The Finnish Ministry of Agriculture and Forestry became responsible for this large agri-environmental programme, and it has been administrated and controlled by the regional and local rural officials subject to the supervision of the Ministry (MAF, 1996). Thus, not surprisingly, the present core idea held by the agricultural policy players is characterised by a fairly pronounced satisfaction with the way of combining environmental goals with agricultural policies and practices. According to them, the main lines of Finnish agri-environmental policy-making had been well established already in the early 1990s and, thus, the 'Europeanisation' could not bring any major innovations or changes. However, in the early 1990s, when the discussion on Finnish EU membership emerged, in the environmental state agency much faith was placed in European farm pollution control (Jokinen, 1995). It was expected in the Ministry of the Environment that the coming of new supranational agri-environmental rules would enable the use of legal instruments, which would also considerably strengthen the position of environmental policy actors in the control of agricultural practices. From the perspective of environmental policy-makers, thus, the main rationale of the prevailing Finnish agri-environmental regulation has appeared somewhat ambivalent: among the supranational policy and increased integration of policies, there certainly is a (financially) remarkable policy response to the urgent agri-environmental problems, the environmental goals and effectiveness of which, however, should be greatly tightened. Actually, and also somewhat paradoxically, the environmental policy players are at the same time supported by the supra-national agri-environmental regulation and pressured by their own increased involvement in the agricultural income guarantee through the implementation of the agri-environmental subsidy system.

CASE 2: NATIONAL IMPLEMENTATION OF THE EUROPEAN NATURE CONSERVATION NETWORK

To put it briefly, the EU 'Natura 2000' nature conservation network aims to conserve natural resources through a programme of habitat surveillance, evaluation and conservation. In Finland, its implementation appeared unexpectedly to be the most profound environmental conflict of the 1990s. The preparatory work was done in 1996–1997 by the Ministry of the Environment, but it received a total of approximately 14,000 written (official) complaints from land-owners, whose mobilisation was impressively supported by the farmers' association.

In the first place, here the traditional explanation through conflict of interests can surely be seen as relevant. The Natura Programme touched the traditional 'basic rights' of farmers, which is the strong emphasis on the property rights and the sense of independence in land use issues. Sairinen (2000) has even called this conflict the Finnish case of 'green backlash': indeed, for the farmers, the EU nature conservation programme embodied unjustified EU regulation, economic problems of agriculture due to the European market, and cultural resistance to nature conservation. In this case, the Ministry of the Environment found itself in a surprising position: the environmental policy-makers had to pay a major part of the political bill for farmers' dissatisfaction with the more market-led EU era.

However, the open conflict about EU-based nature conservation was also symptomatic of a more general characteristic of Finnish environmental policy style: environmental policies still seem to go back very much to nature conservation thinking and natural scientific expertise-based rationality, which results in difficulties in dealing with the various vertical and horizontal scales of action. The Ministry of the Environment neglected the social side of environmental policy by making serious mistakes in the hearing stage and, thus, it was legitimately blamed for being totally unable to negotiate with the land-owners concerned. This means that the challenges by reflexive political modernisation have proved to be, so far, too large-scale for the narrowly grounded sector policy for the environment.

DISCUSSION

The examination of the Finnish agri-environmental case confirms the importance of supranational EU regulation in the formation of environment-related policies. In the Finnish case some immediate authority has been transferred from the nation-state to the 'supra-state' and internationalisation has affected the relationship between the domestic agri-environmental state policy players. However, support is also lent to the idea that EU agri-environmental regulation manifests itself at the national level through political re-definitions of the agri-environmental issue, instead of having a homogenising effect on policy. Agri-environmental policy throws together differing policy definitions as well as differing organisational rationalities and interests, and the redefinition of the transnational rules has also advanced through the conflicts on the main principles of the policy.

In the Finnish case, overall, both the agricultural policy sector and the environmental policy sector are involved in agri-environmental issues and, thus, contribute to the development of policy. Somewhat surprisingly, however, as a result of Europeanisation the national agricultural policy actors (instead of national environmental policy actors) have become more influential in agri-environmental regulation, and agri-environmental policy seems to have been trampled on by the income and production policy objectives. As has been elaborated in more detail elsewhere (Jokinen, 2000), this is mainly due to the concern the agricultural interests felt for the survival of domestic agriculture within the EU. At least temporarily, it reinforced the agrarian and 'agricultural policy community' type of thinking in agri-environmental issues, which, as stated, had ultimately remained within national discretion. Importantly, this resulted in the use of the agri-environmental subsidy scheme as an essential part of the agricultural income policy, which also illustrated the national equalising and re-distributing tradition of 'welfare rationality' in agricultural policy. The traditionally strong position of agriculture and the national tradition of Nordic welfare policy do indeed seem to have acted as intermediating mechanisms between the 'supra-state' and nation-state policy.

The consideration in this paper might be regarded as limited in the sense that Finnish attempts to bring issues at the common EU agenda have hardly been discussed. This is mainly because the very first years of the membership appeared unique: the EU agricultural policy framework Finland had to adopt herself to was given. The national decision-making on the agri-environmental issue was also subordinated to this agricultural framework, and instead of any initiatives to the EU on environmental matters the political focus at the national level was on the re-definition of the issue. Nowadays, since the circumstances of Finnish agriculture in the more market-led era have stabilised after five years, the agri-environmental issue also seems to have been normalised. This is well illustrated by the main principles of the newly approved Finnish agri-environmental programme for 2000–2006, which do not differ significantly from those of the previous scheme. However, the recent preparation process differed from the previous one, because it did not raise any principal debate, to say nothing of conflicts. Similarly, the Finnish implementation of the Natura (the EU nature conservation programme) is now legally valid and, thus, the conflict has departed from the current political arena. As regards current Finnish interests within the Common Agricultural Policy, regional issues (for instance, instead of environmental issues) are prioritised; on the grounds of her own proposal, Finland has recently become the only EU country whose entire arable area is covered by EU support for 'less favoured agricultural area'.

REFERENCES

Alanen, I. (1995). Finland as a Peasant Society and the Agrarian Reforms. In: L. Granberg & J. Nikula (Eds), *The Peasant State*. Lapin yliopisto: Rovaniemi.

Baker, S. (1997). The Evolution of the European Union Environmental Policy: From Growth to Sustainable Development?. In: S. Baker, M. Kousis, D. Richardson & S. C. Young (Eds), *Sustainable Development: Theory, Policy and Practice in the European Union*. London: Routledge.

Baker, S., Kousis, M., Richardson, D., & Young, S. (1997). Introduction. The Theory and Practice of Sustainable Development in EU Perspective. In: S. Baker, M. Kousis, D. Richardson & S. C. Young (Eds), *Sustainable Development: Theory, Policy and Practice in the European Union*. London: Routledge.

Baldock, D., & Lowe, P. (1996). The Development of European Agri-environmental Policy. In: M. Whitby (Ed.), *The European Environment and CAP Reform. Policies and Prospects for Conservation*. Guilford: CAB International.

Billaud, J., Bruckmeier, K., Patricio, T., & Pinton, F. (1997). Social Construction of the Rural Environment. In: H. De Haan, B. Kasimis & M. Redclift (Eds), *Sustainable Rural Development*. Aldershot: Ashgate.

Brouwer, F., & Lowe, P. (1998). CAP Reform and the Environment. In: F. Brouwer & P. Lowe (Eds), *CAP and the Rural Environment in Transition. A Panorama of National Perspectives*. Wageningen: Wageningen Pers.

Buller, H., Lowe, P., & Flynn, A. (1995). National Responses to the Europeanisation of Environmental Policy: a Selective Review of Comparative Research. In: J. D. Liefferink, P. D. Lowe & A. P. J. Mol (Eds), *European Integration and Environmental Policy*. Wiltshire: John Wiley & Sons.

Castells, M. (1996). *The Information Age. The Rise of the Network Society*. Cornwall: Blackwell.

Christiansen, P. M., & Lundqvist, L. (1996). Conclusions: A Nordic Environmental Policy Model? In: P. M. Christiansen (Ed.), *Governing the Environment: Politics, Policy, and Organization in the Nordic Countries*. Copenhagen: Nordic Council of Ministers.

Cobb, D., Dolman, P., & O'Riordan, T. (1999). Interpretations of Sustainable Agriculture in the U.K. *Progress in Human Geography*, *23*(2), 209–235.

Curry, N., & Stucki, E. (1997). Swiss Agricultural Policy and the Environment: An Example for the Rest of Europe to Follow? *Journal of Environmental Planning and Management*, *40*(4), 465–482.

Daugbjerg, C. (1999). The Nature of Environmental Policy Making: A Comparison of Danish and Swedish Agri-environmental Policy. In: M. Joas & A. Hermanson (Eds), *The Nordic Environments: Comparing Political, Administrative, and Policy Aspects*. Aldershot: Ashgate.

Ebbinghaus, B. (1999). Europe Through the Looking-Glass: Comparative and Multi-Level Perspectives. *Acta Sociologica*, *41*(4), 301–314.

Epstein, P. J. (1997). Beyond Policy Community: French Agriculture and the GATT. *Journal of European Public Policy*, *4*(3), 355–372.

Granberg, L. (1995). A Break in Agriculture. From Peasant Values to Welfare Rationality. In: L. Granberg & J. Nikula (Eds), *The Peasant State*. Lapin yliopisto: Rovaniemi.

Granberg., L. (1999). The Emergence of Welfare State Rationality in Finnish Agricultural Policy. *Sociologia Ruralis*, *39*(3), 311–327.

Jamison, A., & Baark, E. (1999). National Shades of Green: Comparing the Swedish and Danish Styles in Ecological Modernisation. *Environmental Values*, *8*(2), 199–218.

Jokinen, P. (1995). The Development of Agricultural Pollution Control in Finland. *Sociologia Ruralis*, *35*(2), 206–227.

Jokinen, P. (1997). Agricultural Policy Community and the Challenge of Greening. The Case of the Finnish Agri-environmental Policy. *Environmental Politics*, *6*(2), 48–71.

Jokinen, P. (2000). Europeanisation and Ecological Modernisation: Agri-Environmental Policy and Practices in Finland. *Environmental Politics*, *9*(1), 138–167.

Katajamäki, H. (1999). Historical Transformations of Rural Finland. *New Rural Policy*, *7*(2), 11–21.

Konttinen, E. (1999). Environmental Challenges in Finnish Countryside in the 1990s. In: E. Konttinen, T. Litmanen, M. Nieminen & M. Ylönen (Eds), *All Shades of Green. The Environmentalization of Finnish Society*. SoPhi. Jyväskylä.

Kosonen, P. (1993). The Scandinavian Welfare Model in the New Europe. In: T. P. Boje & S. E. Olsson (Eds), *Scandinavia in a New Europe*. Oslo: University Press.

Liberatore, A. (1997). The Integration of Sustainable Development Objectives into EU Policy-making. In: S. Baker, M. Kousis, D. Richardson & S. C. Young (Eds), *Sustainable Development: Theory, Policy and Practice in the European Union*. London: Routledge.

Lundqvist, L. J. (1999). Nordic Environmental Policy in Transition: Ecological Modernisation and Beyond. In: M. Joas & A. Hermanson (Eds), *The Nordic Environments: Comparing Political, Administrative, and Policy Aspects*. Aldershot: Ashgate.

Macnaghten, P., & J. Urry (1998). *Contested Natures*. London: Sage.

MAF (1996). Ministry of Agriculture and Forestry. *The Agri-environmental Programme in Finland*.

Marsden, T., Murdoch, J., Lowe, P., Munton, R., & Flynn, A. (1993). Constructing the Countryside. London: UCL Press.

Miettinen, A. (1998). Finland. In: F. Brouwer & P. Lowe (Eds), *CAP and the Rural Environment in Transition. A Panorama of National Perspectives*. Wageningen: Wageningen Pers.

Mjoset, L. (1992). The Nordic Model Never Existed, but Does it Have a Future? *Scandinavian Studies*, *64*(4), 652–671.

Mol, A., & Sonnenfeld, D. (2000). *Ecological Modernisation around the World: an Introduction*. In: A. P. J. Mol & D. A. Sonnenfeld (Eds), *Ecological Modernisation around the World: Perspectives and Critical Debates*. London: Frank Cass.

Niemi-Iilahti, A., & Jokinen, P. (1999). Three Years' Experience of EU Integration: the Case of the CAP and Agri-environmental Subsidies in Finland. In: M. Joas & A. Hermanson (Eds), *The Nordic Environments: Comparing Political, Administrative, and Policy Aspects*. Aldershot: Ashgate.

Oksa, J., & Rannikko, P. (1996). The Changing Meanings of Rurality Challenge Rural Policies. *New Rural Policy*, *3*, 3–14.

Rannikko, P. (1999). Combining Social and Ecological Sustainability in the Nordic Forest Periphery. *Sociologia Ruralis*, *39*(3), 394–410.

Sairinen, R. (2000). *Regulatory Reform of Finnish Environmental Policy*. Centre for Urban and Regional Studies: Espoo.

Van Tatenhove, J. (1999). Political Modernisation and the Institutionalisation of Environmental Policy. In: M. Wissenburg, G. Orhan & U. Collier (Eds), *European Discourses on Environmental Policy*. Aldershot: Ashgate.

Walby, S. (1999). The New Regulatory State: The Social Powers of the European Union. British *Journal of Sociology*, *50*(1), 118–140.

Wilson, G. A., Petersen, J., & Höll, A. (1999). EU Member State Responses to Agri-Environmental Regulation 2078/92/EEC – towards a Conceptual Framework. *Geoforum*, *30*(2), 185–202.

Winter, M. (1996). *Rural Politics. Policies for Agriculture, Forestry & the Environment*. London: Routledge.

Winter, M. (2000). Strong Policy or Weak Policy? The Environmental Impact of the 1992 Reforms to the CAP Arable Land Regime in Great Britain. *Journal of Rural Studies*, *16*(1), 47–59.

Yearley, S., Baker, S., & Milton, K. (1994), Environmental Policy and Peripheral Regions of the European Union: an Introduction. In: S. Baker, K. Milton & S. Yearley (Eds), *Protecting the Periphery. Environmental Policy in Peripheral Regions of the European Union*. Essex: Frank Cass.

Young. O. (1995). The Problem of Scale in Human/Environment Relationships. In: R. Keohane & E. Ostrom (Eds), *Local Commons and Global Interdependence. Heterogeneity and Cooperation in Two Domains*. London: Sage.

ENVIRONMENTAL DISCOURSE AND THE STATE: A SOCIAL ANALYSIS OF DEBATES ON TRANSPORT AND ENVIRONMENT IN PORTUGAL AND THE NETHERLANDS

C. S. A. (Kris) Van Koppen

INTRODUCTION

Characteristically, the state has occupied a central place in environmental policy theory. The arguments for this position seemed obvious: the physical environment was considered to be a public good and a legacy to future generations, which could not be left to individual preferences and market mechanisms; there was little trust in the environmental motives and capacities of other sectors of society, such as industry; and environmental policy was closely associated with traditional responsibilities of the state such as public health, physical planning, infrastructure, and forestry. Especially since the mid-1980s, however, the position of the state with respect to environmental protection has been under attack, for reasons of both *effectiveness* and *legitimacy*.

In the course of the development of national environmental policies, it became clear that there are limits to the *effectiveness of direct regulation*. Market mechanisms and self-regulation of industry appeared to be necessary

The Environmental State Under Pressure, Volume 10, pages 121–146.

ISBN: 0-7623-0854-0

complements to legal and administrative regulation by the state. In addition, critics of the state have pointed out that the *scale level of the state* prevents it from dealing effectively with environmental problems. The state level is considered to be either too high (which prompts the call for a regionalization of environmental protection) or too low (by many analysts stressing the transboundary nature of environmental problems and the globalization of the driving forces of environmental degradation). Moreover, the *legitimacy of the state* as the central institution for coping with environmental degradation is at stake. As Beck and Giddens emphasize, the emergence of new arrangements that can be said to "work around" the formal politics of the state – *subpolitics* in the wording of Beck – is related to a decline in the legitimacy of conventional politics under conditions of reflexive modernization (Hogenboom et al., 1999).[1]

Despite such criticism, the position of the state in environmental protection is still strong, not only in practice, but also in environmental sociology.[2] There is no certainty about the direction of future developments. Neither is there an unequivocal answer to the question of which theoretical approach – or, citing Weale (1992), what "idiom of analysis" – would be most adequate to better understand and anticipate these developments.

One way of further exploring this theme – a way followed in this article – is to analyze the structure of societal debates on specific environmental controversies. What role is claimed by the national government? What role do other actors attribute to the state, and what roles do they attribute to themselves and other non-state actors? What sort of arguments are put forward by actor coalitions to defend their interests? How do different coalitions influence the outcome of the debate? With regard to the different aspects of the position of the state, this approach implies that the emphasis will be on legitimacy, though we must bear in mind that legitimacy is not independent of effectiveness. With regard to the idiom of analysis, my approach will be close to what Weale (1992, p. 55 ff.) identifies as the "policy discourse idiom."

The article originates from the EU research project "Transport and Risk Communication" in which the author participated. Most of the empirical material presented here is derived from the project report (Mormont et al., 1997). My aim here is to further articulate the theoretical framework developed in the project, and to illustrate it with a brief account of two cases of large transport infrastructure projects: the planning of a new bridge over the Tagus river in Portugal and the planning of a new freight railway line across the Netherlands.[3] Both Portugal and the Netherlands are small EU member countries, and in each one transport infrastructure is considered to be a vital condition for economic development. In both cases, the infrastructure projects generated heated public debate on transport, environment, and the economy.

A THEORETICAL FRAMEWORK

The environmental debates central to this article concern large and complex projects. Large implies that they are deemed to be of such importance and size that they become part of a substantial political decision-making process. Complex means that they affect many interest groups in different ways, and have multiple environmental and socio-economic consequences, many of which are difficult or impossible to assess. The infrastructure projects used as cases are examples of this type of project. The political debate on these projects typically develops across different channels and issues. Interest groups may use lobbying, lawsuits, policy procedures, public demonstrations, media publicity and other means of promoting their objectives. The environment is only one of issues at stake and has to be balanced against other major issues. This type of project, in short, draws heavily on a society's capacity for decision making.

Many social science studies have been devoted to clarifying and improving these decision-making processes. Analyses have been made from different angles, such as environmental impact assessment, multi-criteria analysis, local protest (e.g. NIMBY-studies), participatory decision making, and risk communication. The concept of risk in particular has spawned a vast body of literature linking environmental impacts, public perception, and political decision making. This article builds on these studies of risk assessment and risk communication.[4] It should be noted that the concept of risk, as I use it here, has a broad meaning, encompassing low probability/high consequence risks (such as calamities caused by transport of dangerous substances) as well as high probability/low consequence risks (such as traffic noise). In other words, the term "environmental risk" has a large overlap with "environmental impact."

At the heart this article are the concepts of political debate and discourse. By political debate, I understand the whole of publicity, open discussion and political decision making concerning a certain project. I will focus more specifically on environmental risk debates; that is, political debates in which environmental issues play a substantial (though rarely an exclusive) role. As I said, such debates may involve a variety of arguments and communication channels and they generally elude a precise demarcation in space and time. Their course is contingent on all sorts of events and their outcome is often unpredictable. Still, they are subject to characteristic social patterns that enable us to conceptualize them as social structures. I distinguish 3 sorts of structural aspects that characterize a political debate:

(1) rules of discourse, determining which normative principles and modes of argumentation are valid and legitimate;
(2) organizational platforms situating the debate, such as a public hearing, a court of justice, or a national parliament;
(3) specific resources connected to the debate, such as access to the media, executive power, or command of financial budgets.

Here, I will concentrate on the rules of discourse. What is their importance in political debates? Boltanski and Thevenot, who investigated discourses in political philosophy and organizational management, motivate their effort in these words.

> If one is attentive to the development of debates, one sees that they are not limited to a direct expression of interests, nor to an anarchistic and pointless confrontation of diverging world views . . .. On the contrary, provided that violence is avoided, the development of debates demonstrates that there are strong constraints in the search for well-founded and solidly proven arguments, and thus shows that, even at the heart of dispute, there are efforts towards convergence (Boltanski & Thevenot, 1991, p. 26, *author's translation*).

As Boltanski and Thevenot demonstrate for discourses in political philosophy and management, the constraints can be ordered according to a limited set of discursive structures, each with its own normative principles and rules. While the course of political debates is often malleable and unpredictable, these discursive structures are of a much more general and stable character. Boltanski and Thevenot call them "states" or "worlds"; other authors, in other contexts, use words like "paradigms"; "logics", or "rationalities" to convey roughly the same meaning. I will use the word *discourse*, to indicate that it represents a discursive structure, with an internal consistency and meaning that transcend the specific situation in which it is used. This interpretation, indebted in some ways to the work of Foucault, confers a certain autonomy on a discourse, without detaching it from its social and historical context (Foucault, 1969).

The concept of discourse is subject to an extensive theoretical debate, which I will not enter into here.[5] However, a few brief remarks may help to outline the concept as I will use it here. To understand the status of discourse, it is important to distinguish between the discourse, the discursive, and the non-discursive (cf. Torfing, 1999, p. 90 ff.). A discourse is situated in a discursive field of meanings, propositions, arguments etc. that are relevant to it. It structures this discursive field, but it does not totally cover or fix it. The debate, in other words, is much richer and more ambiguous than the discourse. This makes it possible, for one thing, that competing discourses are articulated within the same debate. Like Foucault in his earlier work, I also distinguish between a discourse and its non-discursive conditions. Non-discursive is to say that they are outside the discursive field that is meaningful to the discourse (though, of course, they may be meaningful in other discursive fields). Events outside of a technological discourse, for instance – a political event, an economic shift – may still influence its structure. Moreover (and unlike Foucault) I interpret the structure of the discourse in accordance with what Giddens (1984, p. 25 ff.) calls the duality of structure: it is produced and reproduced in social practices. Actors not only adapt to the rules and principles that constitute the structure of the discourse, they also make use of them and try to modify them. Even if the influence of separate groups of actors is limited, discourses may change in content and importance in a relatively short time, as is illustrated by the establishment of environmental protection as a political argument, or by the emergence of participation as a principle of democracy.[6]

Several authors have used the "discourse idiom" (Weale, 1992) to analyze environmental controversies and environmental politics (e.g. Litfin, 1994; Hajer, 1995; Eder, 1996; Dryzek, 1997; Jasanoff, 1999). Two of them are of particular interest here. Hajer (1995) analyzes the rise of ecological modernization as an environmental discourse in the United Kingdom and the Netherlands. His concept of discourse, also drawing on Foucault and Giddens, is quite close to the one in this article. Following Boltanski and Thevenot, however, this article puts a greater emphasis on the coherence of a discourse (cf. Hajer, 1995, p. 44). Dryzek (1997) analyses both radical and more conventional positions in environmental politics. His analysis of conventional positions is to some extent comparable with the discourses of direction that will be distinguished below. While both Hajer's and Dryzek's studies cover a much longer period and a wider array of environmental debates than the EU project, and their studies were not directly used as input to the theoretical framework of the EU project, it is interesting to note these aspects of convergence.

Discourses of Interests

The analysis of discourses in environmental risk debates, as presented in this article, starts from a sample of risk literature. Several categories of considerations are identified in studies of public debates on risks, a few typical examples of which are mentioned here. In a social-psychological perspective Wilke (1989, 1991) distinguishes three motives which govern people's decisions on risk-bearing public projects: *greed* (personal benefits), *efficiency* (the efficient use of common goods), and *fairness* (conformity to what is regarded as generally fair). Kunreuther (1992), who approaches the management of risk from an economic angle, identifies two main types of considerations: *efficiency* (the optimal allocation of resources for society as a whole, across all interested parties) and *equity* (the balanced distribution of differential impact among the interested parties). Rayner (1992), representing a cultural approach to risk, proposes a concept of risk management in which risk is seen as a combination of the engineering aspect (probability * magnitude of consequences) and the social aspect. The social aspect consists of three principles: *trust* (towards the institutions that manage and regulate the technology), *liability* (the principle used to apportion liabilities for undesired consequences to those affected), and *consent* (the acceptability of the procedures by which collective consent for a course of action is obtained). As to these procedures, he outlines three reasoning styles: the *hierarchy*, *market*, and *collective* style. In the sociological approach of Wynne (1987, 1992a, b) a crucial distinction is that between *local knowledge*, related to local practices, and *scientific* or *technocratic* risk assessment, related to the bureaucratic procedures of governmental policy. He stresses the importance of integrating local knowledge in risk management, in what he calls a *social learning approach.* The sociologists Freudenburg and Pastor (1992) identify three basic perspectives on public protest against locally unwanted land uses: the public as *ignorant or irrational* (a perspective which they consider inadequate), the public as *selfish* (defending what they see as their private interests), and the public as *prudent* (contributing to better decision making for society as a whole).

Although these categorizations stem from very different theoretical approaches, we can identify similar principles in them. Two quite obvious sets of principles are those related to private or *local interests* and those related to the good of society as a whole, or *general interests.*

Interventions based on *local interests* of the actors are a common trait of environmental risk debates. Quite often, these interventions are referred to as NIMBY (Not In My Back Yard) protest, usually with negative connotations (Wolsink, 1994). It is important to note, however, that "selfish" resistance to activities because of their negative local effects is in many respects considered justified (Freudenburg & Pastor, 1992). As long as individuals and organizations comply with legitimate political and juridical procedures and acceptable methods of non-violent protest, they have the right to intervene in decision-making processes that affect their interests and to maximize their personal benefit. The normative principles that govern this discourse of local interests are related to the *protection of the physical, social and economic well-being of citizens,* to *civil rights* and to *equity.*[7] Protection of well-being implies, for instance, that noise nuisance or ambient air pollution should not exceed established threshold values. Civil rights involve the protection of private property.

The principle of equity (or fairness) implies that the achievement of a public aim should not inflict disproportionate damage on one group of people. Possible damage includes financial losses, but also unequal distribution of environmental effects. If such damage is unavoidable, then the groups involved should be at least compensated in a fair way.

The major part of the arguments in environmental risk debates are based on *general interests*. As was illustrated by the examples above, these general interests are often referred to as *efficiency*. In environmental debates concerning large projects we find two major discourses under this heading: the *environmental effectiveness* discourse and the *economic efficiency* discourse. When interested parties present balances of environmental gains and losses that will result from a project, they enter the *environmental effectiveness* discourse. Unlike the environmental arguments in the local interests discourse, the arguments in the environmental effectiveness discourse are based on the interests of broader categories of people, including future generations; they may even be based on the assumed interests of non-human beings. Arguments concerning environmental effectiveness may refer to a wide variety of problems, ranging from local contamination of the soil and regional degradation of natural areas to world resource depletion and global warming. The *economic efficiency* discourse – dealing with the economic costs and benefits for the "society as a whole" – is a structuring factor to almost every controversial political issue. One of the most common and strongest lines of argument in political controversies is that the societal costs of a project will exceed the benefits, or the same societal benefits could be attained at lower costs. Economic efficiency and environmental effectiveness constitute the main arenas where environmental risk debates are fought and decided. Though local interests are usually acknowledged, environmental risk debates are predominantly framed as general interest debates, that is, as arguments concerning the common good. The negative connotations of the NIMBY qualification have precisely to do with this point. It is not so much that it blames protest groups for defending their own interests, but that it denies them the right to engage in the – much more powerful – debates on the common good.

Usually, these general interests discourses focus on the level of the nation-state. The public interests and aims that are central to the arguments are often related to national economy and national environmental policy. But this is not necessarily so. In order to conceptualize the common good, actors may also refer to higher scale levels, such as the world economy or the planetary biosphere. From these global points of view the national interests would appear to be local interests. The dividing line between the local and the general is therefore not a fixed one. However, it is not primarily the economic or physical scale of the problem under discussion that determines the level of the general interest discourse; the key question is which authority is held to legitimately represent the interests of all.

Discourses of Direction

The previous section presented some examples of the risk debate in the literature. The ordering of local interests and general interests discourses in the previous section covers only a part of the arguments in literature. Many of the considerations in the publications mentioned above – as well as in more recent literature, e.g. Grove-White (1996), Jasanoff (1999) – do not concern the issues and interests at stake, but the political *approaches* (Wynne, 1992b) or *reasoning styles* (Rayner, 1992) by which these issues are resolved. To take these considerations into account we need to turn to another domain of discourse, the discourses on legitimate ways of directing society. Reviewing the aforementioned risk literature and comparing this literature with broader studies of political legitimacy (Habermas, 1968; Boltanski & Thevenot, 1991; Hisschemöller, 1993) we can distinguish different styles of political reasoning. These styles of reasoning can be interpreted as discourses. As a consequence of this interpretation, reasoning styles are not linked to specific groups of actors, like for instance Wynne (1992b) and Rayner (1992) do. In principle, any group can engage in any discourse, as far as it has the means of having its arguments heard. Although the social positions, interests, and value orientations of the groups involved play an important role in disputes, it is first of all the discourse itself, according to this interpretation, that is structuring the ways of reasoning in policy debates.[8] Most of the different positions on the direction of society that we encounter in risk literature can be captured in four discourses.

(1) The *decisionist* discourse. This discourse is often also referred to as hierarchical or authoritarian. I will use the term *decisionist* to avoid the suggestion that this mode of reasoning is undemocratic or centralist *per se*. It corresponds to Weber's theory of political power, according to which political decisions are justified by the position of the political leader, not by rational discourse (Habermas, 1968). Decision-making power can be located centrally or delegated to decentral levels. But in either case there is no open debate at the core of decision making. The decision-making process can only be changed by electing new representatives, appointing new officials or modifying their powers. In the decisionist discourse, the

focus of debate is not so much on the decisions themselves, but rather on the conditions of legitimacy: the competence and legality of the decision-making authorities.

(2) The *market* discourse. In this discourse political controversies are not to be resolved by political decisions, but by the interplay of market forces. It might seem strange to speak of a discourse here, since the market system is often depicted as being beyond the communicative sphere. However, as Boltanski and Thévenot (1991) point out, the market approach is in fact embedded in normative rules concerning the way in which the sum of individual choices will serve a common good (such as equal access to the market, fair pricing and limitation of the market forces where they clearly violate principles of utility). While the day-to-day decisions are scattered among the individual actors, the legitimate functioning of the market in accordance with these normative rules, remains a public issue and can become subject of political debate.

(3) The *technocratic* discourse aims at framing political problems into scientific or technological questions and consequently solving these problems by means of scientific advice or technological solutions. Parties in a controversy may engage in this discourse by bringing in expertise and counter-expertise. In a technocratic approach, each conclusion must be argued for in an open debate, but this debate is confined to scientific arguments and it is the consensus of the scientific forum that is decisive. A technocratic mode of reasoning typically starts from normative goals, set outside the domain of science, that constitute the premises of the scientific or technological argument. Being essential conditions of a technocratic approach, both the scientific consensus and the normative premises are often the targets of criticism in legitimacy debates (cf. Rip, 1992).

(4) The *participatory* discourse considers political decision-making processes as open debates in which the stakeholders, with diverging interests and varying types of knowledge, negotiate and try to come to agreement. We may also call this a *consensual* approach, but negotiations, package deals and compromises are as much part of it as is consensus in a strict sense. Wynne's process of social learning, as well as Rayner's collective reasoning style relate to this discourse. Many other contemporary contributions to the social analysis of risk also underline the importance of a participatory approach to understanding risk (cf. Jasanoff, 1999; Grove-White, 1996). Since the structure of the debate itself is in principle very open, the demarcation of the debate – which individuals or group representatives can legitimately participate – is of great importance in this discourse.

Dynamics of Debates: Uncertainty and Closure

Large projects, such as the transport cases discussed here, bring threats and opportunities to a wide array of groups: local residents, economic interest groups, government officials, politicians, and environmental organizations. In the public debate that is likely to emerge around such projects, the participants are compelled to produce strong and valid arguments that advance their own position and undermine adverse positions. As I have hypothesized, these arguments are structured according to two sets of discourses: the *issues and interests* put forward are predominantly informed by the discourses of economic efficiency, environmental effectiveness, and local interest; whereas the *styles of political reasoning* are governed by the decisionist, technocratic, market and participatory discourses.

It is worth noting here, that there is no one-to-one relationship between discourses on issues and on reasoning modes; they can come together in different ways. An issue of local interests, for instance, can be put forward in accordance with the decisionist discourse (by stressing the competence of local authorities), the technocratic discourse (by appealing for scientific assessment of local social or environmental impacts) or the participatory discourse (by advocating negotiations between local groups and government officials). With simple risk issues, there may be a clear and generally accepted mode of reasoning (for instance, a technocratic approach for dealing with the safety requirements of a bridge). In environmental risk debates, however, the issues are often much more complex, and actors may slip from one mode of political reasoning into another, depending on the situation (cf. Boltanski & Thevenot, 1991, p. 30).

A central characteristic of environmental risk debates on large projects is uncertainty (e.g. Wynne, 1987). This uncertainty is caused by the complexity of the issues at stake, as well as by the dynamics of the debate. In their search for arguments, parties involved will be inclined to broaden and upscale the debate, for instance by introducing new technological options, by appealing to other authorities, or by questioning the legitimacy of unfavorable modes of political reasoning. Whenever possible, new arenas that might offer better positions and stronger resources will be opened, for instance when local groups start to address issues on the level of national interests. These processes tend to heighten the complexity of the problems and the uncertainties that surround the decision-making processes. When uncertainties appear to be persistent and pose an obstacle to a legitimate outcome of the controversy, they are likely to move towards the center of the debate. To proceed with the decision-making process, these central uncertainties have to be dealt with. Uncertainties can be regarded as closed when they no longer obstruct a legitimate decision-making process. This does not mean that uncertainties no longer exist, but it means that there is sufficient consent about the way they are handled to avoid political disintegration and violence. This closure of uncertainties is an important movement in the dynamics of environmental risk debates, paralleling and interacting with the actual establishment of a political decision.

Since uncertainties normally obstruct a decisive argument on the issues involved, the modes of political reasoning are very important in this process of closure. In correspondence with the discourses of direction, I distinguish four modes of closure (cf. Dryzek, 1997).

(1) "Let the authority handle it." According to the decisionist approach, the uncertainties are left to an authority that is legally entitled to deal with them – having been elected or formally appointed for this task – without further argument.
(2) "Leave it to the market." The market approach is based on the assumption that, by virtue of the market forces, the uncertainties will translate into opportunity and risk costs that will bring about an optimal allocation of resources.
(3) "Let experts handle it." The technocratic approach tries to cope with uncertainties by a scientific assessment of environmental risks as well as costs and benefits. The assessment results are aggregated and weighed by means of objectifying decision-making techniques such as multi-criteria analysis.
(4) "Discuss it among the stakeholders." The participatory approach consists in launching a debate in which the stakeholding parties try to come to an agreement on how to deal with the uncertainties.

We will now turn from the theoretical discussion to the case studies. Both cases concern infrastructure project plans that generated widely resonating policy debates with substantial environmental aspects. In the case of Portugal, the subject of dispute was the location of a new bridge over the Tagus River, in the Netherlands it was the construction of a new railway line. For each case, I will first give a brief description of the development of the debate and then analyze the debate according to the theoretical framework presented above.

THE CASE OF THE TAGUS BRIDGE IN PORTUGAL

The case of the Tagus Bridge concerns the planning of a new crossing of the Tagus River in the Lisbon region.[9] One of the largest of its kind in the world, this project had a significant infrastructural impact at the regional and national levels, as well as on international transport. It was the first infrastructural project in Portugal to generate a heated public debate. This debate, launched by Portuguese environmental organizations, did not question the need for a river crossing, but focused on the choice of site.

Before the building of the new bridge, there was only one bridge (the April 25th Bridge) connecting the central and northern parts of the Lisbon metropolitan area with the south bank of the river. The old bridge was more and more frequently blocked by traffic jams, and in 1990 the Minister of Public Works, Transports and Communications, Ferreira do Amaral, announced the construction of a new bridge. In 1991 a "Working Group for the Tagus River Crossing in Lisbon" (Gabinete para a Travessia do Tejo em Lisboa – GATTEL) was created under the aegis of the Ministry of Public Works, with representatives from the ministries responsible for finances, physical planning, and environment. GATTEL delivered a comparative study to the Minister, that identified two feasible locations for the bridge: a "central corridor" and an "eastern corridor." It was on these alternatives that the debate focused.

From the very start of the decision-making process, the Minister of Public Works had expressed his intention to locate the bridge at the eastern corridor. Of the two alternatives, this one called the Montijo-Sacavém option presented the greatest risks to the environment. The south bank of the crossing is a rural area with salt basins and marshes which are valuable for harboring various species of birds, mollusks, crustaceans and fish. There is also a Special Protection Zone for Bird Life (ZPE) on this side of the Tagus estuary, as well as other nature reserves. When in the course of 1991 it became clear that the choice would be the Montijo-Sacavém option, Portuguese environmental associations started a wave of protests.[10]

At first this protest was mainly channeled towards the European Union. The strategy was to mobilize legal means at the European level, most notably the European directive on bird life protection, to influence the decision-making process. Soon, however, the environmentalists broadened their arguments to the issues of physical planning surrounding the choice of location. In the perspective of socio-economic development, the Montijo-Sacavèm option would give a major impulse to private road transport, while the central corridor option (providing for light rail on the April 25th Bridge) would stimulate collective transport and urban rehabilitation. For these reasons several organizations and authorities – among which were the ministries responsible for physical planning and environment – favored the central corridor option. But unlike the environmental organizations, none of these actors voiced strong protests. By widening the debate, the environmental organizations succeeded in generating much more media attention, even though they never managed to entirely cast off the image of "bird freaks."

In July 1992, while the Minister of Environment was on holiday, the Council of Ministers formally decided to construct the bridge in Montijo. Various reactions ensued. Montijo and its neighboring county celebrated the decision, but several mayors of municipalities in the south that would have benefited from the central corridor option criticized the central government for their exclusion from the decision-making process. In parliament, the small Ecological Party protested against the way decision making had taken place, but, in spite of strong pressure from the environmental organizations, the influential Socialist Party and Communist Party kept silent. The main criticism from those who did raise their voice in public centered on the lack of solid foundations for the choice of location and the obvious weakness of the arguments of the Ministry of Public Works. This criticism concerned both the ecological and the economic uncertainties looming over the project.

An Environmental Impact Assessment of the new bridge was completed in 1994. Though heavily criticized by environmentalists for its scientific flaws, it was approved by the European Commission. The European Commission also agreed with the construction of the bridge within the ZPE bird conservation zone, on condition of compensating conservation measures (even though such an agreement is only legitimate if there is no alternative location). The indirect economic aspects of the bridge generated the most intense public concern. While a substantial amount of the bridge's cost was covered by EU funding and loans and by national funds, another part of the financing had to be secured by raising the tolls on the April 25th Bridge. In the summer of 1994, public protest against these tolls cumulated in four days of "businão"(honking) protests on the April 25th Bridge, followed by a blockade that was violently repressed by the police. Representatives of the environmental organizations played along with these economic uncertainties, among other things by sending letters to the companies participating in the bridge consortium to warn them of the investment risks. Information on the "financial engineering" of the bridge was not provided and even the City Government of Lisbon stated it "had never received the studies of an economic-financial nature that the government based its choice upon" (Barros et al., 1997, p. 128).

However, all these protests did not affect the governmental decision. Construction was started in 1995 and in 1998 the imposing bridge – crossing 8 km of land and 10 km of water, with a 47 m high main span mounted on 148 m high pylon towers – was opened as the "Vasco da Gama Bridge."

Analysis: The Opening of a Decisionist Position

The Tagus Bridge has become the center of a debate on questions of transportation, environment, and spatial planning, of a size and scope that had never been seen in Portuguese society. During the entire debate, the government's approach was clearly decisionist, and the environmental movement continuously attempted to open other arenas for debate. On the one hand they appealed – unsuccessfully – to higher levels of authority, namely the EU; on the other hand they tried – with more success – to arouse a public debate in Portugal. Their approach can to a large extent be characterized as technocratic: they opposed the location mainly by stressing the lack of clarity and scientific argumentation in the decision-making process. As one respondent of the Ecological Party said: "For a long time, our war horse was to demand transparency in processes, to know what criteria, what options, what studies would serve as the basis for the decisions to be taken on the matter" (Barros et al., 1997, p. 108). Another feature is the widening of the debate, from issues of nature protection to issues of physical planning and socio-economic development. There were no suitable platforms and resources to further discuss these issues, but in the course of the public debate it became clear that the uncertainties surrounding them were not adequately accounted for, and that the choice for the location was being made in an overtly authoritarian style. A Lisbon city official summarizes: "It was an authentic I want, I can, and I order it to be done, by the Minister" (Barros et al., 1997, p. 122). This decisionist approach was rejected by environmental movement representatives: "We do not accept that decisions be made in a unilateral manner and entirely closed off from everything" (Barros et al., 1997, p. 119). But most other parties involved considered the decision-making style to be legitimate, even if they remained opposed to the location. In the words of an opponent from the Socialist Party: "But that was a decision of a Government that enjoyed popular legitimacy – the decision was legitimate." (Barros et al., 1997, p. 119). The personal charisma of the Minister, Ferreira do Amaral, added to that legitimacy.

Portugal is a country that has been rapidly transforming in the past decades "from a State used to imposing its will despotically into one now obliged to account for itself" (Mónica, 1996, p. 42, translation by Barros et al., 1997, p. 133). In the idiom of this article, this transition implies that political decision making is no longer exclusively governed by the decisionist discourse. New spaces for public and scientific debate are opening up, structured by technocratic and participatory discourses. Though not successful in influencing the actual decision, the efforts of the environmental movement have undoubtedly stimulated this process, and they have contributed to the articulation of issues of environment, physical planning, and economic development within the emerging discursive spaces. These changes in political discourse were felt by most of the actors involved – whether opponent or supporter of the decision – and expressed in the shared view that "nothing will be like it was before the bridge" (Barros et al., 1997, p. 133).

THE CASE OF THE BETUWE LINE IN THE NETHERLANDS

Apart from the expansion of Schiphol Airport, there has not been any infrastructure project in the 1990s that has been so intensely debated in Dutch society as the Betuwe Line.[11] The Betuwe Line (in Dutch: Betuweroute) is a railway line dedicated to freight transport from the port of Rotterdam into Germany. In 1990 the project was incorporated in the national policy plans for two main reasons: upgrading good transport from Rotterdam to the German "hinterland" and mitigating the environmental impacts of road transport by a shift to rail freight. The Dutch Railways (Nederlandse Spoorwegen) jumped on the project and in 1991 published a Notification of Intent that was the formal starting point of the decision-making procedure. At the same time, a round of consultations was started in which the plans of the Dutch Railways were presented to the municipal authorities involved.

The initially positive or neutral attitude of the municipalities shifted when it became clear that Dutch Railways were not inclined to adapt the route variants contained in the Notification to their suggestions. They then insisted on a strict observation of environmental conditions (mainly: noise nuisance and risks from hazardous substances), to be dealt with in the Environmental Impact Assessment required for the project. The local populations reacted even more critically when confronted with the plans. Pressure groups emerged in most of the 28 municipalities situated along the projected line. The aim of these groups was to prevent the line from crossing their municipality. Many of them combined forces in the National Betuwe Line Association (Vereniging Landelijk Overleg Betuweroute – VLOB). From the outset, the VLOB took the position that the need for the Betuwe Line, both in economic and in environmental terms, had not been demonstrated.

In 1992 the Dutch Railways published a Project Memorandum. This report presented a rationale for the Betuwe Line, underpinned with arguments of national economy, environment, and infrastructure capacity. It included the Environmental Impact Statement and identified the optimum route variant according to economic and environmental criteria. This variant was taken over by the government and subsequently entered into a mandatory procedure of consultation and advice from stakeholders. During this period, the local protests grew into a public debate on a national scale. Local actors gained increasing support from advisory bodies and university experts for their criticism of the Betuwe Line. The standards for noise nuisance that had been applied in the Environmental Impact Assessment were disputed. In cooperation with experts in underground construction, pressure groups and lower-level authorities promoted the alternative of completely tunneling the Betuwe Line, in order to avoid all local impacts. At the same time, and again with the help of scientists, the pressure groups joined in the VLOB successfully pointed out the uncertainties on the economic and environmental benefits. The government itself acknowledged the insufficiency of the strategic underpinning of the project in the Project Memorandum and commissioned additional research.

In the spring of 1993, however, the government agreed to the construction of the Betuwe Line and stated that it was in line with national environmental policy, that aboveground construction was fully acceptable and that the route – which was now defined within narrow margins – had been situated with consideration for the local consequences. Local actors, of course, were disappointed, but pinned their hopes on the political debate in parliament. The VLOB organized a national conference, in cooperation with a scientific society of physical planners, to stimulate a fundamental debate on the issues involved (NIROV/VLOB, 1993). The environmental organizations had initially accepted the railway line on the condition that the plans would be adapted to environmental requirements, but now decided to withdraw their support.[12]

When, at the end of 1993, the issue was decided in parliament, both the right-wing liberals and two parties on the green end of the political spectrum voted against the Betuwe Line for reasons of economic and environmental uncertainties. In spite of that, the project was accepted, albeit with several modifications. Most of these modifications were meant to mitigate local problems (e.g. by local tunneling); some of them were so-called "flanking policy measures" to stimulate sustainable transport by economic and regulatory means (e.g. by taxes). However, political consensus remained low, and after a change of government the new (right-wing liberal) Minister of Transport suspended the decision. To overcome the deadlock, she installed the "Betuwe Line Commission" (Commissie Betuweroute) to reassess the alternatives and construction variants. The Betuwe Line Commission consisted of politicians from the governing and opposition parties and experts in the fields of finance, technology, logistics, and environment. Quite unexpectedly, and to the relief of the business world and Dutch Railways, the Commission concluded that the Betuwe Line was an adequate answer to the future need for rail facilities. This conclusion marked a turning point in the decision-making process. At the national level, the debate on the necessity of the project and possible strategic alternatives faded. In accordance with the policy procedure for this category of planning decisions, a new round of consultation with local authorities was initiated, with the aim of removing local bottlenecks. This resulted in a set of adjustments in the government proposal, which was then once again passed in parliament in 1995.

Currently, the economic efficiency and environmental effectiveness of the Betuweroute remain unclear. In 1999 a group of transport economists stated in the media that the Betuwe Line would never be cost-effective. New calculations of the major Dutch environmental research institute published that same year were said to prove that the environmental benefits of Betuwe Line rail transport as compared to road transport are being overrated. Some municipalities are still in conflict with the national government over the local construction of the line. But the preparations of the Betuwe Line – delayed by the decision-making procedures – are in full progress now and there seems to be sufficient consent among the political parties and the local communities involved to keep this process going.

Analysis: Decision Making in a Consensus Society

Perhaps the most striking feature of the Betuwe Line debate is the rapid shift from local interests debates at a municipal level to a general interests debate at the national level. As I described, local actors joined forces and successfully stimulated debates at the national level, for instance by proposing the option of complete tunneling or by questioning the long-term economic efficiency of the line. The primary motivation to do so clearly came from the threat to local interests and the frustration of local consultations due to the top-down approach of the Dutch Railways and the Ministry of Transport and Water Management. As the Mayor of Gorinchem (a prominent municipality in the debate) stated: "Had there been a sincere and generous approach to the assessment of noise nuisance and the like, it might never have come to a tunneling debate" (Krommendijk & Van Koppen, 1997, p. 203). If the protests had initially been motivated by local interests, the national debates they generated revealed serious flaws in the general economic and environmental underpinning of the project. To stimulate these debates, the VLOB and the local authorities made use of a technocratic approach, engaging experts to criticize the argumentation of government and the Dutch Railways and develop alternative options.

Though subject to several expert assessments, the central questions of economic efficiency and environmental effectiveness proved too complex for a scientific solution. Many of the uncertainties have not been resolved, and the scientific debate continues to date. For the political decision-making process, however, the discussion had to be closed. This closure was brought about in a decisionist manner, by a government sticking to its intentions and eventually obtaining a majority in parliament. But two factors appear to have contributed decisively to the political and public consent. First, there was the Betuwe Line Commission, representing an interesting mix of a participatory approach (aiming at a consensus of all participating representatives) and a technocratic approach (membership of experts). The advice of this Commission was instrumental in obtaining sufficient parliamentary support. Then, there were the renewed consultations with the local authorities, after the decision, which were conducted in a much more open and participatory manner. In the words of a municipal spokesman: "what you see, really, is that we went back from the action trail . . . to the normal consultation trail" (Krommendijk & Van Koppen, 1997, p. 196).

A remarkable feature of the case is the low profile of the environmental organizations in the debate. One reason was that, at the time, the environmentalists lacked a clear position on the issue of the Betuwe Line, which required a much more complex assessment than a simple "yes to rail" and "no to cars." Perhaps another reason was the fear to engage in what was considered by many to be NIMBY protest of local pressure groups. Ironically, it was these local pressure groups that eventually aroused a fundamental debate on the environmental benefits of the Betuwe Line; a debate revealing that the environmental (as well as economic) efficiency depends heavily on the national policies towards other transport modes, and on developments at a supranational level.

The European level is nearly absent in the debate, in spite of its clear relevance. It would seem obvious, for instance, to compare the economic efficiency of the Betuwe Line with alternative connections to Germany through other countries (there actually is an unused railway track, called the "Iron Rhine", running parallel to the Betuwe Line through Belgium). But these arguments played hardly any role in the debate. The efficiency debates centered on the level which offered the best organizational platforms and resources for decision making, and which was apparently considered to be the most legitimate. This was the national level of the Dutch State.

CONCLUSIONS AND DISCUSSION

What conclusions can we draw when comparing these cases against the background of the theoretical framework?

Portugal is an industrializing country where environmental problems are low on the political agenda, and which has only recently made the transition from an authoritarian regime to an open society. In the highly industrialized

Netherlands environmental issues have high public and political priority, and the political system is geared to consultation and consensual decision making. But in spite of these differences, we can see common characteristics in the dynamics of the debates. In both countries, we find that the debates grew from specific (local or environmental) issues into debates that addressed the environmental effectiveness as well as the economic efficiency of the projects in dispute. The uncertainties that arose from those debates were not resolved, but closed in a prevailingly decisionist way. To obtain sufficient consent, however, other approaches were needed in addition to the decisionist approach. The discourses as we found them in the cases were not a priori linked to specific actor groups. Environmental organizations in Portugal and local interests groups in the Netherlands eventually engaged in roughly the same kinds of general interests discourses. During the debates, groups switched from one discourse to another: from environmental to socio-economic issues, from decisionist to technocratic and participatory reasoning styles, and back.

As the cases show, not only the central government, but also environmental organizations, local authorities and pressure groups employ technocratic arguments to defend their interest. The *technocratic* discourse, as I have defined it here, is therefore not linked to a centralist, top-down approach to decision making – in contrast, for instance, to what was found in studies by Wynne (1992a, 1992b).[13] Indeed, engaging expertise to criticize decisions seems to be a particularly useful tool for breaking up decisionist positions. In both investigated cases, however, technocratic arguments did not provide sufficient grounds for a final decision on the controversy. The Environmental Impact Assessment is a central element in the scientific evaluation of environmental effectiveness. Though the results of EIAs were influential in the environmental debates, and contributed to the selection of feasible options, they were not effective in closing the debate on environmental uncertainties. The EIA conclusions were intensely disputed, as were other scientific studies into the environmental and economic aspects of the controversy.

The *market* discourse was largely absent in the cases presented here. This is obviously due to the circumstance that the infrastructure projects were commonly regarded as a government responsibility. Some of the uncertainties regarding the financing of the projects were framed in a market discourse: public-private structures were developed for both projects to arrange the financial engineering of the construction and exploitation. Still, large parts of the financing are directly or indirectly provided by the state, and therefore the emphasis lies on the role of the state.

A *participatory* discourse structured some parts of the debates, especially in the Dutch decision-making process, which offered specific organizational platforms for participatory debates. These platforms were found on a local level, but also on a higher level, as was the case with the national Betuwe Line Commission. A participatory approach appears to be especially suited to establish a consensus, but only if the parties involved have a feeling that the participants constitute a fair representation of the stakeholders and if there is room for a genuine negotiating process. If that is not the case, its effects on the consent of the participants can be adverse, as was the case in the first consultation round of the Betuwe Line.

Furthermore, the cases show that the interventions of pressure groups in an environmental risk debate tend to make this debate more complex, but also tend to improve the quality and scope of argumentation in the decision-making process. Both in Portugal and in the Netherlands the pressure groups contributed to the understanding (mostly by revealing the lack of it) of the economic and environmental costs and benefits of the projects. It might even be argued that they added to the quality of the discourses themselves and thus contributed to better decision making in the future. In other words, the cases confirm what Freudenburg and Pastor (1992) call the "prudent" perspective. It seems fruitful not to judge the contribution of groups in environmental risk debates by what is supposedly motivating them (e.g. as NIMBY protest), but rather by the quality of their arguments in relation to the discourse they want to engage in.

ENVIRONMENT, PARTICIPATION AND THE STATE

At the beginning of this article, I have raised the question of the position of the state with respect to environmental protection. What can we say about this question in the perspective of this article? Our cases corroborate the view that, besides the decisionist discourse (of a liberal representative democracy), there are other discourses gaining importance: a technocratic discourse (of expert decision systems), a market discourse (of deregulation), a participatory discourse (of dialogic democracy, or subpolitics). On the evidence of this article, however, these discourses should be interpreted as an extension rather than a substitution of decisionist approaches. One reason for the continued relevance of a decisionist discourse is the need to take decisions in circumstances of uncertainty. Uncertainties are a typical feature of complex decision making, and political debates will often tend to amplify rather than take away these uncertainties. Generally speaking, none of the other approaches will be capable of closing these uncertainties. The reach of scientific assessment, like EIA, is limited. A market approach is not relevant in many cases. Neither can a participatory approach be relied upon to yield a final decision on uncertainties. Stakeholders may withdraw from the consultation and shift to other discourses once they feel they cannot hold on to their interests. Investigations in this area show that it is questionable whether a participatory debate in itself can remove obstacles in the decision-making process.[14] A final decision by parliament or other authorities will often remain necessary. However, as a result of a consensual approach, this "decision in dissensus" may be more legitimate (cf. Van den Daele & Neidhardt, 1996).

As our study illustrates, the state is clearly regarded as the appropriate level of debate in such substantive questions as large infrastructure projects. Even where the issues of environmental and economic efficiency would be more adequately dealt with on a supranational scale, the debates centered on the national level. There are some plausible non-discursive reasons for this. Most resources (in terms of decision-making power and budgets) were in the hands of the state. Also, the major platforms for debate were situated at the state level. But the state was also the appropriate level in terms of discursive legitimacy: hardly any of the groups involved questioned the legitimate right of the state to decide. Compared to the views of Giddens and Beck, our study suggests that a sphere of subpolitics or dialogic democracy is indeed emerging, but in addition to, rather than at the cost of the legitimacy of conventional state politics. In the infrastructure debates we investigated, it is hard to find signs of an eroding legitimacy of science, as it is thematized by Beck (1986, p. 254 ff.).We may speak of a politicization of science, but then in the sense that science and technology are utilized by different parties.

Against this background of multiplying and intensifying societal debates, the question of how to deal with decision making on large projects becomes even more central. Many policy studies and debates have been devoted to solving the dilemma of how to involve local actors in decision making without blocking the progress of the project as a whole. In the Netherlands, this dispute has led to widespread criticism on the top-down approach of government, but at the same time it has led to the adoption of new legislation to speed up the decision-making process. Policy studies have suggested several structural options for improvement. Two of such options are to carry out a *strategic impact assessment* at the beginning of the project, and to obtain an *agreement in principle* from the stakeholders (WRR, 1994, Spaargaren & Krommendijk, 1997). In the terms employed in this article, this means initializing both a technocratic and a participatory debate at the very start of the decision-making process. Though it would probably make sense to implement such options, they cannot be expected to produce more than limited results. If a quantitative assessment of the economic and environmental impacts of a particular plan cannot bring about a satisfactory conclusion in the course of a project, it would seem even less likely to achieve that result beforehand. Moreover, many of the actors are not involved in the debate from the very outset but will only appear as stakeholders in the course of the process (Niekerk & Voogd, 1999). It is only when it becomes clear that the project, as it is operationalized, will directly affect the interests of actors, that these actors will start intervening in the debate and bring in new issues, new scientific questions, and new claims on decision-making procedures. Similar limitations apply to another option for improvement proposed by Hajer (1995: 288 ff), among others: to organize a "societal inquiry" as a platform of civic debate, parallel to the conventional decision-making processes. Hajer argues that such a societal inquiry, provided it is open to the arguments of the different groups involved, can illuminate implicit cultural and political choices and show what other courses of action might be taken. However, experience of mixed panels of experts and lay people and open discussion meetings of stakeholders has shown that, as long these platforms are not directly linked to concrete decisions affecting concrete interests, it is difficult to assess their political impact and it is often hard to obtain a commitment from more than just a small group of specifically interested persons.

The best way, in the perspective of this article, to deal with these complex processes of decision making is to accept the interventions of new stakeholders arriving on the scene and the continuation of debates; to anticipate on the prospect that a decisionist procedure is needed to close the uncertainties; and to confer on this procedure as much legitimacy as possible by creating organizational platforms for debate which are maximally linked to concrete steps in the decision-making sequence. The structure of such platforms should be geared to achieving high-quality debates. In this context, Weale speaks of the design of a richer set of institutional conditions, to increase the "capacity of discursive rationality" (Weale, 1992, p. 222). He especially emphasizes the need for institutional structures at the international level. On the evidence of the cases discussed here, we can underline this need. If there had been adequate platforms for a debate on transport and environment on an EU level, the debates on economic and environmental costs and benefits might have moved beyond the national level. However, it is to be expected that the success of platforms on the local, national and international levels will be closely related to the actual decision-making capacities and resources at these different levels. The findings of this article also indicate that it would be important to structure such platforms in accordance with the type of discourse that they are aimed at. As is testified by the case studies and many other experiences in public debates, the entanglement of different types of discourse – local and general interests arguments; decisionist, technocratic, and participative reasoning styles – can easily obscure the issues at stake and lead to misunderstanding and unnecessary conflicts. Examples of such entanglement are: stakeholders expecting a participative debate at a public hearing organized by authorities within a decisionist framework; experts dominating a participative debate by imposing a technocratic discursive frame; governmental authorities failing to distinguish between a decisionist and a technocratic discourse (and imposing characteristics that are only legitimate in a decisionist position, such as confidentiality of information and personal evaluation of alternatives, on a technocratic discourse). To avoid such entanglement, it would be vital to clearly set out the aims of the discourse and bring it into line with the choice of participants, place, rules of debate, and decision-making consequences. The typology of discourses that was presented in the article may be helpful to the further development of procedures to meet this goal.

To avoid misunderstanding: none of such procedures can safeguard the movement of debates against interest conflicts, struggles for hegemony, manipulation, and conceit. The structure and quality of debates remain deeply influenced by power relations. Discourse theory, however, helps us to see that the reverse is equally true: power relations can be substantially influenced by the structure and quality of debates.

NOTES

1. In this context, Giddens points at the emergence of an alternative, participatory conception of democracy which he calls "dialogic democracy" (Giddens, 1994, p. 112 ff.). Beck stresses the politicization and moralization of science, technology and economy (Beck, 1986, p. 304 ff.).

2. To illustrate this point: Jänicke, who was one of the first authors who sharply criticized the position of the state, nonetheless uses the nation-state as the basic unit of comparison in his recent studies on society's capacity for environmental protection (Jänicke, 1986, Jänicke & Weidner, 1996).

3. The theoretical framework builds on a theoretical chapter in the project report (Van Koppen & Mormont, 1997), albeit with some conceptual modifications. Next to the Dutch and Portuguese cases, the report also contains a Belgian case, which is omitted here.

4. For a good introduction to and overview of these studies, see Krimsky and Golding (1992). For more recent social-theoretical elaborations of risk and environment see e.g. Lash, Szerszynski and Wynne eds. (1996) and the *Environmental Values* Vol. 8 No. 2 (1999) special issue on risk.

5. For reviews from two different angles, see Schiffrin (1994) and Torfing (1999).

6. Yet, it should be noted that the kinds of discourses identified in this article have a long standing in history. Many of the characteristics of the contemporary environmental discourse can be found in environmental arguments of the 19th century and earlier, e.g. George Perkins Marsh's *Man and Nature* (1864) and John Evelyn's *Fumifugium* (1661). A participatory concept of democracy, in certain respects, can be traced back to the classical republicanism of the Athenian city-state (Held, 1995, p. 5 ff).

7. The local interests discourse, as we have labeled it, could be further analysed as composed of different elements, each of which is part of other discourses (such as the civil rights discourse). This observation, that discourses can be subdivided into different discourses, which are in turn part of other discourses, does not contradict our conception of discourse. Tracing these discourses and demarcating them would be an important way to further investigate the contents of a discourse. See for instance Hajer (1995) for the development of the environmental effectiveness discourse and its relation to the economic efficiency discourse. Rather than elaborating on the contents and the demarcation of discourses, however, this article focuses on identifying the main discourses in environmental risk debates and analyzing their interplay in political debate.

8. For an elaboration, see Hajer's explanation of his "argumentative approach" to discourses (1995, p. 59 ff).

9. The Tagus Bridge case is more extensively described in Barros et al. (1997). It was investigated by means of a systematic research of available reports, articles in press and speciality magazines, and other written statements in the period from 1991 to 1996. Also, 41 open interviews were carried out in 1995 with local, regional and national officials, representatives of political parties, environmental organizations and the transport sector, and various experts involved in the case.

10. At the time, there were three national ecological associations actively co-operating in the protest against the location: the Study Group for Territorial Planning and Environment (GEOTA); the League for the Protection of Nature (LPN); and the National Association for the Preservation of Nature (Quercus).

11. The Betuwe Line case is described in Krommendijk and Van Koppen (1997). The secondary sources consisted of available reports, articles in journals and magazines, and policy documents (mainly in the period from 1990 to 1996). Some 30 semi-structured interviews were carried out in 1995 with representatives of pressure groups, municipalities, provinces, environmental organizations, and commercial interests.

12. The Foundation for Nature and Environment (Stichting Natuur and Milieu) was the most prominent participant among the nationally operating environmental organizations. The Dutch branch of Friends of the Earth (Vereniging Milieudefensie), which normally is very keen on issues of infrastructure and environment (e.g. Schiphol), did not actively engage in the general debate. Neither did the provincial environmental federations (though these federations played an important role in mitigating local nature management bottle-necks).

13. It should be noted, that Wynne's studies do not focus on infrastructure projects. It is obvious that access to technological expertise will be different according to the issues, arenas and groups involved.

14. Tukker (1998, p. 188 ff) demonstrates this in the case of the Dutch chlorine debate. For German research into these limits of the participatory approach, see Van den Daele and Neidhardt (1996) and Bora et al. (1998).

REFERENCES

Barros, A. de, Gomes, S., & Joachim, G. (1997). Portugal: The Tagus Bridge. In: Mormont et al. (Eds), *Transport and Risk Communication. Belgium, Portugal and the Netherlands*. Frankfurt a.M.: Peter Lang.

Beck, U. (1986). *Risikogesellschaft. Auf dem Weg in eine andere Moderne.* Frankfurt a.M.: Suhrkamp.

Boltanski, L., & Thévenot, L. (1991). *De la justification. Les économies de la grandeur.* Paris: Gallimard.

Bora, A. et al. (1998). *Die Umsetzung von Technikfolgenabschätzung in Verwaltungsverfahren.* Berlin: WZB.

Dryzek, J. S. (1997). *The politics of the earth. Environmental discourses.* Oxford: Oxford University Press.

Eder, K. (1996). The institionalisation of environmentalism: ecological discourse and the second transformation of the public sphere. In: S. Lash, B. Szerszynski & B. Wynne (Eds), *Risk, Environment and Modernity. Towards a New Ecology* (pp. 203–223). London: Sage.

Foucault, M. (1969). *L'Archéologie du savoir.* Paris: Gallimard.

Freudenburg, W. R., & Pastor, S. K. (1992). NIMBYs and LULUs: stalking the syndromes. *Journal of Social Issues, 48*(4), 39–61.

Giddens, A. (1984). *The Constitution of Society.* Cambridge: Polity Press.

Grove-White, R. (1996). Environmental knowledge and public policy needs: on humanising the research agenda. In: S. Lash, B. Szerszynski & B. Wynne (Eds), *Risk, Environment and Modernity. Towards a New Ecology* (pp. 269–286). London: Sage.

Habermas, J. (1968). *Technik und Wissenschaft als Ídeologie'.* Frankfurt a.M.: Suhrkamp.

Hajer, M. A. (1995). *The Politics of Environmental Discourse. Ecological Modernization and the Policy Process.* Oxford: Clarendon Press.

Held, D. (1995). *Democracy and the Global Order.* Cambridge: Polity Press.

Hogenboom, J., Mol, A. P. J., & Spaargaren, G. (1999). Dealing with environmental risk in reflexive modernity. In: M. Cohen (Ed.), *Risk in the Modern Age. Social Theory, Science and Environmental Decision Making.* Basingstoke: MacMillan.

Jänicke, M. (1986). *Staatsversagen. Die Ohnmacht der Politik in der Industriegesellschaft.* München: Piper.

Jänicke, M., & Weidner, H. (Eds) (1996). *National Environmental Policies. A Comparative Study of Capacity-building.* Berlin: Springer.

Jasanoff, S. (1999). The songlines of risk. *Environmental Values, 8,* 135–152.

Hisschemöller, M. (1993). *De democratie van problemen.* Amsterdam: VU Uitgeverij.

Krimsky, W., & Golding, D. (Eds) (1992). *Social Theories of Risk.* Westport: Praeger.

Krommendijk, E., & Van Koppen, C. S. A. (1997). The Betuwe Route as case study. In: M. Mormont et al. (Eds), *Transport and Risk Communication. Belgium, Portugal and the Netherlands.* Frankfurt a.M.: Peter Lang.

Kunreuther, H. (1992). A conceptual framework for managing low-probability events. In: S. Krimsky & D. Golding (Eds), *Social Theories of Risk.* Westport: Praeger.

Lash, S., Szerszynski, B., & Wynne, B. (Eds) (1996). *Risk, Environment and Modernity. Towards a New Ecology.* London: Sage.

Litfin, K. T. (1994). *Ozone Discourses: Science and Politics in Global Environmental Cooperation.* New York: Columbia University Press.

Monica, M. F. (1996). Os costumes em Portugal. In: A. Barreto (Ed.), *A situação em Portugal 1960–1995.* Lisboa: Edition Banco Português do Investimento.

Mormont, M., Spaargaren, G., & Gomes, S. (Eds) (1997). *Transport and Risk Communication. Belgium, Portugal and the Netherlands.* Frankfurt a.M.: Peter Lang.

Niekerk, F., & Voogd, H. (1999). Impact assessment for infrastructure planning: Some Dutch dilemmas. *Environmental Impact Assessment Review, 19,* 21–36.

Rayner, S. (1992). Cultural theory and risk analysis. In: W. Krimsky & D. Golding (Eds), *Social Theories of Risk*. Westport: Praeger.

Rip, A. (1992). Risicocontroverses en de verwevenheid van wetenschap en politiek. *Kennis en methode* 1992, (1), 63–80.

Schriffin, D. (1994). *Approaches to Discourse*. Oxford: Blackwell.

Spaargaren, G., & Krommendijk, E. (1997). The Betuwe Route and the Dutch discourse on transport and the environment. In: Mormont et al. (Eds), *Transport and Risk Communication. Belgium, Portugal and the Netherlands*. Frankfurt a.M.: Peter Lang.

Torfing, J. (1999). *New Theories of Discourse. Laclau, Mouffe and Zizek*. Oxford: Blackwell.

Tukker, A. (1998). *Frames in the Toxicity Controversy. Based on the Dutch Chlorine Debate and the Swedish PVC Debate*. Tilburg: Thesis KUB.

Van Koppen, C. S. A., & Mormont, M. (1997). Analysing risk communication. In: M. Mormont et al. (Eds), *Transport and Risk Communication. Belgium, Portugal and the Netherlands*. Frankfurt a.M.: Peter Lang.

Van den Daele, W., & Neidhardt, F. (1996). 'Regierung durch Diskussion' – Über Versuche, mit Argumenten Politik zu machen. In: *Kommunikation und Entscheidung*. Berlin: Edition Sigma.

Weale, A. (1992). *The New Politics of Pollution*. Manchester: Manchester University Press.

Wilke, H. A. M. (1989). Promoting personal decisions supporting the achievement of risky public goods. In: Vlek & Cvetkovich, *Social Decision Methodology for Technological Projects*. Dordrecht.

Wilke, H. A. M. (1991). Greed, efficiency and fairness in resource management situations. *European Review of Social Psychology*, *2*, 165–187.

WRR (Scientific Council for Government Policy) (1994). *Besluiten over grote projecten*. Den Haag: Sdu.

Wolsink, M. (1994). Entanglement of interests and motives: assumptions behind the NIMBY-theory on facility siting. *Urban Studies*, *31*(6), 851–866.

Wynne, B. (Ed.) (1987). *Risk Management and Hazardous Waste. Implementation and the Dialectics of Credibility*. Berlin: Springer Verlag.

Wynne, B. (1992a). Sheep farming after Chernobyl. In: Lewenstein (Ed.), *When Science Meets the Public*. Washington: American Association for the Advancement of Science.

Wynne, B. (1992b). Risk and social learning: from reification to engagement. In: Krimsky & Golding (Eds), *Social Theories of Risk*. Westport: Praeger.

PART III:

THE ENVIRONMENTAL STATE AND DEVELOPMENT PROCESSES IN THE SOUTH

THE ENVIRONMENTAL STATE AND THE FOREST: OF LOOKOUTS, LUMBERJACKS, LEOPARDS, AND LOSERS

Bianca Ambrose-Oji, Tim Allmark, Peter Buckley, Bindi Clements and Graham Woodgate

INTRODUCTION

Contemporary societies are facing the realisation that environmental changes are entering a new phase, one which challenges the old structural order. Whether viewed from the national, regional or international perspective, the modern technologies, institutions and systems of organisation that mediate relationships between people and the environment, have profoundly altered our relationship with the material world, at the same time as affecting how we perceive, understand and attempt to manage environmental resources and services. Consequently, modern life presents worrying contradictions; just as society begins to understand more about the consequences of anthropogenic environmental change, the alliance of science, technology and capitalism seem increasingly to multiply ecological risk.

As a result, we hear calls for bio-economic change by populations demonstrating against environmental degradation and social deprivation. Nevertheless, these same populations resist change to the lifestyle aspirations, which produce the environmental outcomes they fight against. Similarly, states continue to

The Environmental State Under Pressure, Volume 10, pages 149–169.

ISBN: 0-7623-0854-0

promote economic development and nurture corporate business as a source of wealth and power whilst, on the other hand, they adopt legislative frameworks designed to prevent ecological damage and foster environmental protection.

Correspondingly, while developing new perspectives to account for this contradictory 'modern condition', sociology has seen the re-appearance of its own epistemological fault lines and struggled to overcome the contradictions epitomised by the nature/culture and structure/agency debates. The emergent 'environmental sociology' has come some way in incorporating 'nature' into social analysis, and also recognised that the wider global configuration within which these society/environment relationships are ultimately embedded must also form part of the debate. Our aim in this paper is to harness some of the ideas coming from environmental sociology, to describe and examine the nature of the 'environmental state' and the contradictory role it plays in fostering and mitigating environmental problems.

Our discussion focuses on the issue of tropical forest destruction, which has both global and local dimensions and has become an important theme for states in the first and third worlds. Our specific concern with the 'environmental state' places the development of inclusionary governance and management of forest resources, at the heart of our analysis. Discussion throughout this paper is informed by extensive research conducted in the West African tropical forest region of South West Cameroon.

THE ENVIRONMENTAL STATE . . .

The concept of 'globalisation' forces a re-examination of the concept of the state because, at one level, states are defined only in relation to other states, a situation which presupposes globalised relations and now prompts discussion about their power and autonomy relative to other modern global institutions. On a more fundamental level, if we agree that nation states are "either 'too small' to manage regional and global problems or 'too big' to deal with local environmental problems" (Bryant & Bailey, 1997, p. 52), we must also recognise the failings of social theories based on conventional nation state precepts in explaining the dynamic linkages between social phenomena and environmental changes experienced at a local level. How then might we reinterpret the idea of the state and present a more nuanced understanding of the environmental state? We begin by turning to Foucault for insight.[1]

Foucault identifies the emergence of biology as a science, as a defining moment, the "entry of life into history", which precipitated a cleavage from the situation where national polities were driven by "reasons of state", to one where they became driven by the need to control institutions relating to the material and administrative conditions sustaining production and reproduction: in other words, to life itself. In this way he suggests that biosciences have become the crucial instrumental knowledges. The result is a fundamental switch from the state's emphasis on the control of territory as land, to the control of territory as people, populations and resources.

Since the emergence of modern nation states on the global stage, state-sponsored bioscience has played a major role in driving the twin processes of industrialisation and capital accumulation, aiding the transformation of nature into ever more managed environments,[2] and reformulating traditional, nationally-bound relations of production into globally fluid conditions of production "where everything is treated as a commodity, even if it is not produced as a commodity" (Escobar, 1996, p. 54). Thus, what Foucault termed 'bio-power' grew out of the dual position of life as "outside history, in its biological environment, and inside human historicity, penetrated by the latter's techniques of knowledge and power" (Foucault, 1976, p. 146).

The role of the state in securing the material well being and reproductive capacity of its population has not changed. However, two of what Giddens (1990) identifies as the four central institutions of modernity, capitalism and industrialisation, have by and large been appropriated and dominated by global business. This changes the very nature of the state; not only does it become decentred, it is forced to consider a new dimension, transnational security threats in the form of ecological risk. The old order of state-based political, scientific and judicial institutions become impotent; the dividing line between domestic and foreign policies becomes fuzzy and the bio-political boundaries between states become blurred. The unpredictability of societal development, lead states to pursue strategies of ecological security which bring them into globalised conflicts over how ecological risks can be distributed, averted, controlled and legitimated (Beck, 1996).

In effect, nation states are transformed into the environmental state, which is far less "a collectivity existing within a clearly demarcated territory, which is . . . subject to a unitary administration, reflexively monitored by both the internal state apparatus and those of other states" (Giddens, 1985, p. 11). Rather, it becomes much more of a complex and dynamically interdependent collectivity of national governments and civil societies that exists bound together *across* political territorial units, and is subject to a bio-political administration composed of national and suprastate economic and legislative agencies. Where the environmental state's concern switches from territory as land, to the control of populations and resources, it becomes more difficult to see a nation's boundaries restricted to geographical space. People are joined through their common utilisation and protection of resources; one person's environmental conduct effects the limits of another's ecological freedom (Luke, 1999), regardless of the specific situation of actors, all form part of the same socio-ecological corpus.

The power of the environmental state does not necessarily diminish, rather it changes form. The structural properties of capitalism and industrialisation are patterned by agencies and organisations such as transnational companies, the World Trade Organisation and the United Nations. The state facilitates these processes at a local level because they remain tied to the material well being of populations. However, for the environmental state a bio-economic understanding of global systems ecology gives rise to new forms of biopolitics, that rely on bio-power "operating upon . . . the 'continuous and multiple relations' between the population, its resources and the environment" (Rutherford, 1999, p. 45). Maintaining dominance in this bio-political realm rests on the exercise of ecological governmentality; where "governmentality is the ensemble formed by institutions, procedures, analyses and reflections, the calculations and tactics that allow the exercise of this very specific albeit complex form of power, which has as its *target population*, as its principle form of knowledge *political economy*, and as its essential means *apparatuses of security*" (Darier, 1999, p. 22).

. . . AND THE FOREST

We turn now to consider the social relations surrounding tropical forests in Cameroon as a real-world example on which to base our theoretical abstractions. Cameroon has a long history of integration into European and global systems of trade and politics. Starting with Portuguese exploration in the Fifteenth and Sixteenth Centuries and then British and German mercantilism during the Eighteenth and Nineteenth Centuries, the forest represented an uncharted wilderness important in supplying slaves, ivory, wild rubber, palm oil, tannin, timber and forest spices to European and world markets (Ardener, 1996; DeLancy & Mokeba, 1990; Njeuma, 1989). During the late Nineteenth and early Twentieth centuries mercantilism was superseded by direct colonial rule. This period saw major changes to social power relations and laid the foundations for contemporary patterns of bio-power. Following Giddens's formulation, power is generated in the reproduction of structures of domination constituted by allocative and authoritative resources. "Any co-ordination of social systems across time and space necessarily involves a definite combination of these two types of resources" (Giddens, 1984, p. 258). For the colonial state the forest represented a significant part of a suite of allocative resources, which had associated with it a complex of authoritative apparatuses.

The conquest of territory in Cameroon saw the development of a system of tenure which declared that all land belonged to the Crown unless effectively occupied by 'natives' or private individuals (Anon, 1900; Ngwasiri, 1995). The test of occupation or ownership was conversion of 'virgin' forest into farmland; the forest effectively became state territory. Coinciding with the appropriation of land, the growing demands of first world industrialisation precipitated a symbolic reconstruction of the forest. Rather than a source of natural wealth, it became a resource ripe for conversion to plantation production (Epale, 1985; Konings, 1995). Economic dominance was assured by two means: trade in forest products was taken out of the hands of African businessmen, while new administrative procedures effectively made illegal native plantations of industrial commodities.

Authoritative dominance was consolidated through the application of rational knowledge and systems of bioscience. These explored, charted, measured, and inventoried the forest, and in many areas modified it as managed plantations. The forest's human populations were mapped, subjected to anthropological classification and incorporated into administrative management through the reinterpretation of social tradition and the invention of chieftancy (CNAB, 1916; CNAB, 1921; CNAB, 1923; CNAB, 1934; Geschiere, 1993). The importation of huge numbers of indentured labourers for the plantations, destabilised and further marginalised forest communities.

In the period covering independence from Britain and France, from the late 1950s to the early 1970s, the forest was symbolically transformed once more. This time it became the site of 'progress' and 'development', the seat of modern nationhood (Victoria Centenary Committee, 1958), and was subject to relatively intensive timber extraction as a source of foreign capital to fund the state's provision of basic infrastructure and welfare services. After 1972 the colonial administration was progressively replaced with a totalitarian regime, and society was urged to attain the goals of the five-year National Development Plans. Central to these was further forest clearance and the improvement of peasant agriculture to produce commodities for world markets.

However, the need to reserve the forest and forested land for public purposes was recognised from the earliest years; timber production reserves and 'conservation' areas were proposed and partially established between 1900 and the 1980s. Following the colonial approach, 'conservation areas' were located in mountainous areas (Kearns, 1997; Wiley, 1999). Systems of reservation servicing the needs of forest communities were also established during the British colonial period, where community control over land and forest resources was vested in the 'Native Authority'.

It is from these historical economic, political, social and conservationist roots that the most recent transformation of the forest, as a risk mitigating resource for the environmental state, has come into being. So, how does our concept of the environmental state equate with the current situation of Cameroon and its tropical forest resource?

THE ENVIRONMENTAL STATE IN THE FOREST

During the late 1980s and early 1990s, under the auspices of the World Bank and IMF the economic autonomy of Cameroon was lost to transnational corporations and the macro-economic policies of suprastate organisations. The instigation of a structural adjustment programme in 1992 pealed the death knell for the last of the government controlled parastatal plantation and processing agri-businesses and prompted a dramatic currency devaluation. Once again all eyes turned to the forest.

Whilst recognising the global importance of the forest's flora and fauna, the World Bank and ITTO[3] identified Cameroon's forests as natural capital ideally suited as security against the risks of debt repayment default.[4] Having projected the amount of income that could be generated from increased logging, the World Bank and the ITTO effectively laid plans to 'mine' the forest if the economic situation of the country worsened (Anon, 1991; Arentz, 1993). Facing declining terms of trade for agricultural commodities and reduced revenues from oil, the Cameroon government responded to external pressure, and promulgated a new Forest Law in 1994 (see Forje, 1993).

The environmental state signed up to forest destruction. The Cameroon government consequently became involved in supporting policies and projects that involved the transformation of natural capital into financial capital. In many cases it was assisted in realising forest policy by ex-colonial interests such as the U.K., French and German governments. The U.K. government was also instrumental in providing the largest employer in the country, the Cameroon Development Corporation, with expertise and materials to restructure and expand forest operations in the run-up to privatisation. Operationalisation of these economic risk mitigating activities was carried out by situated environmental professionals drawn from the relevant Cameroon line ministries, as well as expatriate representatives of business and government. For much of Cameroonian civil society the forest became a refuge from financial and other livelihood risks stemming from the harsh economic climate (Ndoye & Kaimowitz, 1998). For these situated actors the forest represents livelihood security: a 'free' source of land and exploitable resources (Demenou, 1997; Gockowski, 1997). For local community elites and entrepreneurs with larger capital endowments the forest presents development opportunities often by subcontracting to transnational companies.

In contrast to the ideology of 'globalism' (Beck, 1998, p. 28) that had driven structural adjustment, the parallel phenomenon of 'globality' produced a series of countervailing power effects that penetrated the social relations surrounding Cameroon's forests. According to Beck, globality represents the alternative politics of globalisation. It stands in stark contrast to the de-politicised economic dimension of globalism, and refers to global social order structured by social relations which are neither integrated in the politics of the nation state nor determinable by the politics of the nation state (Woodgate et al., 1999). The shared values of this 'world society' include ethnic diversity and environmental quality and resonate with the problematic of 'tropical deforestation', that had captured government and public attention in both donor nations and Cameroon. Constructed as problems of global environmental risk, 'climate change' and 'biodiversity loss' were quickly linked to forest destruction. Similarly, globality has helped to coach more sophisticated understandings of environmental issues, leading to the social construction of the environment in the third world as a livelihood issue, thus tapping into discourse around indigenous rights and the pursuit of sustainable forest livelihoods.

Reacting to these pressures, as well as those from suprastate organisations, such as UNCED and WWF, the environmental state conceded an important addition to Cameroon's new Forest Law. Clauses were introduced which allowed greater involvement in resource management for forest communities. The environmental state – the same expatriate government donor agencies and Cameroonian line ministries that were involved in forest destruction – began implementing or supporting participatory, Integrated Conservation and Development Programmes (ICDPs). These were to be implemented by environmental professionals drawn from the same pool of personnel involved in commercial exploitation.

Figure 1 illustrates schematically these dynamic connections and inter-relationships as they converge in participatory interventions. The environmental state is linked to situated actors as the 'risk population', which must be taken "into account in all its observations and savoirs, in order to be able to govern effectively in a rational and conscious manner' (Foucault, 1991 quoted in Burchell et al., 1991, pp. 144–145). Suprastate agencies and organisations of global capital are linked as the 'global agenda setting community'.

Each set of actors reflexively monitors changes in the social practices of the others, as well as environmental conditions in the material world. Perceived changes in either practice or conditions, prompt reactions from each group of actors, which in turn, alter patterns of agency and environmental possibilities. In this way the forest is refashioned physically as well as cognitively (c.f. Woodgate & Redclift, 1998).

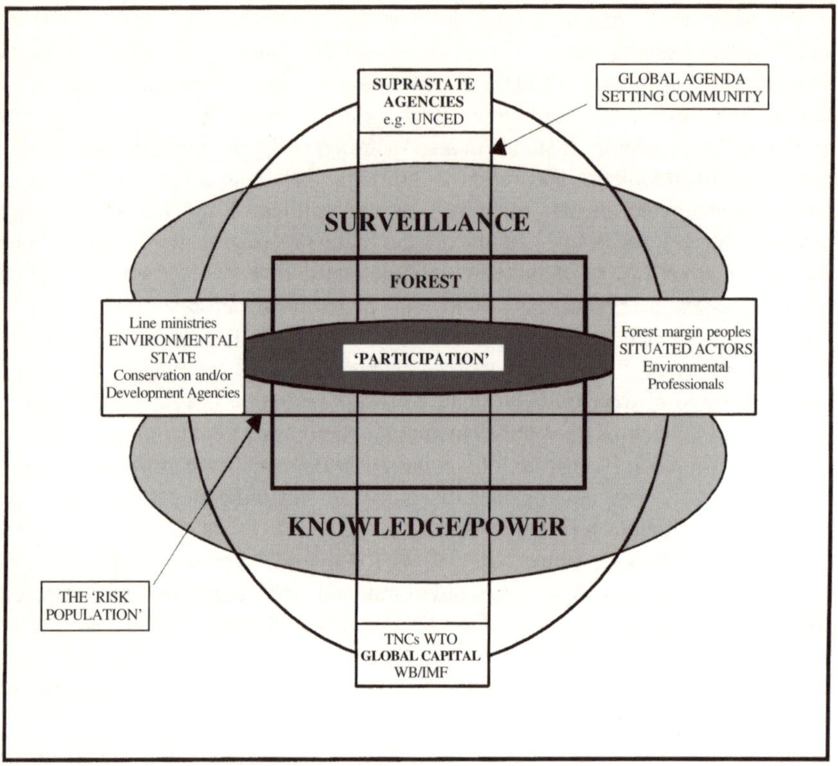

Fig. 1. Schematic of the Dynamic Social Interrelationships Surrounding the Forest.

The ability to monitor reflexively and initiate change depends on two crucial components of social practice. One of these is what Giddens (1990) identifies as a third institutional dimension of modernity – surveillance (control of information and social supervision), or what Foucault may have called apparatuses of state security (the essential means of governmentality). The other is what Foucault saw as the knowledge/power complex, a fused grid or network of relations expressed through action. Different capabilities concerning surveillance and the knowledge/power complex are associated with each set of actors. Each group employs these components of social practice to further its own agenda. For 'suprastate agencies' such as UNCED and GEF (a World Bank environment fund), the agenda is global ecological regulation as well as the promotion of sustainable livelihoods. For the institutions of 'global capital' e.g. transnationals and the World Bank, the agenda is the maximisation of profit based on neoliberal ideology. As for the situated actors, the forest margin communities are concerned with minimising livelihood risk and maximising security; and the environmental professionals, as representatives of nation states, have conservation and development agendas. The environmental state, Cameroon and donor country line ministries, and conservation/development organisations, aim to minimise ecological and livelihood risks, and build national economic security.

Having outlined how the global 'agenda setting community' and the 'risk population' come together within the wider material world and meet in the tropical forest, it is to this conjunction of the knowledge/power complex and surveillance we now turn to expose the power effects related to the operation of the environmental state.

OF LOOKOUTS

From our thumbnail sketch tracking the history and development of the environmental state in the forest, it becomes clear how previous modes of environmental protection have come under severe pressure. Reflexive monitoring by all actors of one anothers' activities, coupled with the shift of economic power to the hand of business, meant that old models of forest protection became untenable for two reasons. First, resources for maintaining 'quasi-military' style exclusionary conservation operations[5] disappeared, whilst at the same time civil resistance and incursion into the forests increased, making effective control impossible. Second, the environmental state was forced to minister to the risks perceived by the population (indigenous rights to self development and secure livelihoods), and those the state perceived as affecting the social body (global environmental quality and national economic capacity); whilst satisfying the edicts of the global agenda setting community (e.g. structural adjustment, ratification of UNCED's Forest Principles, Biodiversity and Climate Change Conventions, and Agenda 21 priorities).

Participatory approaches to conservation, in which communities were 'empowered' to direct their own 'development' were pushed forward as a credible alternative to exclusionary modes of conservation. The environmental state has adopted and normalised this discourse, and used it to legitimise the contradictory functions of forest protection and exploitation demanded by local and global interests. However, the discourse of 'participation' as theory and practice is subject to its own fundamental contradictions. As Brown (1997, pp. 13–14) explains, on the one hand populism suggests that the poor already have the qualities needed for their 'development' and the proper job of environmental professionals is to liberate them from structures of domination whilst, on the other hand, it also suggests that the structures of domination have so altered the consciousness of the poor that they no longer possess these qualities. Thus the task is to re-educate and re-instate a valid 'consciousness'.

A number of important points can be drawn from this contradiction. Both positions invest environmental professionals with an increased authority to monitor and investigate rural communities; tracking patterns of forest resource use, uncovering the political economy constituting their daily lives, and probing their environmental consciousness through the elicitation of indigenous knowledge (cf. Neumann, 1997, p. 560). Participatory techniques rely on the collection and exposure of large quantities of this kind of information, which environmental professionals then use to facilitate liberation or re-education projects.

These interventions at once claim to build the reflexive capacity of local communities, whilst continuing to vest authority in the environmental professionals who may themselves deny the ability of local communities to do this. Either way "the political and institutional dimensions of the situation are consistently discounted, and the argument is diverted from structural relationships to individual responsibilities" (Brown, 1997, p. 14), so that participatory processes facilitate the shifting of responsibility for bearing risk, from the state to individuals.

In this sense participation becomes a form of Foucauldian 'confession' and we can understand the emerging conservation orthodoxy as a form of surveillance. Rather like Foucault's 'panoptican' or watchtower, the environmental state constructs, through the discourse of 'participation', a lookout from which it can extend its gaze over the forest and its natural resources and into the lifeworlds of forest and forest margin communities. Through surveillance the knowledge/power complex is exposed as central to processes of participation. Following through Foucault's ideas of confession, he states that it is "not only confession of madness, but also the patient's own recognition of madness, [that are] the essential dimension[s] of the cure" (Foucault, quoted in Novellino, 1997, p. 55). In other words, once confessed, knowledge and lifeworld become objectified and subject to examination and appropriation by bioscience. Authority remains with the environmental professionals who control the process of analysis "stop[ping] short of advocating a full surrender of authority" to local people (Brown, 1997, p. 14). Therefore, as participatory conservation operates at global and local levels it raises important questions over whose environmental agendas and bio-power are being furthered.

OF LUMBERJACKS

The way in which surveillance and the knowledge/power complex are contained within the participatory process, satisfies the utilitarian projects of first world and third world elements of the environmental state. We have suggested that the environmental state is forced to minister to the 'risk population' whilst satisfying the edicts of the 'global agenda setting community'. Contradictions exist for the environmental state in that the risk population demands livelihood security predicated on forest development, and ecological security dependent upon forest conservation.

By and large, for the first world 'conservation-through-participation' serves a protective function by developing investments in 'risk-mitigating resources'. Here the environmental state focuses on the tropical forest as an 'sink' for CO_2 emissions, and as a source of novel species and genes with potential for mitigating risks inherent to industrially transformed and managed ecosystems. The financial investment by donors into Cameroon's forest conservation and management sector is not insubstantial, one estimate of bilateral aid alone, runs to over U.S.$100 million between 1990 and 1997. The first world is thereby afforded significant status whilst seeking a tangible return on its investment.

The processes of time-space compression that reorganise social relations and condition the permeable boundaries between first world and third world elements of the environmental state, depend, according to Giddens (1990), on 'disembedding mechanisms'. These 'lift out' social activity from localised contexts, and are mediated by two different kinds of encounter, what Giddens (*ibid.*) terms 'faceless commitments' and 'facework commitments'. The faceless commitments in our example relate to the structures, institutions and discourses which make up the agenda of the environmental state. Giddens shows how faceless commitments are dependent on the development of trust in abstract systems. Giddens makes the point that faceless commitments are either sustained or transformed by facework commitments at 'access points'.

Participation, and the surveillance/knowledge/power complex it encompasses, can be understood as a disembedding mechanism, where the expert knowledges of bioscience and risk constitute the abstract system. The expert system calculates benefits and risks of the actions of the environmental state, but also creates a universe of events by implementation of that knowledge. The access points of abstract systems involve individuals as representatives; in our example, the situated environmental professionals.

At these access points facework commitments directed by the environmental professionals tie the forest and forest margin communities into trust relationships. Even though the trust is with the abstract system rather than the individuals who represent it, "access points carry a reminder that it is flesh and blood people who are its operators. Face work commitments tend to be heavily dependent upon what might be called the *demeanour* of system representatives" (emphasis added Giddens, 1990, p. 85). Demeanour here relates to the neo-populist narrative of liberation. These encounters pull local communities into the first world project and into participatory conservation interventions.

Participation as praxis represents a semiotic conquest of local knowledges. 'Saving nature' demands the valuation of local knowledges of sustaining nature where "knowledge is seen as something existing in the minds of individual persons (shamans or elders) about external 'objects' (plants, species), the medical or economic 'utility' of which their bearers are supposed to transmit to us" (Escobar, 1996, p. 57). Participation separates out knowledge from power, and in the process of disembedding loses the context from which knowledge of resources emanates. Additionally, the philosophical base of participation assumes the possibility of self-development based on Habermasian views of consensus-seeking civil society. As Rutherford (1999, p. 44) stresses "not only is knowledge pivotal to practices of power; it is central to *the constitution of the objects upon which power operates* – that is to the making up of *both people and things*".

Sustaining faceless commitments also relies on re-embedding processes (Giddens, 1990). These processes complete the binding of people and institutions across space-time, and serve to hide the weaknesses, problems and uncertainties of the expert systems. The central concern of the first world for resources, identified by a 'gaze' that looks 'through' people, provides the channels not only for disembedding but also for re-embedding social relations. In this way knowledge and power are reinvented and reinserted into the forest milieu.

Through its focus on resources and its targeting of population, the environmental state of the first world is thus incorporated into social practice implying 'action at a distance' (Latour, 1992). The environmental state produces in essence, a situation that can be likened to O'Connor's (1989) notion of 'combined development' – or perhaps more accurately 'combined conservation' – where the first world's project of protecting risk mitigating resources relies on situated forest margin actors fulfilling a predetermined agenda. The environmental state as the Cameroon government, has the twin objectives of satisfying livelihood goals and facilitating national development. However, in bringing the surveillance and knowledge/power complex to bear on the forest, the spotlight on forest peoples and the extended gaze into the forest itself, create opportunities for coercive development of political capital, predicated on forest destruction.

What has to be impressed here is that, in Cameroon, the boundaries between the state as government, the state as line ministry, community elites, and civil society are not sharply defined. Civil organisations are often linked to state organisations, elites to government and so on. The practical consequence of this is that since Independence any relation involving the forest, *has to be* understood in terms of the power relations enmeshed within the national political economy.

We have already shown how at every major historical change of rulership the forest became a site of transformation, and how the forest's own history became part of political history. The strong ties between the forest and politics continue into the present day. The forest continues, for those competing for political position, to be a site to mobilise political support and achieve community representation. The economically well-to-do of forest and forest margin communities may also be representatives of line ministries, or agents of transnational companies. Participatory approaches provide an efficient means by which they can co-opt situated actors onto their personal agendas.

Those seeking political elevation often mediate between conservation/ development organisations and local communities, influencing the projects of the first world with demands for prerequisites (e.g. health facilities, new roads, etc.) to community participation. The same individuals may also become active in the NGO sector where they have sought control over the exploitation of particular forest resources and promised community benefits. In other areas they may be supporting logging companies, fixing terms between the community and business concerning royalties and the provision of services. For these local representatives of line ministries and government, knowledge of the discourse and discursive practices of local and global communities is vital. Local communities are engaged with the language of development and progress, whilst the same initiatives are presented to first world actors as 'sustainable community development', or 'indigenous rights' issues.

OF LEOPARDS

As we reach this point in the discussion, it is clear that the ecological discourse of the environmental state is not simply about the tropical forest environment, the key question concerns which social projects are furthered under the flags of resource and livelihood protection. The social relations surrounding the forest in Cameroon involve a number of powerful 'discourse coalitions' (Hajer, 1995), which struggle to stake their claims over forest resources and peoples.

This creates a situation that Burnham (1994) describes as the 'operational carve-up of zones of influence' between conservation and development interests, where each coalition effectively closes its eyes to the activities of the other, in return for being able to mark their territory successfully. In practice, vast swathes of the forest in Southern Cameroon have been identified as current and potential logging concessions, whereas in the South West conservation areas such as Korup National Park, vie for position with plantation agribusiness.

There is a further layer of contradiction introduced by the way that the discursive communities and policy coalitions, are overlain by epistemic fraternities subscribing to two different interpretations of what Hajer (1995) terms 'ecological modernisation'. One is based on institutional learning, the other on the creation of new institutions and political forms. The institutional learning perspective believes that ecological considerations should be treated as an added component for consideration within existing institutions. In contrast, the alternative view is that appropriation of ecological discourse by current institutions merely perpetuates the status quo, plunging the environmental state and the human species body into deeper crisis; the path to less destructive social practice lying in the emergence of new biopolitical institutions.

Putting all these elements of complexity and layers of incongruity together, it becomes easier to see how the environmental state remains in a position of constant tension, pressure and contradictory reality. It is easier to accept the means by which conventional and ecological forms of capitalization can "co-exist schizophrenically in the same geographical and cultural region" (Escobar, 1996, p. 56), where 'traditional', 'modern', and emerging institutions are caught in a maelstrom of contradictory, facilitative and exclusionary relationships.

OF LOSERS?

So what are the implications for the everyday people living in and around the forest on whom the environmental state focuses its gaze? Our starting point is that the notion of 'risk' is perceived differently by local populations compared with the other groups of actors in our discussion. As Jasanoff (1999, p. 150) puts it, risk is "experienced by experts and laypeople alike . . . [but risk] . . . is culturally embedded and has texture and meaning that vary from one social grouping to another". She goes on to say that "against this background, it makes very little sense to regulate risk on the basis of centralised institutional authority . . . and claims to superior expertise" (*ibid.*).

The livelihood strategies of the local population are structured in response to different types and 'textures' of risk than those perceived by the groups that maintain authority over environmental discourse. It is the local populations themselves, who are the expertly skilled actors in interpreting and responding to the risks present in their own lifeworlds. Consequently, their agency may not easily be turned towards achieving the goals of forest conservation or forest development in the way envisaged by environmental professionals.

A second observation, supported by the historical analysis presented earlier in this paper, is that the discourse and praxis of 'participation' resembles many of the social practices and power relations of the colonial and post-colonial past. For many individuals in the forest zone of South West Cameroon suspicion of the motives of environmental professionals is real and tangible. Many people perceive and believe that the "new forms of intervention . . . tend to represent a continuity with, rather than a cleavage from, past practices" (Neumann, 1997, p. 56). The trust so essential to the processes of disembedding and re-embedding social relations, and to the construction of the authoritative gaze, is not easily won. Access points remain places of extreme vulnerability for the environmental state.

Here we come back to Foucault, and underline how his notion of the 'panoptican', was very different to Weber's iron cage of subjugation and control. To Foucault liberty is not the absence of domination but "an expression of individuals' very own existence in the specificity of power relations" and that "liberation from 'oppression', . . . is a delusion because power is not exclusively repressive, . . . [but] 'capillary', diffused and everywhere" (Darier, 1999, p. 19). This position interprets power as 'constitutive' and 'enabling' (*ibid.*). In other words, the field of power may constrain the options open to the agency of individuals and groups, yet they maintain the capacity either to accept or challenge them. This idea of the limiting of options, accords with Giddens' analysis of the enabling and constraining features of social structure, and the " 'dialectic of control' – the space that exists, even when [authoritative and allocative] resources are not equally available to all parties in a relationship, for some sort of struggle to take place" (Craib, 1992, p. 50).

In the same way that participation presents opportunities for the environmental state to further its agenda of risk mitigation, it presents situated actors with similar reflexive means to pursue their goals and objectives of livelihood security. So, for the authoritative dimensions of the environmental state and the ontological security of environmental practitioners committed to the participatory project, the uncomfortable reality is that their "objectifying gaze at the black . . . is haunted by the suppressed recognition that the glance could be returned" (Kearns, 1997, p. 451). Knowledge concerning forest resources and the local political economy, as well as expert knowledge held by environmental professionals exposed during participatory exercises, is open to scrutiny and exploitation by forest people.

Where conservation projects are perceived to further their own objectives, situated actors may subscribe to participatory interventions. They may also be willing to provide information as part of participation in practice but, nonetheless, what and how much information to provide is subject to skilled calculations concerning the risk of providing that information: the gaze of the state can be distorted by 'selected extracts'. The emphasis given to resources by those leading the participatory project provides a restricted rather than holistic view of the forest, which, when subjected to the power effects of the local political economy, means that participation is very often destructive rather than protective.

Individuals and groups may also agree to certain courses of protective action, and even develop systems of sanctions against offenders, whilst the reality of what they are actually doing 'backstage' outside the objectifying gaze may be very different. Resistance to the agendas of the environmental state comes in many forms. Many villages and individuals in the conservation zone of the South West have opted out of conservation interventions all together. In some examples not wishing to be 'emancipated' they simply choose not to confess. In other places the discourse of participation is reflected back at environmental professionals and used to expel them.

Around the Mount Cameroon area for example, there are a number of indigenous villages which, unwilling to countenance changes to livelihood security based on hunting, have resisted any meaningful contact with personnel from projects. Others have physically removed environmental professionals from their land, because they felt their objectives were being manipulated rather than facilitated by participatory projects concerning medicinal plants.

Acts of resistance also take more subtle forms. In another instance forest communities agreed to participate in inventorying the quantity, and mapping the location of a valuable species, with a view to what the project staff understood to be future sustainable exploitation directed by them. However, after the exercise was completed, replete with knowledge that strengthened their bargaining position, villagers negotiated exploitation concessions direct with an international company. Participatory inventories and forest mapping have also provided a route for people to identify and then open new areas for agriculture within the forest. Similarly, small scale community-based timber exploiters have been able to locate valuable trees and assess the extent of each others claims, moving in to cut trees ahead of their rivals in a race to realise profits. In all these instances; the benefits to either forest or biodiversity protection are debatable, but the importance in mitigating local risks and to local livelihood security is clear.

The protective and destructive contradictions inherent to 'participation', and the expert knowledge of local economy and risk held by situated actors, is nowhere more apparent that at Giddens' 'access points'. Keen to engender trust and elicit information, the agency of environmental professionals can be co-opted by situated actors. The vulnerability of facework has seen agency staff take an active role in supporting local livelihood activities, by transporting timber exploiters and their equipment into the forest to fell, or hunters into the forest to hunt, or by sharing meals of endangered species. The environmental professionals are helpless to shout out, fearing the collapse of the building of trust. Through all of this lies an implicit sanction by the environmental state, that people must secure their livelihoods at all costs, that the local political economy is the 'politics of the belly'.

Hence, there are unintended ecological consequences of action/resistance as well as unintended power effects of social knowledge, such that, "[t]he concept of normalisation/resistance cannot be understood as a fixed meta-narrative describing 'power' in the abstract, but, on the contrary, should be approached as a constant recontextualisation of power relations as lived and experienced by humans" (Darier, 1999, p. 18). This suggests that processes of 'modernization' and 'globalization' are woven together with local action to create institutions and practices which synthesize the 'traditional' and the 'modern' in previously unimagined ways.

TO CONCLUDE

The environmental state simultaneously employs a three-pronged strategy: it creates conditions favourable for capital accumulation and economic growth yet it maintains legitimacy by symbolically tending to the needs of the exploited and protecting the ecological capital on which we all depend. Participatory conservation is, in this sense, a process of symbolic legitimation which tends to the needs of the exploited 'peasant' as well as the exploited forest. However, it also provides the means whereby the target of the state, the population, exposes the knowledge/power complex constituting their political ecology, in a way that strengthens apparatuses of state security. Manipulating the allocative and authoritative resources implicated in the knowledge/power complex using diverse calculations, tactics, and manoeuvres, the environmental state furthers its risk mitigating agendas by seeing deeper into the forest and the lifeworlds of its inhabitants.

The ability of actors reflexively to monitor each other's actions, introduces the possibility of unintended outcomes arising from the exercise of either local or global agency. Participation is thus an activity which may transform social practice with protective functions into destructive consequences. In addition, aiming for forest protection through participatory discourse comes close to echoing historic patterns of social power relations, and creates conditions where "the overextension of post-modern ideas . . . could also be characterised as a kind of cryptocolonial discourse effectively masking the commercial exploitation of knowledge, culture and biotic resources (Gandy, 1996, p. 34); the danger being that communities are given symbolic stewardship over forest management only in so far as it meets the aims of the environmental state.

The environmental state will likely face increasing pressure to minister to risk populations in different geographic locales, bound together across permeable boundaries situated in compressed space-time. For the environmental state, the challenge remains one of developing institutional forms that can "accommodate the increase of cognitive reflectivity, argumentation and social choice" (Hajer, 1996, p. 266) of all those tied together as the risk population. Whether institutional learning, or the emergence of completely new biopolitical institutions is the route to fulfilling this challenge, the role of participation as a process and a discourse needs to be assessed critically. In whatever form, unintended consequences are likely to continue to produce contradictory effects on the material and social worlds. The fate of the forest and of 'nature' more generally are hard to predict. All we can be sure of are further surprises.

NOTES

1. We are aware of the difficulties in applying Foucault within sociological analysis and to environmental sociology in particular (for a useful critique see Fox, 1998). Foucault passed through three broad phases in his thinking and writing, which give rise to the contradictions in his work, as he continued to develop his ideas over time. Even though Foucault never looked at the question of the environment, some of his ideas concerning the nature of the state and of knowledge/power offer useful additions to any analysis of the environmental state.
2. For useful reviews see Giddens, 1990; Goodman and Redclift, 1991; Norgaard, 1994.
3. International Tropical Timber Organisation.
4. In 1991 Cameroon's debt as a percentage of GNP was 57.5% (World Bank, 1993).
5. This style of conservation has been popular the world over, but is particularly prominent in Africa. It is based on the demarcation of reserve boundaries and the action of Forest Department personnel patrolling sometimes vast tracks of forest, to prevent entry and resource exploitation by local populations.

REFERENCES

Anon (1900). All Highest Ordinance with regard to empowering the Governor of the Kamerun to issue Ordinances for the Protection of the Forest. *Imperial Gazette.*

Anon (1991). World Bank targets African greens. *Africa Analysis.*

Ardener, S. (1996). *Kingdom on Mount Cameroon; Studies in the History of the Cameroon Coast, 1500–1970.* Oxford, U.K.: Berghahn Books.

Arentz, F. (1993). Country Profile – Cameroon. *Tropical Forest Update, 3,* 18–19.

Bass, S., Dalal-Clayton, B., & Pretty, J. (1995). *Participation in Strategies for Sustainable Development.* London: IIED.

Batterbury, S., Forsyth, T., & Thompson, K. (1997). Environmental transformations in developing countries: hybrid research and democratic policy. *The Geographical Journal, 163,* 126–132.

Beck, U. (1996). Risk Society and the Provident State. In: S. Lash, B. Szerszynski & B. Wynne (Eds), *Risk, Environment and Modernity: Towards a New Ecology*. London: Sage Publications.

Beck, U. (1998). *¿Qué es la Globalización? Falacias del Globalismo, Respuestas a la Globalización*. Barcelona: Paidos.

Brown, D. (1997). Professionalism, participation, and the public good: issues of arbitration in development management and the critique of the neo-populist approach. *Public Sector Management for the Next Century*. University of Manchester, Manchester, 29th June – 2nd July: University of Manchester.

Bryant, R., & Bailey, S. (1997). *Third World Political Ecology*. London: Routledge.

Burchell, G., Gordon, C., & Miller, P. (1991). *The Foucault Effect: Studies in Governmentality*: Harvester Wheatsheaf.

Burnham, P. (1994). The Cultural Context of Rainforest Conservation in Cameroon. *Thirty-Sixth Annual Meeting of the African Studies Association*. Boston, USA, December 1993: African Studies Association.

CNAB (1916). Qh/a/1916/1: Preliminary Report on the Forests of the British Sphere of the Cameroons. A.H. Unwin.

CNAB (1921). Ag4: Intelligence Report on the Clans and Village Groups in Victoria Division.

CNAB (1923). Ag7: Preliminary Assessment Report on the Bambuko People Victoria Division.

CNAB (1934). 1462/Ae22: Intelligence Report on the Bambuko Clan of the Kumba Division, British Cameroons Clans and Village Groups in Victoria Division : F. A. Goodliffe, Assistant District Officer.

Craib, I. (1992). *Anthony Giddens*. London: Routledge.

Darier, M. (1999). Foucault and the Environment. In: M. Darier (Ed.), *Discourses of the Environment*. London: Routledge.

DeLancy, M. W., & Mokeba, H., M. (1990). *Historical Dictionary of the Republic of Cameroon*. London: The Scarecrow Press.

Demenou, A. P. (1997). La Place du Bois de Fue dans un Sisteme Agroforestier: Rapport Final. Yaounde, Cameroon: CIFOR.

Dreyfus, H., & Rabinow, P. (1982). *Michel Foucault: Beyond Structuralism and Hermeneutics*. Chicago IL: University of Chicago Press.

Epale, S. J. (1985). *Plantations and Development in Western Cameroon, 1885–1975: A Study in Agrarian Capitalism*. New York: Vantage Press.

Escobar, A. (1996). Constructing Nature: Elements for a poststructural political ecology. In: D. Peet & M. Watts (Ed.), *Liberation Ecologies: Environment, Development, Social Movements*. London: Routledge.

Forje, J. W. (1993). *Legal and Policy Dimensions for Biodiversity Conservation and Resources Management in Cameroon*. Yaounde, Cameroon: Centre for Action Oriented Research on African Development.

Foucault, M. (1976). *The History of Sexuality*. New York: Panthenon Books.

Foucault, M. (1977). *Discipline and Punish: the Birth of the Prison*. London: Allen Lane.

Fox, N. J. (1998). Foucault, Foucauldians and sociology. *British Journal of Sociology*, *49*, 415–433.

Gandy, M. (1996). Crumbling land: the postmodernity debate and the analysis of environmental problems. *Progress in Human Geography*, *20*, 23–40.

Geschiere, P. (1993). Chiefs and Colonial Rule in Cameroon: Inventing Chieftancy, French and British Style. *Africa*, *63*(2), 153–175.

Giddens, A. (1984). *The Constitution of Society: Outline of the Theory of Structuration*. London: Polity Press.

Giddens, A. (1985). *The Nation State and Violence*. Cambridge: Polity Press.

Giddens, A. (1990). *The Consequences of Modernity*. Cambridge: Polity Press.

Gockowski, J. (1997). *An Analytical Model of Deforestation Effects in Related Markets: the Case of Cocoa, Plantain, and Cocoyam Production in the ASB Cameroon*. Benchmark.

Goodman, D., & Redclift, M. R. (1991). *Refashioning Nature: Food, Ecology and Culture*. London: Routledge.

Hajer, M. A. (1995). *The Politics of Environmental Discourse: Ecological Modernization and the Policy Process*. Oxford: Clarendon Press.

Hajer, M. A. (1996). Ecological Modernisation as Cultural Politics. In: S. Lash, B. Szerszynski & B. Wynne (Eds), *Risk, Environment and Modernity: Towards a New Ecology*. London: Sage Publications.

Hughes, C., Hawthorne, W., & Bass, S. (1998). *Forests, Biodiversity and Livelihoods: Linking Policy and Practice*. London: Department for International Development.

Jasanoff, S. (1999). The Songlines of Risk. *Environmental Values*, *8*(2), 135–152.

Kearns, G. (1997). The imperial subject: geography and travel in the work of Mary Kingsley and Halford Mackinder. *Transactions of the Institute of British Geographers*, *63*, 450–472.

Konings, P. (1995). Plantation Labour and Economic Crisis in Cameroon. *Development and Change*, *26*, 525–549.

Latour, B. (1992). *Science in Action*. London: Harvard University Press.

Luke, T. W. (1999). Environmentality as Green Governmentality. In: M. Darier (Ed.), *Discourses of the Environment*. London: Routledge.

Marshall, B. K. (1999). Globalisation, Environmental Degradation and Ulrich Beck's Risk Society. *Environmental Values*, *8*, 253–275.

Messerschmidt, D. A. (1995). *Rapid Appraisal for Community Forestry: The RA Process and Rapid Diagnostic Tools*. London: IIED.

Ndoye, O., & Kaimowitz, D. (1998). Economics, Markets, and the Humid Forests of Cameroon. Research Mailing List, CIFOR.

Nelson, N., & Wright, S. (1995). *Power and Participatory Development: Theory and Practice*. London: Intermediate Technology Publications.

Neumann, R. P. (1997). Primitive Ideas: Protected Area Buffer Zones and the Politics of Land in Africa. *Development and Change*, *28*, 559–582.

Ngwasiri, C. N. (1995). *Land Tenure in the Mount Cameroon Region?* Buea, Cameroon: University of Buea.

Njeuma, M. (1989). *Introduction to the History of Cameroon in the Nineteenth and Twentieth Centuries*. London: Macmillan.

Norgaard, R. B. (1989). The case for methodological pluralism. *Ecological Economics*, *1*, 37–57.

Norgaard, R. B. (1994). *Development Betrayed: The End of Progress and a Coevolutionary Revisioning of the Future*. London: Routledge.

Novellino, D. (1997). *The Relevance of Social Capital in Theory and Practice: The Case of Palawan (The Phillipines)*. Rome: Food and Agriculture Organisation of the United Nations.

O'Connor, J. (1989). Uneven and combined development and ecological crisis: a theoretical introduction. *Race and Class*, *30*, 1–11.

Rutherford, P. (1999). The Entry of Life into History. In: M. Darier (Ed.), *Discourses of the Environment*. London: Routledge.

Scoones, I. (1997). The Dynamics of Soil Fertility Change: historical perspectives on environmental transformation from Zimbabwe. *The Geographical Journal*, *163*, 161–169.

Stockdale, M., & Ambrose, B. (1996). Mapping and NTFP Inventory: Participatory Assessment Methods for Forest-dwelling Communities in East Kalimantan, Indonesia. In: J. Carter (Ed.), *Rural Development Forestry Study Guide: Recent Approach to Participatory Forest Resource Assessment*. London: Overseas Development Institute.

Victoria Centenary Committee (1958). *Victoria Southern Cameroons, 1858–1958*. Victoria, Southern Cameroons: Victoria Centenary Committee by Basel Mission Book Depot.

Wiley, L. (1999). Moving Forward in African Community Forestry: Trading Power, Not Use Rights. *Society and Natural Resources*, *12*, 49–61.

Woodgate, G., Ambrose-Oji, B., Fernandez Durán, R., Guzmán, G., & Sevilla Guzmán, E. (1999). Alternative Food and Agriculture Networks: an Agroecological Perspective on Responses to Economic Globalisation and the 'New' Agrarian Question. Keynote paper to the European Union COST Social Science Working Group on Rural Innovations, Córdoba, Spain, June 1999.

Woodgate, G. R., & Redclift, M. R. (1998). From a "Sociology of Nature" to Environmental Sociology: Beyond Social Construction. *Environmental Values*, *7*, 3–24.

World Bank (1993). *World Development Report*. Oxford: Oxford University Press.

Zarate Hernandez, J. E. (1998). Ethnography, Cultural Change and Local Power. *Journal of Historical Sociology*, *11*, 138–149.

Zimmerer, K. S. (1994). Human Geography and the 'New Ecology': The Prospect and Promise of Integration. *Annals of the Association of Human Geographers*, *84*, 108–125.

THE GLOBAL IN THE LOCAL: THE ENVIRONMENTAL STATE AND THE MANAGEMENT OF THE NILE PERCH FISHERY ON LAKE VICTORIA

Douglas C. Wilson

INTRODUCTION

Lake Victoria, shared by Kenya, Uganda and Tanzania, is the world's second largest freshwater lake. The Nile perch (*Lates niloticus*), was introduced into the lake in the 1950s and its population exploded in the late 1970s. Predation by this expanding population was the main cause of the extinction or near extinction of an estimated 300 fish species (Barel, 1986). The Nile perch is a large, white, meaty fish which finds a ready international market. Thus, an immediate consequence of this vast change in species composition was a dramatic manifestation of the "treadmill of production" (Schnaiberg, 1980) on the lake's shores. A processing and export industry appeared in Kenya and Uganda during the 1980s and spread to Tanzania during the early 1990s. Between 1986 and 1994 exports from Tanzania increased five levels of magnitude to 53,000 metric tons. Now, many signs indicate that the Nile perch is being overfished (Pitcher & Bundy, 1995).

The Tanzanian State faces a complex policy environment as it seeks ways to manage the new fishery. Agencies responsible for economic growth

The Environmental State Under Pressure, Volume 10, pages 171–192.

ISBN: 0-7623-0854-0

and structural adjustment encourage the fish export industry. The agencies responsible for fisheries research and management, however, are more immediately affected by a second kind of globalization: an intense interest in the lake from international scientific, environmental and development groups. The funding that has followed this interest has meant that a large portion of these agencies' budgets stems from external sources within a loosely configured network of people interested in management policy on the lake. Local and regional fish traders, consumers, and fishers that are not tied to the export industry, resist fisheries management measures that are designed to respond to these external political and economic demands.

Fisheries management on Lake Victoria is an interesting case study of the environmental state. Resource management and conservation in Africa is central to the problem of structural adjustment because pressures to increase exports fall most heavily on agriculture and natural resources. Tanzania has been a poster child for cooperation with multi-lateral agencies over the past decade and a half. At the same time, this lake has become a poster child for environmental degradation in Africa.[1] The Tanzanian state is a relatively weak, dependent state trying to maintain coherent policies in the midst of these pressures.

This case study reports data collected by a team of researchers from the Tanzanian Fisheries Research Institute and Michigan State University in field work that extended from June 1992 through December 1994. Qualitative interviews were held with fisheries management professionals, fish processing plant managers, and others who work in the fisheries sector. Field research was done between January 1993 and November 1994 in nine beaches where fish are landed and sold. A survey (Wilson & Medard, 1994) was conducted with stratified random samples of boat management ($n = 145$) and crew ($n = 241$), riparian households ($n = 178$), and fish processors and traders ($n = 95$). In addition, participant observation, focus groups and in-depth interviews were done with the same populations during the approximately two weeks that the research team stayed on each beach.[2]

The Theoretical Problem: The Treadmill of Production and Ecological Modernization

The Lake Victoria case addresses several questions in the debate between conceptualizing the environmental state as the coordinator of the treadmill of production and the more recent idea of an ecological modernization that seeks to bring "human interaction with the subsistence base under rational ecological control" (Spaargaren & Mol, 1992, p. 323). One is the degree to which these approaches are mutually compatible. This case suggests that they are, if the trends pointed to by ecological modernization are understood as attempts to rationalize and control ecological obstacles in support of the treadmill rather than as a new historical phase of industrial society (Huber, 1982, 1985 cited in Spaargaren & Mol, 1992). Another question is whether the concept of ecological modernization is applicable to Southern contexts. This supposed inapplicability is suggested by more than one theorist (Blowers, 1997; Spaargaren & Mol, 1992), but the present study describes a Southern state operating in a context in which Northern priorities have a great deal of influence. This case also suggests that areas where ecological and social "irrationalities" resist modernization offer occasions for resistance to the injustices that accompany the treadmill.

Schnaiberg's (1980) concept of the treadmill applies systems reasoning to the relationship between society and the environment. The treadmill of production is the logic of the modern social system in which the constant expansion of production is in the immediate interest of all sectors of society: companies, workers and governments. Constant competitive pressure on firms to invest in new technology, and displace workers in the process, creates a political need for more economic development to create jobs and support a welfare state. "The net result of these processes is an increasing necessity for ever greater ecological withdraws and additions in order to sustain a given level of social welfare" (Schnaiberg & Gould, 1994, p. 69). On Lake Victoria the rapid and broadly supported creation of a fish export industry in response to the Nile perch has been a dramatic case in point, as will be demonstrated in detail below.

Habermas's systems theory as it appears in *Legitimation Crisis* (1973) and his *Theory of Communicative Action* (1987) are complementary to the treadmill of production and help illuminate how it relates to ecological modernization. In his basic framework (Habermas, 1973) the political-administrative system provides coordinating services to the economic system while receiving fiscal support, and provides social welfare to the socio-cultural system while receiving mass loyalty. He argues that both the class structure and periodic economic crises exert constant pressure on the state to renew political legitimacy. Its coordinating functions cannot be seen in decisions for which it is accountable because then it would be responsible for compensation. While seeking to renew political legitimacy while maintaining this coordination role the state faces the constraint that there can be no "administrative production of meaning" (1973, p. 70). The cultural traditions on which the state's legitimacy depends weaken when they are perceived to be strategically employed to protect narrow interests.

While the environment plays a marginal role in Habermas' own work, this model is applicable to the environmental state. At the center of the state's economic coordination role is the maintenance of economic institutions, particularly property rights (Marchak, 1987) and these property rights are pivotal within human ecology. They not only mediate economic relations between people, they are a, perhaps the, primary way in which the social system defines and relates to its natural environment. The state, through creating and enforcing property rights and other economic institutions, determines who shall receive both the benefit streams and the negative impacts that result from unsound uses of nature (Bromley, 1991). Issues of environmental protection, conservation, and justice are a particularly acute expression of the crises in political legitimacy that Habermas describes because they involve basic survival norms (Beck, 1995).[3] The present case is an excellent example as the Tanzanian state is caught between the export industry, other resource users, the conservation movement, and a steady decline of the resource.

As the Lake Victoria case also demonstrates, however, no unitary account of the state is empirically adequate. States are large organizations made up of smaller units with their own priorities, perspectives and incentive structures (Skocpol, 1979). Furthermore, each of these units is linked to constituencies outside the state making up units that Knoke (1990) refers to as policy domains. Pluralism, i.e. conceiving of the state as a balance between pressure groups, is the differentiated concept of the state with the longest tradition. Pluralism, however, is a theoretically weak approach because of the essentialism reflected in categorizing actors into groups and then assuming that some sort of balance will emerge between these categories. The categories of actors, and whatever policy struggle is argued to reflect the emerging balance, end up defining each other.

Network approaches avoid this pitfall because they maintain an "anticategorical imperative" (Emirbayer & Goodwin, 1994) and place individual actors within concrete sets of relationships, hence unveiling what network researchers (e.g. Granovetter, 1985, Burt, 1992) think of as the social structure. Knoke (1990, 1993) is prominent among those who have applied the network structure approach to the state. He analyzes concrete relationships between rational political actors in networks characterized by influence and domination. The weakness of network approaches is an atomism that leads to limited applications beyond a micro level and their related failure to capture the structural dynamics of social change.

Emirbayer and Goodwin (1994) argue that the anticategorical imperative does not require atomism. The idioms found within cultural discourses and narratives are also a non-categorical level of organization that patterns activities. Hajer (1995) points out that individual interests are intersubjectively constituted through discourse in actual speech situations. The same is true of identities and other determinants of behavior – including policy positions. Hence, it makes a difference what communicative idioms are available in these speech situations.

Analyses linking networks and discourses in the formation of environmental policy have been done successfully (e.g. Hajer, 1995; Redclift, 1984). One of the best examples is Haas' (1989) analysis of the creation of an international agreement to regulate pollution in the Mediterranean. He used the concept of "epistemic" community, meaning people who share certain assumptions about how environmental issues should be defined. The Mediterranean agreement came about through the actions of members of an international epistemic community who shared a common definition of the problem and worked through the environmental ministries of their countries to bring about the agreement.

Discourse and network analyses, however, remain descriptive unless linked to a concept of the social system. The treadmill of production argument makes this link by assuming that individual incentives are determined by the system and those discourses reflect these incentives (Schnaiberg & Gould, 1994). While this is a useful assumption, Habermas' (1987) system theory gives us some tools to illuminate a richer relationship between the social system, networks, and discourses. He relates idiomatic communications to political and economic systems using the idea of the "lifeworld," which is the set of background assumptions that give meaning to communications. Communications between individuals depend on references to shared lifeworlds. He conceives of markets and bureaucracies as systems using mechanisms for shortcutting communications by defining how interactions can come to closure while relying only minimally on shared lifeworlds. The economy depends on money, through which interactions are defined by the decision to take or leave an offer. Bureaucracies depend on the authoritative power that attaches to offices and minimizes the need for creating a mutual understanding about how a decision will be finalized (Habermas, 1987; Wilson, 1998).

These social systems affect discourses in three ways (Wilson et al., 1999). First, it is commonplace to observe that the claims people make in communications are influenced by their seeking increased money and power. This is the link between the system and discourses based on incentives, mentioned above, and it is clearly the appropriate starting point. On Lake Victoria all actors raise claims about fisheries management from the perspective of their own interests. Our survey of attitudes shows that it is a rare fisher who supports restrictions on his or her own gear (Wilson, 1996). The filleting plants call for certain sized gill nets to be the dominant gear because they need fish of a certain size. The approach used in this case study, however, takes us deeper, however, than just analyzing incentives.

Second, background assumptions are partially derived from positions within the competitive systems. As political and economic systems become more complex and differentiated they reduce the degree to which lifeworlds are shared. This growing differentiation of shared lifeworlds can be observed on Lake Victoria (Wilson et al., 1999). For example, a growing group of fishers are fishing full time, in contrast to the majority who fish as one part of the sustenance strategy of an agricultural household. These fishers tend to be more migratory, and hence less associated with fishing communities, and more integrated into the international market. In interviews and discussions with our team, those who were more specialized and migratory drew on a more commodified and short-term view of the lake as an arena of investment to be rationally managed and exploited, while those who are still part-time fishers drew on a more traditional, permanent, and place-based view (Wilson et al., 1999).

Finally, Habermas (1987) argues that communications can be "distorted" and that lifeworlds can be "colonized" by social systems. This means that situations become defined by the political and economic systems. The imperatives of these systems become the basis of validity, privileging some perspectives over others. Values that depend on more complex communications and shared meanings (i.e. meanings more complex than 'take it or leave it' and 'because I said so') are excluded from having a role in coordinating social life.

On Lake Victoria the management measures being actively considered are the ones that fit into the needs of the export industry and the externally-oriented management bureaucracy. Gear restrictions that fit the priorities of the export community are actively discussed and promulgated. Other measures, such as closed areas, seasons, fisheries co-management, and limits on access, which may be equally or more effective for maintaining a sustainable fishery, receive much less attention. This is in spite of the fact that many people in the Tanzanian state and environmental policy networks are not supporters of the export industry (Wilson et al., 1999).

It is this last idea of systematically distorted communications that helps us to understand ecological modernization. Most of the people reading this paper are engaged in one way or another in seeking to reduce the damage of ecological irrationality. We do ecological modernization. Furthermore, our incentives are often not directly linked to the expansionist pressures of the treadmill and, as we shall see, this is also true of many of the actors on Lake Victoria. What this case study also shows, however, is that the treadmill system channels ecological modernization discourses by constraining the meaning of the claims raised in these discourses.

THE TREADMILL OF PRODUCTION ON LAKE VICTORIA

Pre-colonial Lake Victoria was a grand bounty for riparian peoples. Shallow, tropical lakes produce immense amounts of food, rivaling that of intensive agriculture. While there was some trade, pre-colonial riparian people fished mainly for subsistence. Elders today relate that their grandparents would fish for a few hours and then have to give away most of their catch. Neither the demand for fish nor the available fishing technologies posed any threat of depletion. Indeed, in Tanzania there is no evidence or recollection of any of the pre-colonial fisheries management regimes that existed elsewhere in Africa. This bounty came to an end with the building of the Uganda railroad at the turn of the century. Fish from the lake were an important source of food for the railway workers and, subsequent to the railroad's arrival, long distance trade in fish began to expand rapidly.

Areas of Lake Victoria have suffered from over-fishing ever since. Fishing regulations date back to 1908, but reports of declines in catch-per-unit-effort, an important measure of fish abundance, are almost as old (Dobbs, 1927). The same amount of fishing effort that caught 50–100 fish in 1905, caught just half a fish in 1972 (Kudhongania & Cordone, 1974). The advent of the Nile perch came as the previous fisheries were in rapid decline. Indeed, when it first arrived the fishers named the perch *Mkombozi,* meaning Savior.

Until 1990, the major markets for fish from the Tanzanian side were local consumers and a regional trade within East Africa. Now, the most important buyers are processing plants that export frozen fillets. In the early 1990s, the ten major processing factories produced twice the value of the regional production of cotton, the primary cash crop (Musendo, 1993b). Tanzania exported five metric tons of whole Nile perch in 1986 and 820 tons in 1989 (Maembe, 1990). In interviews in 1994, plants reported exporting the fillets of 53,000 tons, of whole fish and had an estimated capacity of 138,000 tons (Wilson, 1996). These exports were worth approximately 50 million dollars.[4] If we use the best estimate of annual maximum sustainable yield (MSY) for the whole lake, 295,000 tons (Pitcher & Bundy, 1995), these plants were using 36% of the MSY for the Tanzanian half of the lake. They are capable of using 87%.

These plants are much more important than just their production capacity. Where they have penetrated they are the driving force of the industry. There is a very intense competition for fish, which are exported for an average of four times the price paid to the fishers.[5] The main strategies they use to gather fish are offering higher prices than other buyers and using loans, usually in the form of actual fishing gear, to get commitments of supply from individual fishers.

The loans also allow the plants to control the type of fishing gear being used. One plant manager described his relationship to the fishers as "sharecropping." The plants coordinate among themselves to keep their internal competition from inflating the price paid to the fishers, while simultaneously keeping the price high enough to substantially reduce competition from the local and regional fish trade. The following incident illustrates the dynamic of this trade.

When bodies from the Rwandan civil war were floating down the Kagera River into the lake, there was a period of about three weeks when Europeans halted their buying of Lake Victoria Nile perch. The factory agents working on Rubiri Island, the landing beach we visited that was most deeply involved in supplying the filleting plants, announced that the factories could not export and wanted to lower the prices they were offering the fishers from $0.25 to $0.20 a kilogram. The fishers decided that rather than stop fishing they would continue with the lower price. After ten days the fishers became suspicious because the factories continued to buy, even though they were saying that they could not sell. The fishers decided to organize. They held a meeting and then demanded $0.30 or they would look for alternative markets. When the response came it was an offer of $0.24. Despite threats by fishers to pay back their loans and leave for other beaches, the factories held firm at $0.24 and the fishers eventually agreed. When we interviewed him, one organizer still dreamt of organizing a fishers' union. Some other fishers, however, who had been sympathetic had since received soft loans and discontinued their support.

This incident illustrates several things. The plant managers are close together in towns and can communicate easily with one another while the fishers face high organizing costs even on one beach. The large profit margins enjoyed by the plants makes them very flexible in their ability to change prices. The system of providing gear to the fishers on credit not only gives them a steady supply of fish, but it gives them leverage to break down cooperation among the fishers.

Social Effects of the Treadmill of Production

The export trade has had a profound effect on social relations in riparian communities. While these effects are critical for understanding the conditions under which environmental policy is being made, they are described in more detail elsewhere (Wilson, 1996; Wilson, 1998; Wilson et al., 1999), and I offer here only a brief outline. Their importance for fisheries policy stems from the inability of the state to effectively manage the fishery without the cooperation of riparian people. Changes in the social structure of these communities, and in their access to the fishery resources, have direct implications for how local people will perceive and respond to state policies. A local workforce emerged that is supportive of the expansion of the treadmill of production while other groups have been marginalized. These groups not only have different incentives, the way they understand and talk about the lake are also quite different (Wilson et al., 1999).

The filleting factories reduce the amount of fish available to others simply because they are able to outbid them. Many women, disproportionately single heads-of-household, have small fish processing and trading businesses. Where the factories have established themselves they turn to the small Nile perch that the factories do not want. Access to the fish is important to these women. This is certainly true for single women, who have little or no agricultural land. We also found that married women with fish-related small businesses tend to have more control, vis-a-vis their husbands, over the proceeds of their enterprise than women in other types of businesses (Medard & Wilson, 1996). Young men on bicycles want larger fish to sell in the interior. They must wait, or bicycle farther and farther to escape the factory agents. Many of them have found a niche gathering fish from the smaller beaches and bringing them to the larger beaches to sell to the agents (Wilson et al., 1999).

The export market is increasing the stratification in the fishing industry. Evidence of this can be found in data on both meters of gill net owned and value of a fisher's operation, i.e. the overall value of his or her boats, engines, and fishing gear. Our research took place when many beaches were still relatively unaffected by the export market, so we are able to make comparisons between "central" beaches, defined as a beach where more than 30% of the fish sold in the week before our survey was destined for the international market, and "isolated" beaches. On isolated beaches considered alone, the average fisher in the top quartile of gill net ownership owned 15 times as much gill net as the average fisher in the bottom quartile, so clearly there is a good deal of stratification in the fishery that has nothing to do with the international market. This ratio increases to 40 on central beaches (Wilson et al., 1999). The size of operation measure reveals the same pattern. On isolated beaches the ratio of top quartile to bottom quartile is 18, while on central beaches it is 27. In both cases the major leap in magnitude happens between the third and fourth quartiles. Thus the main source of the stratification is a small number of well endowed fishers who are driving up the figures in the highest quartile (Wilson et al., 1999).

The mechanisms driving this stratification are variable access to both inputs and market opportunities. The loans schemes are critical. These schemes tend to aid larger operations more because they have a record of successful fishing and are a better risk, they can supply more fish, and they can handle larger loans which reduce the overhead of the lenders. Market access is also an important mechanism. Once a fisher has an engine, or a large sail driven transport boat, he or she has direct access to the processing plants. They can transport their own fish, and they can buy and transport other fishers' fish.

On central beaches crew members are experiencing increasing economic distance between themselves and the boat and gear owners. The expectation is that a good crew member, a concept which comprises both skill and character, will move up by a traditional path. First they will buy a small net, then a larger one, and finally a boat. Because of increasingly expensive gear and decreasing relative remuneration, opportunities for advancement for the crew members are becoming more difficult.

The Processing Industry and the Tanzanian State

The filleting plants want Nile perch ranging in size from three to nine kilograms. Fish smaller than three kilograms cannot be filleted efficiently. Fish larger than nine kilograms have too much dark meat for optimum marketing. Gill nets are selective for size because fish that are too small swim all the way through them and fish that are too large to be caught in them at all. As a result, the filleting plants want only gill nets that catch the fish of the size they want to be used in the fishery. Such nets have mesh sizes from 6.5″ to 10.5″ (Ligtvoet & Mkumbo, 1990). The nets that the filleting plants make available to fishers through their credit schemes are in the lower end of this range as small mesh sizes catch more fish. Eighty-seven% of the gill nets being used in the fishery fall between 6″ and 7.5″ (Wilson, 1996). In interviews, the managers of the plants expressed a great deal of concern about the use of beach seines and small-mesh nets by fishers and were angry that the government was "doing nothing about it." The factories also want restrictions placed on the types of gear used, not on fishing effort. The more people fishing, of course, the more the sale of fish at the lake shore becomes a buyers market. Finally, the existing plants would very much like to see a freeze on the construction of new plants.

The treadmill of production model emphasizes the complementary incentives of private firms and the state in increasing ecological withdrawals. Tanzanian structural adjustment policies driven by the foreign exchange that the plants generate, reflect this model well. At the time of our research, all but one of the filleting plants had been certified by the Investment Promotion Center in Dar es Salaam. This is a government agency concerned with increasing Tanzania's exports. This certification means that they had received tax breaks through individually negotiated agreements in return for attracting foreign investment.

Most of the plants were excused from paying all taxes beyond a 5% export royalty.

In February 1993, in response to complaints from the processing plants to the "highest levels of government" (Musendo, 1993a), a ban was clamped on the export of whole fish. Whole fish had been going to Kenya to be filleted in plants there and the Tanzanian processors were claiming that there was a scarcity of fish for their operations. The sub-text was that there was a scarcity of fish at conveniently located beaches at the prices they wanted to pay. The immediate effect of this ban was to push the ex-vessel price of Nile perch down 30%. Predictably, the hue and cry raised by the fishers was extensive and the story got a great deal of play in the newspapers. A high-level team led by the director of the Tanzania Fisheries Division (TFD) came out from Dar es Salaam and held a meeting with fisheries officials, industrial processors, and "prominent fishers." Prominent, according to one official, meant 20 boats or more, so only the wealthiest fishers were given a voice. All that resulted from all this discussion, however, was a 45 day postponement of the ban.

The government had several reasons of its own to impose the ban. One is that export taxes are easier to collect from the factories than they are from trucks that go directly from the beaches to the Kenyan border. Another is that the whole fish trade used mainly local currencies and so Kenya was gaining most of the foreign exchange benefits. A third reason was the value added by filleting was accruing entirely to Kenya.

The influence of the filleting plants on the state is by no means determinate. Indeed, some important people in the management agencies are distinctly unsympathetic to them. Biologists at the Tanzania Fisheries Research Institute (TAFIRI) are very concerned about the degree of investment in industrial processing. Professor Bwathondi, the director of TAFIRI, has been quoted in newspapers as saying "If all these plants start operating next year, there will be no fish for the ordinary people and two years later Lake Victoria will be dry of fish" (Musendo, 1992). As I will argue below, the strongest "influence" of the plants may be the background assumption in policy debates that fisheries management must assume the continued dominance of the export sector (Wilson et al., 1999).

The government of the European Union may be as important to the Lake Victoria fishing industry as the Tanzanian government. The European market is becoming more and more demanding in their sanitation requirements. Beaches are required to have concrete fish handling areas, sources of clean water, and latrines (Musoke, 1997) and the filleting plants must also meet EU hygiene requirements (Goulding, 1997). In 1996, an EU inspection team found an unacceptable level of contamination in fish from all three countries that share Lake

Victoria and, as a result, they now require examinations for all Nile perch imports from the region (Goulding, 1997). Tanzania now has only five approved exporters (Goulding, 1997), but others processors may be able to remain in business by export their fish through the approved ones.

FISHERIES MANAGEMENT AND THE ENVIRONMENTAL STATE IN TANZANIA

Tanzanian Fisheries Management Structures

Tanzanian fisheries management consists of two agencies, the Tanzanian Fisheries Research Institute (TAFIRI) and the Tanzanian Fisheries Division (TFD). TAFIRI is responsible for biological and socio-economic research while the TFD is responsible for management activities. In 1972 the Tanzanian government decided to pursue a radical decentralization of its policy apparatus, including the development and management of the fisheries. TFD personnel, from District[6] Fisheries Officers down, were assigned to report to District Councils rather than the TFD (RTF1, 1995). They became part of the local government and were assigned duties on that basis. Perhaps the most problematic result of this was the assignment of those who were to gather catch statistics to also gather taxes on the very same fish landings that they were charged to accurately count for scientific purposes. This structure, and a general lack of information interchange, has made it difficult for TAFIRI research to influence policy (Nhwani, 1992). We asked respondents in both government agencies and private concerns about their use of fisheries science and never found any that had used TAFIRI. Furthermore, TAFIRI biologists reported that they have never received requests for information from anyone investing in the fishery.

TFD agents, referred to locally as Bwana Samaki or Mr. Fish, are an important presence on the small number of more important beaches where they are stationed. The fishers look to them for leadership. One survey question was "when you want help or advice concerning fishing or fishing related activities whom do you ask?" On four beaches where officers were stationed, 34% answered that they would go to him, this was higher than family (26%), no one (14%), boss (11%), and friends or neighbors (7%) (Wilson, 1996). However, the fishers often expressed worry about corruption. Some feel that these are patronage jobs. Corruption is also evident in the enforcement process (Medard, 1996).

Both of these agencies are starved for resources. The TFD has only 7% of the lake shore personnel that Kenya has (RFT1, 1995) to monitor half of the lake's shoreline. The employees of these agencies are poorly paid and get few operating funds for research or administration from the government treasury. A top executive in a government unit involved in fisheries management receives a salary of less than $100.00 a month, while the lowest level professional on his or her staff receives $30.00. While housing is included, these are not living wages and they are often forced to pursue other part-time sources of income. The only way these people can afford to do research, extension, and management activities of any magnitude is if someone from the outside provides them with the resources to do so. This means that their research agendas are driven by outsiders, or at the very least, defined through negotiations in which outsiders have a great deal of leverage. Research designs are not independent of considerations of the economic situation of the researcher.

The implications of this powerful outside influence on the content of policy is complex. There are many international development agencies and environmental organizations involved with Lake Victoria. Harris (1997) suggests that there are three major epistemic communities with distinct policy goals for the lake. These "communities" are hermeneutic categories. They are not hard and fast groups, nor would a person pursuing one of these goals necessarily disagree with the other goals. The communities reflect differing discursive themes and areas of emphasis.

The first community is concerned with the economic rationalization of the fishing industry. This includes promoting new products, seeking more efficient fishing gears, and trying to balance fishing and fish processing capacity with the productive capacity of the lake. This community's strongest institutional embodiment is in the lake-wide cooperative management efforts organized by FAO and supported by the World Bank and the European Union. This group emphasizes rationalizing systems for international cooperation between the three riparian countries. They work to harmonize management legislation, build comparable statistical systems, control the number of filleting plants, assess specific management measures, and improve product quality control (RFT1, 1995). These goals assume the continued primacy of the export industry are clearly pushing the riparian states toward ecological modernization.

The second community is concerned with meeting the basic human needs of local people (Harris, 1997). This perspective is also present within the World Bank and EU efforts and even more strongly in the work of IDRC. They support many of the rationalizing efforts at the level of management structures that the first community does. They also want research on riparian nutritional needs and management that ensures local sustenance. They have a strong programmatic concern with political rationalization in the form of increasing stakeholder participation. "Stakeholder participation" in fisheries management has been widely advocated within the international development community. FAO published a local management manual in 1985 (Ben-Yami & Anderson, 1985) and other donor agencies such as IDRC, UNDP and the World Bank are encouraging participation in fisheries programs that they support (IBRD, 1996).

One of the main tensions between the Tanzanian state and the outside groups has been over who the stakeholders are that should be involved in managing the fisheries. Tanzanian management officials formally recognize that participation by local fishers in the formation and enforcement of the regulations would be a good thing (Ssentongo, 1992) but there are no mechanisms for participation. Ad hoc mechanisms, such as the meeting about the whole fish export ban, include only the wealthiest fishers. The management professionals exaggerate fishers' ignorance of management reasoning (Wilson, 1996). In interviews and planning documents, fisher's participation in management is conceived of almost exclusively in educational terms (e.g. RTF1, 1995). The experts will tell the fishers what they should know and what they will do, and the fishers will participate by complying. Hence, participation is defined in a way that reinforces, rather than moderates, top-down bureaucratic authority.

Harris' (1997) third epistemic community, those seeking to save the pre-Nile perch diversity of the lake, is made up of environmentalists, and scientists from the conservation biology and evolutionary ecology communities. Its institutional personification is mainly in academic and scientific groups such as the International Limnological Society. These groups are seeking ways, such as protected areas and satellite lakes and ponds, to move Lake Victoria closer to its historic distribution of fish species. While this community has generated quite a bit of research funding, its influence on fisheries policy has been limited. Many of their ideas are expensive and difficult and it has proved difficult for their arguments to have practical effect in the policy debate. Their greatest impact has been in public perceptions. Proponents of this construction have sought, with some success, to paint the lake as "dying" in the popular press (e.g. Okie, 1993). Frustration with the continued dominance of the construction of Lake Victoria as primarily an economic resource may be part of the reason why some in the environmental community have resorted to exaggerating the lake's problems (e.g. Chege, 1995).

Fisheries Management Measures

Few good data on fish growth, catch, and fishing effort are available (Nhwani, 1992). Recent estimates of Nile perch MSY are in the 300,000 tonne range for the whole lake (Pitcher & Bundy, 1995), while the, also rough, official statistics report a catch in the Tanzanian half of the lake of between 146,000 and 213,000 tons per year between 1988 and 1993 (CIFA, 1994). All informal observations that we solicited from 1992 to 1994, from both fishers and fishery professionals, indicate that the CPUE for Nile perch has fallen from its high point in 1988. Statistics, confirmed by personal observation and the reports of fishers, also indicate that mean size of the Nile perch is falling (IFIP, 1990). Many fish processors reported rarely seeing fish eggs. All of these facts suggest overfishing.

The Tanzanian biological experts' recommendations emphasize control of gear rather than controls on fishing effort. Gill nets have developed a terrible reputation among lay people, but a small-scale, nylon, gill net fishery, has real advantages in fisheries management. As discussed above, gill nets are very selective for size. Ligtvoet and Mkumbo (1990) found that in the Mwanza Gulf in Tanzanian waters, on average, female Nile perch become sexually mature at 40″. Their data on the selectivity of gill nets indicates that if one wanted to ensure that half the catch of females had reached sexual maturity (and therefore have had a chance to spawn) one would want to use a mesh size of 11.5 inches. Less than 1% of the gill nets being used are this size or larger (Wilson, 1996). TAFIRI recommends nets of seven to eight inches for the Nile perch fishery (Bwathondi, 1992) and currently 83% are in this range (Wilson, 1996).

The government has banned beach seines, the use of mosquito nets for fishing, and fishing with trawlers. There is a legal minimum of five inches for the mesh size in gill nets. Because of the nets provided by the filleting plants currently 96% of the gill nets targeting Nile perch are greater then five inches. Thus, this ban is aimed at fishers of tilapia and other species and/or sizes outside of the Nile perch export market. Mosquito nets are rarely used because of the quality of the catch. The bans on trawlers and beach seines were both advocated by the international community and were a chance for the government to demonstrate to its funders that it was ready and able to take action. Trawlers were already being converted by owners into fish transport boats because the profits are greater. Beach seines do catch some fish for the export market but they mainly supply local and regional trades. A ban on beach seines is much easier to enforce than a ban on other gear because they are large and used on shore.

The beach seine ban is very controversial. They are expensive gears that tend to be owned by locally prominent people. Privately, some fisheries officers do not support the ban. They argue that the beach seines may be destructive where they are used, but that there are so few places on the Tanzanian lake shore where they can be used because of rocks and vegetation that their destructiveness is insignificant. Beach seines play another role. The pullers of the seines are young men and boys who work for fish. Local families who do not have fishing gear have the option of sending their children down to the beach for a few hours to pull a seine and bring home high quality protein. People complained to us that when the seines were gone many families would lose the best access they had to the fishery resource. Without fishing equipment of their own, their only sources of fish would be cash purchases or angling, which is both less sure and less productive.

In summary, the structures and outcomes of fisheries management on Lake Victoria reflect efforts to rationalize the management system in ways that respond to pressures that originate at the international level. The economic rationalization of the fishery is driven by the filleting plants on the one hand, and development agencies concerned with modernizing fisheries management on the other. In an example of systematically distorted communications, the underlying assumption has been that fisheries management must reflect the needs of the export industry, which has led to an emphasis on controlling fishing gear, particularly those less involved in supplying that market, rather than fishing effort. The beach seine ban, a centerpiece of this policy, is a measure of questionable value that has been to the direct detriment of poorer riparian households. The outsider-driven effort at the political rationalization of management through greater participation, on the other hand, has been redefined and gutted by agency personnel who have little to gain from more people in the decision making process.

The result has been resistance to management measures in the riparian communities. Many local people support fisheries management in principle. Half of them responded that they are worried about having enough fish in the future (Wilson, 1996). They are willing to support and even enforce rules they believe in, for example the ban on fishing using poison. But they are resisting other management efforts. Most commonly, this resistance takes the form of not paying attention. Only 7% of all fishers are aware that there is any regulation concerning mesh sizes (Wilson, 1996). In the first region where it was implemented, only 11% of the fishers were aware of the newly promulgated rule banning beach seines (Wilson, 1996). Awareness increases, of course, when there is active enforcement. Medard (1996) studied an area where there has been active enforcement of the beach seine ban and found that through a combination of stealth and bribery beach seines have continued to be used.

The lake fishery cannot be managed under these conditions. Cooperation by both the filleting plants, because of their enormous influence on fishing operations, and the riparian people is necessary. The government must be willing to work with these groups, and working with them means seeking ways to balance their interests in ways that are perceived as fair.

THE ENVIRONMENTAL STATE, ECOLOGICAL MODERNIZATION, AND RESISTANCE

Perhaps the first question this case raises about the "environmental state" is what the meaningful unit of analysis really is. This environmental state has amorphous boundaries. The direct influence of the EU government on Lake Victoria fisheries is nearly as great as that of the Tanzanian. The significant influence of foreign entities, both public and private, within the policy networks that affect the lake raises the same question. This is partly a function of Lake Victoria being shared by three countries. It is mainly a result, however, of the global nature of both markets and policy networks. In a real sense the "environmental state" is a global state in formation.

This raises questions about whether or not the Tanzanian state can produce coherent environmental policy. Indeed, this question's own coherence is debatable because it presumes an identifiable subject that may not exist. If the question is whether or not the TFD is able to make independent and objective decisions the answer is no. The TFD and TAFIRI, however, are very much a part of an conservation community which has representatives in the three riparian countries and strong international backing. This community may eventually be able to articulate coherent policies and facilitate their implementation.

This is the reason that ecological modernization, which was developed as a way to explain European states, is relevant here. Hajer (1995) defines ecological modernization as "the discourse that recognizes the structural character of the environmental problematic but none the less assumes that existing political, economic, and social institutions can internalize the care for the environment" (p. 25). It seeks to make ecological degradation calculable, to define environmental protection as a positive sum game, and assumes that economic growth and the resolution of ecological problems can be reconciled. Ecological modernization also has a political version. Scholars such as Sirianni and Friedland (1995) suggest that the growth of "civic environmentalism," stemming in large part from legal reforms that have given the environmental community greater influence on policy. This trend, along with other forms of "citizen participation," is argued to reflect a new, reformist, political rationality which is more responsive to environmental concerns (Wartenberg & Chess, 1993).

The trends described by ecological modernization are attempts to rationalize and control ecological processes in response to the crises of political legitimacy raised by environmental problems. Rationalization through bureaucratic power requires clear, observable, enforceable, and quantitative decision rules. Complex ecological realities, and the social formations related to them, resist such simple definitions. The beach seine ban is one example of how bureaucratic needs will trump biological and social ones. It was a biologically questionable measure driven by ease of enforcement and oriented more to an external policy environment rather than the needs of either a sustainable fishery or local people.

Habermas' (1987) model of systematically distorted communications helps us understand how discourses surrounding state responses to environmental degradation relate to the treadmill of production. On Lake Victoria ecological modernization, in the form of the economic rationalization discourse, is focused on managing the lake's ecology for the treadmill. Potential management measures that do not fit the treadmill get little attention. Ecological modernization, in the form of the basic needs discourse, lends support to most of the same goals, while its own particular emphasis on stakeholder participation becomes redefined as education in order to protect the bureaucratic authority of the state. The restoration discourse gains little traction as it fits neither market nor bureaucratic imperatives.

Crises of political legitimacy are exacerbated, in situations such as capture fisheries, where the establishment of property rights is difficult for either ecological or social reasons. Systemic failures in such cases, the so-called tragedies of the commons, have been established in both theory and in empirical situations for many years (Scott, 1955). When property rights are poorly defined ecological modernization on behalf of the treadmill become much more difficult. The state's first response is to find some way to either mimic property rights or directly control behavior. There are, however, substantial limits to the state's ability to do this. Such limits can arise from the legitimacy of traditional forms of access to resources. Surveillance and enforcement of economic institutions may also be challenging when the geographical scale is large and the ecology variable and uncertain. These problems can make the state dependent on the cooperation and knowledge of local resource users and this, in turn, raises questions of environmental justice. This may lead to resistance to rationalized resource management as it is defined by markets and bureaucracies.

Lake Victoria fisheries management is a case in point, as are other capture fisheries. The resistance of ecological realities to rationalization opens up critical moments in contexts beyond fisheries. Eder (1996) argues that nature itself, as a collective good, can force moral discourses related to distributive justice. Many examples exist of where unclear property rights stemming from new technologies, new environmental concerns, or resource characteristics have created political space for resistance. Such cases have arisen from traditional systems of communal tenure. Biodiversity and genetic resources have offered opportunities to challenge treadmill-based definitions of property rights. Examples abound in the environmental justice literature (e.g. Goldman, 1999). Focusing both theory and research on these discontinuities and opportunities promises to deepen our understanding of the environmental state.

ACKNOWLEDGMENTS

The author gratefully acknowledges the support of: the U.S. Department of Education's Fulbright-Hays Doctoral Dissertation Research Abroad Program; the John T. and Catherine D. MacArthur Foundation; the Michigan State University African Studies Center; National Science Foundation Dissertation Improvement Grant #INT 9320235; the Tanzania Fisheries Research Institute; and the Social Science Research Council International Predissertation Fellowship Program. Without these institutions this research would not have been possible. A great debt of thanks is owed to Joyce Frederick, Modesta Medard, Ramadhani Mhekela, and Bellarmine Zenge for perseverance in data gathering and Charles and Olivia Mkumbo for the same in data entry.

NOTES

1. The lake suffers from a number of environmental problems, particularly pollution and water hyacinth, beyond the overfishing that is the focus of this paper.
2. This data set is described in detail at http://isp.msu.edu/AfricanStudies/Plea/tanset.htm
3. While the Tanzanian state's present need for legitimation does not make it an important point in the present discussion (although certainly the beach seine ban is scientifically justified) it is worth noting that in many contexts the environmental state increasingly turns to science in an attempt at an "administrative production of meaning." State bureaucracies must construct bureaucratically manageable versions of nature, through for example quantitative indicators, that conform to the need to maintain both the treadmill of production and political legitimacy through environmental sustainability.
4. These figures are all estimates based on various sources, none of which have adequate statistical reporting systems. This figure for export value is taken from the estimates of exports given to me by plant managers, which I consider more reliably than official export statistics, and the average price per kilogram of whole fish derived from Goulding (1997).
5. This estimate is based on the whole fish export value discussed in footnote three and the most common ex-vessel price at the time of our survey.
6. Districts are a fairly local government level, comparable to counties in the U.S.

REFERENCES

Barel, C. D. N. (1986). *The Decline of Lake Victoria's Cichlid Species Flock* University of Leiden: Zoologisch Laboratorium.

Beck, U. (1995). Politics in Risk Society. In: *Ecological Enlightenment: Essays on the Politics of the Risk Society Atlantic Highlands,* (pp. 1–18). NJ: Humanities Press.

Ben-Yami, M., & Anderson, A. (1985). *Community fishery centres: guidelines for establishment and cooperation*. FAO Fisheries Technical Paper, No. 264.

Blowers, A. (1997). Environmental Policy: Ecological Modernization or the Risk Society? *Urban Studies*, *34*(5–6), 845–871.

Bromley, D. (1991). *Environment and Economy: Property Rights and Public Policy*. Oxford: Basil Blackwell.

Burt, R. (1982). *Toward a Structural Theory of Action*. New York: Academic Press.

Bwathondi, P. O. F. (1992). The Fishery Resource Base for the Tanzanian Sector of Lake Victoria. Report of a National Seminar on *The Development and Management of Tanzanian Fisheries of Lake Victoria* (pp. 21–29). UNDP/FAO Regional Project for Inland Fisheries Planning (IFIP) RAF/87/099/TD/35/92:86pp.

Chege, N. (1995). Lake Victoria: a sick giant. *People and the Planet*, *4*(2), 14–16.

CIFA (1994). *Report of the Committee for Inland Fisheries of Africa Sub-Committee for the Development and Management of the Fisheries of Lake Victoria*. Seventh Session. Kisumu, Kenya. Rome: FAO.

Dobbs, C. M. (1927). Fishing in the Kavirondo Gulf, Lake Victoria. *Journal of the East Africa and Uganda Natural History Society*, *30*(July), 97–109.

Eder, K. (1996). The Institutionalization of Environmentalism: Ecological Discourse and the Second Transformation of the Public Sphere. In: S. Lash, B. Szerszynski & B. Wynne (Eds), *Risk, Environment and Society,* (pp. 201–223). London: Sage.

Emirbayer, M., & Goodwin, J. (1994). Network analysis, culture, and the problem of agency. *American Journal of Sociology*, *99*, 1411–1454.

Goldman, M. (Ed.) (1998). *Privatizing Nature: Political Struggles for the Global Commons*. New Brunswick NJ: Rutgers University Press.

Goulding, I. (1997). Nile Perch – Marketing Success or Ecological Disaster? *Seafood International* May 1997.

Granovetter, M. (1985). Economic Action and Social Structure: The Problem of Embeddedness. *American Journal of Sociology*, *91*, 481–510.

Haas, P. M. (1989). Do regimes matter? Epistemic communities and Mediterranean pollution control. *International Organization*, *43*, 379–403.

Habermas, J. (1973). *The Legitimation Crisis*. Boston: Beacon Press.

Habermas, J. (1987). The Theory of Communicative Action. *Volume II Lifeworld and System: A Critique of Functionalist Reasoning*. Boston: Beacon Press.

Hajer, M. A. (1995). *The Politics of Environmental Discourse: Ecological Modernization and the Policy Process*. Oxford: Clarendon Press.

Harris, C. K. (1997). Regime formation and community participation in fisheries management. In: T. Pitcher (Ed.), *Reinventing Fisheries Management*. London: Chapman and Hall.

Huber, J. (1982). *Die Verlorene Unschuld der Okologie: Newe Technologien und Superindustrielle Entwicklung*. Frankfurt am Main: Fisher.

Huber, J. (1985). *Die Regenbogengesellschaft. Okologie und Sozialpolitik*. Frankfurt am Main: Fisher.

IFIP. (1990). Report of the Symposium on Socio-economic aspects of Lake Victoria Fisheries. A Symposium organized by the IFIP Project under the framework of the CIFA Sub-committee for Lake Victoria RAF/87/099-TD/10/90. UNDP/FAO Regional Project for Inland Fisheries Planning (IFIP). Rome: FAO.

International Bank for Reconstruction and Development (1996). *Operational Strategy of the Global Environment Facility*. Washington: The World Bank.

Knoke, D. (1990). *Political Networks: The Structural Perspective*. New York: Cambridge University Press.

Kudhongania A., & Cordone, A. J. (1974). Past Trends, Present Stocks and Possible Future State of the Fisheries of the Tanzanian Part of the Lake Victoria. *The African Journal of Tropical Hydrobiology and Fisheries*, *3*, 167–182.

Ligtvoet, W., & Mkumbo, O. C. (1990). Stock assessment of Nile perch in Lake Victoria. *FAO Fish Rep.*, *430*, 35–74.

Maembe, T. W. (1990). A Review of the Main Characteristics of Long Distance Fish Trade from Lake Victoria, Tanzania. In: Proceedings of the *Symposium on Socio-Economic Aspects of Lake Victoria Fisheries* (Vol. 1, pp. 68–100). UNDP/FAO Regional Project for Inland Fisheries Planning (IFIP) RAF/87/099-WP/05/90 114pp.

Marchak, P. (1987). Uncommon Property. In: P. Marchak, N. Guppy & J. McMullan (Eds), *Uncommon Property: The Fishing and Fish- Processing Industries in British Columbia* (pp. 3–32). Toronto: Methuen.

Medard, M. (1996). Report of the *Socio-economic Study of the Fisheries of Mwanza and Speke Gulfs Following the Ban of the Use of Non-selective Gear*. Mwanza: TAFIRI.

Medard, M., & Wilson, D. C. (1996). Changing Economic Problems for Women in the Nile Perch Fishing Communities on Lake Victoria. *Anthropologica* XXXVIII, 149–172.

Musendo, Z. (1992). Lake Victoria Fish in Danger. *Daily News* August 26.

Musendo, Z. (1993a). Control exports of whole fish, urge processors. *Daily News* February 1993.

Musendo, Z. (1993b). Mwanza fish exports raise differing reactions. *Sunday News* February 1993.

Musoke, D. (1997). *European Union Gives Ultimatum On Fish Exports*. Pan-African News Agency, Sept. 30th.

Nhwani, L. B. (1992). Management Issues Options and Strategies for the Lake Victoria Fisheries. In Report of a *National Seminar on The Development and Management of Tanzanian Fisheries of Lake Victoria* (pp. 58–78). UNDP/FAO Regional Project for Inland Fisheries Planning (IFIP) RAF/87/099/TD/35/92:86pp.

Okie, S. (1993). *The Race to Save a Dying Lake*. The Washington Post 7/4/93:A27.

Pitcher, T., & Bundy, A. (1995). Assessment of the Nile Perch fishery in Lake Victoria. In: T. J. Pitcher & P. J. B. Hart (Eds), *The Impact of Species Changes in African* Lakes (pp. 163–180). London: Chapman and Hall, Fish and Fisheries Series No. 18.

Redclift, M. (1984). *Development and the Environmental Crisis: Red or Green Alternatives*. London: Methuen.

RTF1 (Regional Task Force 1) (1995). Report on *Fisheries Management and Water Hyacinth Control*. Lake Victoria Environmental Management Program.

Schnaiberg, A. (1980). *The Environment*. New York: Oxford University Press.

Schnaiberg, A., & Gould, K. A. (1994). *Environment and Society: the Enduring Conflict*. New York: St. Martins Press.

Scott, A. (1955). The Fishery: the Objectives of Sole Ownership. *Journal of Political Economy*, *63*, 116–124.

Skocpol, T. (1979). *States and Social Revolutions*. Cambridge: Cambridge University Press.

Sirianni, C., & Friedland, L. (1995). *Civic Environmentalism*. Online: http://www.cpn.org/sections/topics/environment/civic_perspectives/civic_environmentalismA.html

Spaagaren, G., & Mol, A. P. J. (1992). Sociology, Environment, and Modernity: Ecological Modernization as a Theory of Social Change. *Society and Natural Resources*, *5*, 323–344.

Ssentongo, G. (1992). Report of a *National Seminar on the Development and Management of Tanzanian Fisheries of Lake Victoria*. RAF/87/099/TD/35/92:86P UNDP/FAO Regional Project for Inland Fisheries Planning (IFIP). Rome: FAO.

Wartenberg, D., & Chess, C. (1993). The Risk Wars: Assessing Risk Assessment. *New Solutions*, *3*(2), 16–25.

Wilson, D. C., & Medard, M. (1994). *Programme on the Lakes of East Africa Socio-economic Data Set for Lake Victoria, Tanzania*. Tanzania Fisheries Research Institute, Mwanza Station/African Studies Center, Michigan State University.

Wilson, D. C. (1996). The Critical Human Ecology of the Lake Victoria Fishing Industry. Ph.D. Dissertation, Michigan State University.

Wilson, D. C. (1998). Markets, Networks, and Risk: an Analysis of Labor Remuneration in the Lake Victoria Fishing Industry. *Sociological Forum*, *13*(3), 425–456.

Wilson, D. C., Medard, M., Harris, C. K., & Wiley, D. S. (1999). The Implications for Participatory Fisheries Management of Intensified Commercialization on Lake Victoria. *Rural Sociology*, *64*(4), 554–572.

PART IV:

THE ENVIRONMENTAL STATE IN TRANSITIONAL COUNTRIES

DEFORESTATION, FLOODS, AND STATE REACTIONS IN CHINA AND THAILAND

Graeme Lang

INTRODUCTION

Natural forests are disappearing in developing countries, with fateful long-term consequences for those countries and for the planet. Identifying the causes of deforestation is easy. Finding solutions is much more difficult. The causes are rooted in various combinations of population growth, poverty, and economic development. Solutions are necessarily political, and must be implemented by sovereign states, since no other agency in the contemporary world has the capacity to deal with the causes of deforestation (Bryant & Bailey, 1997).

State action to halt deforestation in developing countries is crucial, but rarely decisive. Under what conditions would a state in a developing society take action to halt unsustainable depletion of natural forests? Have any states achieved this feat? How are those states – or the conditions under which they took effective action – different from other states where such actions have not occurred? Do democratic states take action more effectively, or with better long-term outcomes, than authoritarian states?

The Environmental State Under Pressure, Volume 10, pages 195–220.

ISBN: 0-7623-0854-0

FORESTS AND THE STATE

States differ greatly in their approach to forests and deforestation, depending in part on the state's political economy. As the best country-studies show in detail, regulation of tree-cutting is influenced by economic and political pressures and interests, and the resulting calculations of gain to various parties, including state officials and their clients and patrons. In general, these pressures and interests have led to a non-sustainable level of tree-cutting worldwide during the 20th century (Williams, 2001).

Pressures to conserve forests, however, have also grown in the late 20th century. There is more international support at the dawn of the 21st century than at any time in the past for forest conservation and sustainable forestry. Scientific research has increased the knowledge-base on deforestation, and some of this knowledge has been incorporated into laws, regulations, and the analyses and lobbying of NGOs and conservation-oriented pressure groups. Regimes everywhere are affected by the growing global institutionalization of environmentalism, in proportion to their links to the international development of environmental knowledge and programs (Frank, Hironaka & Schofer, 2000).

Domestic and international organizations collectively generate pressures toward 'ecological modernization' as some societies gradually develop the technological, legal, and institutional apparatus to pursue less ecologically destructive prosperity (Mol, 1995). Thus, forestry regulation in some countries offers a special case of the more general trends described in the theories of ecological modernization and global institutionalization of environmentalism. Indeed, it could be argued that success in managing the national environment is becoming a factor in the assessment of 'good government' and hence in regime-legitimacy, at least in those countries where most of the population feel economically secure.

The 'treadmill of production' model (Schnaiberg & Gould, 1995), however, suggests that forests will be intensively exploited by economic interests which will resist the imposition of forest regulations which seriously inhibit their operations or reduce their profits, and which will be supported by political elites dependent on growth and revenue generated by these economic interests. In the medium term, forests will be exploited on a non-sustainable basis, despite rising pressures for stricter control. The 'ecological modernization' model suggests that forestry interests and forestry regulators will increasingly develop systems which conserve forests over the longer-term and which approach sustainable forestry exploitation. The question of which model is more accurate undoubtedly depends on the economic and political conditions within particular societies, as well as their links with various external forces, including world markets for wood products, and their links with international flows of scientific and conservationist expertise and resources.

There are a number of factors which affect the exploitation and conservation of forests, and which have been described in the literature. The internal factors include land-hunger, the political power of forest-harvesting interests, state regulatory capacities, corruption, and civil monitoring. The internal-external and external factors include markets for various kinds of forest products and forest uses, and the inflow and deployment of conservation-supporting resources. But in addition there is also a little-studied 'wild card': *environmental disaster*.

The impact of environmental disasters has not been assessed in most analysis of environmentalist policies, since such events (although likely to occur frequently in the future) are still rare. But they may be exceptionally important if they stimulate strong state action, and they may have this effect if they threaten regime-legitimacy.

The legitimacy of modern secular regimes seems to rest on public perception of three core competencies: good government, economic prosperity, and national power.[1] If any of these three foundations are seriously damaged, a regime will respond to protect its rule.[2] Extreme environmental degradation could highlight government incompetence, undermine the economy, and erode national power. Thus environmental decline could threaten a regime's legitimacy and hence its survival, and prompt aggressive state responses.

In most developing countries, however, the threat to regime-legitimacy from environmental problems is still small. The longer-term costs of such problems, which are often debatable, usually fall beyond the planning horizon, and there are too many other problems which are more pressing. Government environmental policies are correspondingly moderate and selective. Since economic development is widely perceived to be incompatible with strict environmental controls, the economy usually takes priority over the environment both in government policy and in popular opinion. Environmental bureaus in developing countries are normally too weak to modify policies of other state agencies which promote economic development (Bryant & Bailey, 1997).

It could also be argued, however, that in the longer term, unsustainable environmental exploitation will eventually lead to a crisis of legitimacy for states where environmental destruction reaches a level at which it threatens some or all of the foundations of regime-legitimacy.

It appears that good government, economic prosperity, and national power – the three pillars of legitimacy – do not at present depend much on environmental management in most developing countries, and hence it is not easy to find cases where a regime has acted aggressively in response to the impact of environmental degradation on legitimacy. However, there are a few countries where environmental problems can undermine regime legitimacy for exceptional local reasons, and hence we can learn about the hypothesized connection between the environment, regime legitimacy, and regime responses by analysis of such cases.

Two cases are described in this chapter: the 1988 floods and resulting state action in Thailand, and the 1998 floods and state action in China. China and Thailand are two developing societies which possessed extensive forests at the beginning of the 20th century, suffered severe forest depletion as their populations exploded after World War II, and struggled to find ways to deal with deforestation during the closing decades of the century. In both countries, a combination of *weak proactive* and *strong reactive* state policies can be observed. The weak proactive policies are responsive to a society's political economy. The strong reactive policies occur only when regime legitimacy is threatened by a high-cost disaster attributable to lax or incompetent policy.

It appears that there are differences between the two societies in the effectiveness with which these strong-reactive policies were implemented in subsequent years. The political systems in the two countries help to account for these differences in outcomes in China and Thailand.

After reviewing these cases, I will discuss their implications for discussions of the 'environmental state' and for theories of 'ecological modernization'. I begin each case study with an overview of state regulation of forestry and state responses to deforestation prior to the disasters which precipitated much stronger responses in both countries.

STATE REGULATION AND DEFORESTATION IN CHINA

Deforestation in pre-modern China, a result of the increasing expansion of the population onto hillsides and into mountainous regions during the Qing dynasty, continued during the Republican period after 1911. The new Communist regime came to power in 1949 with a program to build up the country, reform the economic institutions of the society for the collective benefit of citizens rather than for the profit of individuals or private organizations, and take strong action against any exploitation which produced collective losses to serve private gains. Not facing periodic elections, the regime could afford to take a long-term view of policies to promote these goals. This kind of agenda gave the regime a particular interest in collective measures to protect the country's agricultural heartland against longer-term degradation, and the role of forests was clearly identified by at least some of the leaders. Programs to conserve forests and plant trees were therefore initiated by the regime in the 1950s. Most of the afforestation proposed by the government was intended to protect agricultural regions from advancing deserts (Richardson, 1990). A national conference on forestry was held in 1955, and announced the goal of planting 100 million hectares of forests in barren lands and mountainous areas by the late 1960s. The conference was followed by propaganda campaigns accompanied by regulations limiting access to afforestation areas and the establishment of a network of Forest Service Centers to monitor these areas.

Reforestation and forest conservation were periodically disrupted by political campaigns, and the most disastrous period for forests occurred only a few years after the 1955 forestry conference, during the 'Great Leap Forward'. With the goal of rapid industrialization, the 'Great Leap' committed workers across the country to setting up neighbourhood furnaces to make steel (often from melted-down pots and pans), and wasted huge amounts of timber which was used to feed these furnaces (Harkness, 1998). Statistics from the Ministry of Forestry showed a sharp decline in forest cover between 1957 and 1964 attributable mainly to this ill-conceived industrialization campaign (Richardson, 1990).

Nevertheless, major campaigns to plant trees for soil conservation were undertaken during the next few decades using the mass mobilization techniques which the Maoist state was able to employ during that period (Richardson, 1990). These programs produced new forest plantations, and slowed the rate of advance of the deserts. Although the seedlings often had a low rate of survival due to inadequate knowledge or practice, and hence there was considerable waste, the overall impact on forest cover was positive. Other programs involved planting lines or belts of trees to protect fields, villages, roads, and canals. The 'Obligatory Tree Planting Program', adopted in 1981, called for able-bodied citizens to plant three to five trees each year, or depending on local conditions, to do other work such as raising seedlings.

It seems that as a result of these programs, the total forest cover actually increased for China as a whole, at least since the early 1980s (Rozelle et al., 2000). While a few provinces, such as Guangdong, have seen a decline in forest cover since 1976, other provinces saw a rebound through the 1980s as some of the new national policies began to take effect. The government's programs are thus having a significant impact on forest cover, at least if one can judge by the overall statistics (Rozelle et al., 2000). It has been estimated that the forest cover in China in 1949 was about 8.6% of the land area. By the mid-1990s forest cover had been increased to nearly 14% through these major afforestation programs.

However, the net growth in forest cover appears to be largely the result of planting protective forest belts and tree plantations, and masks the considerable reduction in natural or mature forests during the same period (Rozelle et al., 1998). The overall figures also hide episodes of tremendously wasteful forestry practices, and heavy logging of natural forests sanctioned by local officials.

One well-known case involved a plan to clear-cut a large forested region in the habitat of the endangered Yunnan Golden Monkey which had been approved by the local forest bureau. Environmental activists from Yunnan and Beijing lobbied the central government in 1996 to stop the plan, and after the intervention of State Councillor Song Jian, the Ministry of Forestry issued an order to stop the logging. However, the county government evidently ignored the order, on the basis that logging was their main source of revenue. The Ministry of Forestry was eventually forced to compensate the county for lost income (Harkness, 1998). Students at the Beijing Forestry College, who had been involved in lobbying to save the forest, later travelled to Yunnan during the summer and camped in the forest to see whether the logging had actually stopped. The ability of local authorities in China to evade national policies through a variety of measures is well-known.

One problem for central government control over logging is that many of the forests are in autonomous regions and prefectures, where Beijing does not exercise the same degree of control as in other areas. For example, 70% of the forests in Yunnan province, in the southwest, are in minority areas, and in Sichuan, autonomous prefectures contain most of the remaining natural forests. Conservation regulations are evidently enforced less strictly in these areas, for the sake of political stability, and the Forest Law of 1984 specifically exempts the autonomous areas from the regulations which apply to other areas (Richardson, 1990). Even outside of the 'autonomous' areas, however, central government power may be limited, and national policies may be evaded.

The environmental protection agencies or bureaus at provincial and county level are responsible to the higher level environmental protection bureaus, but must also serve the needs of the local governments. These lower-level bureaus also typically depend on the local government for funds, facilities, and career advancement (Alford & Shen, 1998). The decentralization of authority has therefore increased the power of these local governments (Economy, 1997; Brandt & Zhu, 2000), and reduced the ability of higher-level environmental protection bureaus to direct the actions of lower-level environmental-protection bureaus (Rozelle et al., 2000).

The lower level governments have been given more flexibility mainly for the purpose of promoting economic growth (Cannon, 2000), and thereby protecting social and political stability. In effect, local governments are evaluated by how well they perform in producing economic growth. Obviously, this imperative and the resulting reduction of the vertical authority of environmental or forestry agencies over their lower-level counterparts is not conducive to a simultaneous emphasis on environmental protection. The fact that the local governments also pay the bills for the local environmental protection bureaus makes the latter even more dependent on local regimes whose main priorities are economic growth.

One of the key variables in forest management in China is the type of organizations responsible for particular forests. There are three basic types. The first type is the state forest farms, which employed about 500,000 people on 4,000 forest farms by the mid-1980s and were responsible to the Ministry of Forestry through the county forest bureaus. In the northern and northeastern provinces, state forest farms managed or controlled over 90% of the forested areas in the region (Rozelle et al., 1998). The state forests are usually in more sparsely populated areas, and are used mainly for commercial timber.

The second type of organization is the collective forestry units, most of which are in the southern provinces. Collectives managed nearly 90% of the forested areas in the five southern and southeastern provinces (*ibid.*), and mainly supplied timber and fuelwood to local communities (Harkness, 1998). Yunnan and Sichuan containing a mix of both types of organizations. Finally, individual peasant households may own or exploit trees on leased plots or in areas immediately around their villages.

From analysis of two comparable national forest censuses in 1981 and 1988, Rozelle et al. concluded that while reform policies in the 1980s had evidently increased forest cover, they had not halted unsustainable harvesting of mature forests. It had been expected by forestry management officials in China that the collectives, given some tenure rights over forested land, would try to ensure sustainable forestry practices to protect their longer-term investments. Apparently, this did not occur, perhaps because of uncertainty about whether their temporary harvesting rights would continue and consequently their desire to achieve the maximum short-term gains. It also emerged from the statistical analysis that in economically poorer areas with poor land resources in agriculture, forestry was more exploitative than in areas with stronger economic growth (Rozelle et al., 1998).

One problem is that prior to 1998, funding for afforestation has been relatively modest. It has been estimated that the total investment in forest management from 1949 until the 1980s was not much more than the amount spent on water conservation in any year during the late 1970s (Richardson, 1990). The increase in the number of forest reserves in the 1980s, for environmentalist reasons, was also not accompanied by a substantial increase in central funding for maintaining such reserves, most of which are dependent on county and provincial governments for financial support (Harkness, 1998).

The poor funding and weak enforcement in these reserves has also led to an increase in non-sustainable harvesting in areas previously harvested on a more sustainable basis by local collectives. When such forest lands were converted to forest reserves, expropriating the forests from local collectives but leaving the population of the collectives still living in or next to the forest, they responded in some cases by immediately harvesting as much of the forest as possible to avoid losing everything to the state (Harkness, 1998; Elvin, 1998; Muldavin, 2000). It is not clear that local collectives protected their forests sufficiently to harvest on a sustainable basis over the long term, as may be the case with village-managed forests in some parts of India (Poffenberger & McGean, 1996). However, it appears that these rural collectives in China were not rapidly destroying the forests in their own neighborhoods before the forests were reclassified as reserves. Thus, weak state enforcement in the new forest reserves led to a worse outcome than when the forests were still harvested by collectives.

In short, the impressive statistics on the establishment of forest reserves hide major management problems resulting from inadequate funding of the reserves. The major afforestation programs since the 1950s, and the reform and afforestation policies since the 1980s, have increased forest cover, but have not prevented unsustainable harvesting of natural or mature forests (Yin, 1998; Zhang et al., 2000). The central government, of course, was aware of these problems, and the 1990s saw increased efforts to control logging even before the 1998 floods. Some provinces such as Hainan were apparently more proactive than others (Jiang, 1999).

China reduced its annual logging quota by 8% in 1996 in an attempt to conserve the forests. The Ministry of Forestry also announced its intention to take stricter action against illegal logging. The central government was especially concerned about the possibility that excess logging would affect the capacity of the massive Three Gorges Dam project on the Yangtze River. The Dam would produce a reservoir 600 kilometers long behind it, and silting could reduce the water capacity of the reservoir and its ability to control flooding, and could also affect the hydroelectric power plants connected to the dam (Dai, 1998). Consequently, the government announced a plan to add 2 million hectares of forests in the areas around the reservoir, in Hubei and Sichuan provinces (Edmonds, 2000). However, the decline of natural forests continued. Government programs added plantation forests in peripheral regions, and largely ignored extensive, unsustainable, and sometimes illegal logging in mountainous areas around the river valleys. The floods of 1998 quickly led to much more drastic policy announcements.

FLOODS AND THE 1998 LOGGING BAN IN CHINA

In the summer of 1998, floods along the Yangtze River devastated large areas of central China and killed more than 3,600 people (Liang, 1998). This was a small number of deaths by comparison with some of the earlier floods in China during the 20th century, such as the floods in 1954 which killed more than 30,000 people (Suh, 1998). However, the economic consequences of the flooding were severe. The cost in damage to property and fields, lost production, aid to flooded areas, and flood control expenses has been estimated at 248 billion rmb (U.S. $30 billion) (Liang, 1998), with some 5.6 million houses destroyed and 64 million acres of land swamped. The deluge may have affected as many as 240 million people (Suh, 1998).

Analysts asserted that over-logging in areas around the major river systems led to excess runoff of soil into the rivers, raised river levels as the silt was deposited downstream, and thus greatly increased the severity of the flooding. This kind of analysis of the consequences of deforestation was well-documented by research, such as in the Journal of the Beijing Forestry University (eg. Wang, 1996).

Responding to the scale of the disaster and evidently angered that overlogging had worsened the flooding, Premier Zhu Rongji announced that logging of China's natural forests in the upper reaches of the Yellow River and the Yangtze River was henceforth banned. This announcement was followed by a flurry of meetings and pronouncements by forestry officials. In October of 1998, the Minister of the State Forestry Administration, Wang Zhibao, said that by the year 2000, natural forests would no longer be logged in most of China's existing natural forests. About half of these natural forests are in the upper reaches of the Yangtze River and the Yellow River, and these forests comprise over 65% of China's natural forests. The plan was to reduce the annual logging quota, of some 29 million cubic metres in 1997, by about 10 million cubic metres each year (Zhang et al., 2000). At the same time, the logging industry would be required to rely only or mainly on harvesting economic forests rather than natural forests. The plan would also require a major state investment in reforestation, using workers who previously worked in the logging industry to plant trees in heavily logged areas. The Minister indicated that the plan would require nearly 20 billion rmb (U.S. $2.3 billion) in loans or credits to deal with displacement of the logging industry and investment in replanting. For example, in Sichuan, the plan would require displacing 45,000 workers from logging, and shifting them to planting trees.

The central government has always placed a high priority on trying to control the floods and reduce the threat to major cities such as Wuhan, and on demonstrating to the population that effective action was being taken (Richardson, 1990). Such major campaigns to control floods have been carried out since the 1950s. Always highly publicized, they are used to demonstrate that the state is potent and successful in guarding the nation's well-being, or at the very least, is tackling the problems with the massive mobilization of effort which only the Party can achieve.

The Party's capacity for mass mobilization, however, had declined during the past two decades. As a result of economic reforms since 1979, the rural communes were dismantled, and most peasants began to work for themselves on contracted fields or in rural factories. Lacking the power in 1998 to mobilize hundreds of thousands of peasants for the kinds of corvee labor campaigns characteristic of the 1950s and 1960s, the central government set the People's Liberation Army to work bolstering and augmenting dams and dykes along the Yangtze River. Their exertions were highly publicized in the national media, as they rescued villagers, filled sandbags, and sometimes blocked sections of a dyke with their bodies (Fang, 1998).

Central government leaders including Premier Zhu Rongji and President Jiang Zemin also toured areas where crucial flood control work was in progress, accompanied by intensive coverage from the national media.

To emphasize the seriousness of the issue, the government pushed prosecutions of illegal logging and of corruption in the allocation of logging permits, and ensured that some of the prosecutions received sufficient publicity to be widely noticed. In another paper (Lang, forthcoming) I review some of the cases which have been reported in national newspapers or environmentalist publications in China. The prosecutions serve as only a rough indication of the intensity of the government's determination to crack down on illegal logging and on violations of the logging ban. However, they include occasional prosecutions of officials who have colluded in illegal or over-quota logging, and wide publicity for such cases as a warning to other officials. It seems that there is a continuing struggle between the central government's determination to enforce the logging ban and local logging interests which have become accustomed to evading such restrictions. As long as the central government prioritizes this campaign, however, the provincial and county goverments are forced to give the appearance of adhering to the policy, and of prosecuting offenders.

It appears, from recent assessments, that the government's ban on logging in 1998 has greatly reduced logging in the seventeen provinces to which the restrictions were eventually applied (Xu et al., 2000; Zhang et al., 2000; Murray, 2001). In combination with reforestation and afforestation programs, assisted in some cases by the World Bank, these measures have evidently stabilized China's forest cover (Rozelle et al., 2000).

However, the success of the ban has inevitably led to a shortfall in wood for various industries such as construction and the production of paper, and this shortfall has induced Chinese firms to make up the shortfall from other countries in the region, particularly in Southeast Asia. For example, imports of timber and wood products reportedly increased sharply in the year after the ban (*ibid.*), and further increases are expected (Bejing Review, 2000; China Daily, 2000b). The logging ban may have a major long-term impact on Southeast Asian forests (Rozelle et al., 2000; Pearce, 2000).

I now turn to the case of Thailand, where the state also attempted to regulate forestry during the past half-century, without halting the continuing decline in natural forests, and where a logging ban was also implemented after disastrous flooding, for nearly the same reasons.

STATE REGULATION AND DEFORESTATION IN THAILAND

The Royal Forestry Department (RFD), established in 1896, has mainly been concerned during most of the first hundred years of its existence with allocating and regulating logging concessions, particularly for teak in the northern part of the country. Most of the logging concessions for cutting and exporting teak were allocated to Europeans, and the agency was actually headed by a British forestry expert from its establishment until 1932 (Bello et al., 1998). In 1899, the state nationalized all natural forests, which were to be controlled by the RFD. After the 1932 revolution, foreign concessions were gradually replaced by Thai logging interests, but deforestation continued, and several million peasant tenant-farmers from the plains eventually moved into northern forested regions to clear land for agriculture (*ibid.*). With the growing stress on economic development in the 1960s and 1970s, the government and external agencies such as the World Bank encouraged the production of cash-crops in the mountainous regions, which led to further deforestation.

The Forestry Department also collaborated with successive governments' political aims in gaining control over resources and territory in the forests. For example, the regime built roads into some of these areas to improve access for the army in their campaign to deny such areas to Communist insurgents. This opened previously remote forested regions to exploitation by migrants and logging interests from the plains after the threat from Communist insurgents waned in the late 1970s.

Conservation was always a secondary concern. Indeed, Thailand's forest cover declined from about 70% of the country in the 1930s, to about 53% by the 1960s, to no more than 23% by the late 1990s (Blakesley & Elliott, 2000). The most recent estimate of the remaining forested area includes degraded forests and monoculture tree plantations of teak, eucalyptus, and rubber trees.

Attempts to regulate logging prior to the 1990s through concessions and limited harvest quotas were not very effective, and illegal logging was common. For example, analysts noted that Thai sawmills in the late 1970s were processing 6.5 million cubic meters of teak wood annually from a legal annual harvest of only 2.5 million cubic meters, according to the Royal Forestry Department's own published statistics (Hunsaker, 1996). (The RFD subsequently stopped publishing such data.) In the early 1960s, the government announced a goal of preserving a forest cover of 50% of the country (*ibid.*). This proved to be unrealistic, and was not backed by any serious attempts to implement such a goal. Forest Reserves established during the 1960s for the purpose of conservation turned out to be already inhabited by large numbers of forest-dwellers and subsistence farmers. Deforestation continued, with an estimated loss of 12.5 million hectares of forest between the 1960s and the mid-1980s. It has been estimated that the forest loss averaged about 2.5% of total forest area each year during the 1980s (Hunsaker, 1996). While this was less than the average rate of deforestation in the 1970s, it was high enough that the loss of all of Thailand's forests was forseeable within the next two generations.

With increasing attention to deforestation from internal and international agencies and NGOs, and with the prospect of serious consequences from deforestation in the next few decades, Thai government agencies produced a new National Forest Policy, announced in 1985, which proposed that 40% of the country should be forested. The plan was that 25% of this forested area would be for production forests, and 15% for 'conservation forests'. This was revised in 1991 to set aside 25% of the forested area as 'conservation forest' (Blakesley & Elliott, 2000).

It has been claimed that Thailand has one of the best systems for protection of forests in the region (McQuistan, 2000). Thailand is also developing the culture and practice of consultation with stakeholders over environmental issues (Rasmussen, 2000). Nevertheless, Thai forestry policy up to 1989 was only weakly proactive, in the sense that it has not had sufficient impact on illegal logging, or on deforestation, to halt continuing and possibly irreversible loss of natural forests and their ecosystems. The program to monitor forests and prevent illegal logging and other malpractice has also been poorly funded (Hunsaker,

1996). As in China, this weak proactive policy was strengthened only after a disastrous flood.

FLOODS AND THE 1989 LOGGING BAN IN THAILAND

In November of 1988, flooding in the southern province of Nakorn Sitamarat killed some 350 people (Hunsaker, 1996), a death rate, proportional to total population, nearly double the death rate from the 1998 floods in China. The floods also caused an estimated U.S. $120 million in damages to property. This rate of damage was proportionally much less than the damage caused by the 1998 floods in China, mainly because the floods in Thailand did not affect regions as densely populated or as important for agriculture as the areas inundated by the Yangtze floods. Nevertheless, in both countries, the floods were perceived as disasters for the local population and for the local economy.

As in China, the 1988 floods and landslides in Thailand were attributed, in part, to deforestation, leading to much higher runoff of rainwater from hillsides. After a public outcry over the disaster, Prime Minister Chatichai Choonhavan's newly installed government issued a nation-wide ban on logging in January of 1989 (Prudhisan & Maneerat, 1997), stopped the issuing of new logging concessions, and moved to revoke existing permits (McDonald, 1990). Former logging concessions were designated as national parks or wildlife sanctuaries (Blakesley & Elliott, 2000). Thousands of workers were forced out of logging, or into illegal logging (Hunsaker, 1996). Enforcement of the ban led to numerous prosecutions in 1990, during which more than 19,000 illegal logging operations were identified, more than 11,000 illegal loggers were arrested, and 188 saw mills were forced to close (England, 1996).

As in China, one of the immediate consequences of the logging ban was to displace logging for the Thai market into neighboring countries (England, 1996). Within a month of the ban, for example, Thai logging interests had signed agreements with the Myanmar Burmese regime to begin cutting timber in Burma (McDonald, 1990). The Myanmar regime was keen to sell logging concessions to get hard currency, and similar deals, for similar reasons, led to increased exploitation of forests in Laos and Cambodia for the Thai market.

But the 1989 ban on logging in Thailand was only partially effective in controlling deforestation (Laird, 2000), and depletion of forests continued despite the ban. The Thai Government's own Office of Environmental Policy and Planning came to the same conclusion (OEPP, 2000). According to one estimate, the rate of net annual forest loss in the 1990s was about one percent each year (Rasmussen, 2000), mainly due to continued illegal logging and expansion of agriculture (Blakesley & Elliott, 2000). This amounts to more than 100,000 hectares of net deforestation every year. The ban also did not cover mangrove trees in coastal areas, where mangroves continued to be depleted for charcoal and to open up space for prawn farming (Bello et al., 1998). Since the logging ban, it has been estimated that overall forest cover has continued to decline, from about 28% of land area in the late 1980s to about 23% ten years later (McQuistan, 2000). The annual loss of forest cover in the seven years after the logging ban was lower than the rate of loss prior to the ban, but still substantial (Rasmussen, 2000).

In Phetchabun province in north-central Thailand, for example, forest cover had declined from over 70% in 1960 to 19% by 1995, and further deforestation continued between 1995 and 2000, according to an official of the Forest Resource Assessment Division (Samabuddhi, 2001b). The early clear-cutting of forest in these areas in the 1960s was the result of policies to deny shelter to Communist insurgents, and was also due in part to the slash-and-burn activities of Hmong hill-tribes. Reforestation in the area was not very successful, due to the continuing pressures on forested land from agriculture, fruit plantations, and other land uses such as the building of resorts for tourists (*ibid.*).

Some of the continuing pressure on forested land has come from the drive to produce profitable export cash crops such as ginger, which has led to clearing of natural forests in highland areas by Lisu hilltribes and other groups, allegedly with capital from business interests in northern towns such as Chiang Rai (Bangkok Post, 1998b). These groups sometimes threaten Forestry officers trying to monitor or prevent illegal cutting of trees for the ginger plots. Production of legal export crops such as casava, beginning in the 1970s, and of illegal export crops such as opium in mountainous regions, has also led to some destruction or degradation of forested areas (Hunsaker, 1996). Ironically, the government's successful campaign to induce some of the hilltribes to abandon opium production led some of them to migrate into lower regions where their impact on forests to create space for other cash-crops has been greater than if they had continued to grow opium in the highlands (Bello et al., 1998).

The hilltribes can be quite different in their uses of land in forested areas. Some hilltribes such as the Karen have practiced a conservative type of subsistence swidden agriculture which allows them to remain in some forested areas for long periods, while other groups such as the Hmong and Yao have practiced shifting swidden agriculture, in which land is cleared and exploited more intensively and which requires periodic migrations and new land-clearing (Bello et al., 1998). Some of these highland groups also differ in their commitment to clearing forested land for cash-crops for sale into lowland market networks. Thus, we must be cautious in generalizing about the impact of the hilltribes on the forests. Some Thai commentators blame the hilltribes for deforestation problems which are often more strongly linked to migrants from the plains and to illegal logging interests controlled by cliques in northern towns. However, there is no doubt that some of the hilltribes also contribute to deforestation.

By the late 1990s there were an estimated one million households subsisting in National Forest Reserves without legal rights (Rasmussen, 2000), and occupying as much as 20% of Thailand's state-owned forest reserves (Hunsaker, 1996). Some of these squatters are non-Thai migrants. Forest-dwellers without legal title to forested lands are naturally devoted to short-term maximization of profit from nearby forests for their own survival, with little concern for the longer-term future of forests in which they have no legal stake, and from which they may be evicted at any time. Lacking Thai identity documents and land ownership deeds, they are less able to resist attempts to relocate them out of forested areas in order to conserve the forests, or to turn degraded forests into plantations operated by agribusiness interests (Bello et al., 1998). Hence, their lack of legal bases for their land claims increases their propensity to engage in non-legal forms of resistance, and in poaching.

The Thai army has on occasion collaborated with the Forestry Department in patrolling for poachers, particularly around National Parks, setting up checkpoints to try to intercept illegally taken logs and inspecting sawmills for illegal supplies of wood (Sukkasem, 2000). But there have also been allegations that soldiers, Forestry Department officials, Land Department officials, and politicians have been actively involved in the profit from illegal logging (Hunsaker, 1996; Bello et al., 1998; Chongcharoen, 2001; Samabuddhi, 2001a).

The political environment also was not sufficiently stable in the years after the ban for a consistent and strict policy to be enforced. The Prime Minister whose government imposed the original 1989 logging ban, Chatichai Choonhavan, was ousted in a military coup in 1991, only two years after the ban, and the military regime which succeeded him and which appointed the next prime minister, in 1992, was not prepared to challenge military interests, nor the logging operations of their allies among the regional cliques of politicians and bosses (England, 1996).

Complicating the process of monitoring deforestation and implementing reforestation is the state-owned Forestry Industry Organization (FIO), founded in 1947 to manage logging concessions under the overall authority of the Royal Forestry Department. The FIO also carried out logging to clear areas around proposed reservoirs and dams, and sold illegally cut timber which had been confiscated from various parties (Rajesh, 2000). The FIO suffered a substantial loss of revenue as a result of the 1989 logging ban. The organization responded by applying to use terminated logging concessions to expand its tree plantations of teak and eucalyptus and to supply its sawmills.

However, this has led to conflict in areas where local communities are determined to resist the conversion of common forest areas or degraded forests into tree plantations. In effect, the policy of reforestation using monoculture tree plantations often pits government agencies and agribusiness firms against local villagers, who may be displaced into other forested areas, or who have nowhere else to go because there is no remaining agricultural land. Conflict has been particularly serious in the poor northeastern part of the country, where an estimated 4.7 million hectares of forests were cleared between the 1960s and the mid-1980s (Hunsaker, 1996), and where current forest cover may be less than 14% (Bello et al., 1998). The attempt to switch the mission of the Royal Forestry Department from production to plantation reforestation and conservation has actually increased the level of conflict with hilltribes and local communities of subsistence farmers in such areas (Hunsaker, 1996; Rasmussen, 2000). There is vigorous debate within Thailand between those who advocate the rights of peoples who inhabit the forests, and those who want to conserve forests even against measured exploitation by forest-dwellers (Rasmussen, 2000). NGOs and other advocates line up on both sides of the debate, but are particularly vigorous in defending the rights of forest-dwellers.

The Royal Forestry Department has been actively involved in the processes of 'ecological modernization' within Thailand over the past few decades. These processes have included the Department's participation in discussions with environmentalist NGOs and intellectuals, participation of government officials in numerous regional forums in Southeast Asia on environmental issues, collaboration with the World Bank on projects to conserve forests, and the preparation of a progressive environmentalist Thailand National Report to the 1992 UN Conference on Environment and Development in Rio de Janeiro, with the active collaboration of Thailand's environmentalist NGOs (England, 1996).

The Forestry Department's commitments to both conservation and plantation forests, however, have led to increased conflict with forest dwellers and subsistence farmers, and to some political pressure to avoid such costly conflict by mollifying local communities which might otherwise engage in aggressive resistance. At the same time, Forestry Department officials are sometimes implicated in mutually beneficial relationships with commercial or even illegal logging interests.

It is a striking feature of the discourse in Thailand about illegal logging that some of the allegations are made by government departments about other government agencies or politicians. Officials of the Forestry Department, for example, attributed illegal logging in one forest reserve to "influential people linked to politicians" (Chongcharoen, 2001), without feeling confident enough to identify those persons. Even the army sometimes comments on vaguely defined "government authorities" who profit from the illegal felling of trees (Samabuddhi, 2001a). Similarly, the Office of Environmental Policy and Planning noted that environmental problems were often "a result of abuse of power by groups with political and executive power and vested interests" (OEPP, 2000). Particular scandals have involved the use of illegally cut timber by local officials, accepting bribes from illegal logging groups, passing advanced warning of crackdowns on log-poaching to the poachers, and use of impending crackdowns as a device to increase the flow of bribes (Noikorn, 1998; Bangkok Post, 1998a).

Since implementation of the logging ban has been seriously flawed by continued illegal logging and the obtaining of logging rights by corruption, it is not surprising that floods resulting from runoff from deforested hillsides have continued. In May of 2001, for example, flashfloods killed dozens of people in a region known for illegal logging (Samabuddhi, 2001a). In August of 2001, further flash-floods in parts of Phetchabun province killed between 100 and 200 people after heavy rains swept away several villages in valleys below deforested hillsides (Samabuddhi, 2001b). The Prime Minister, Thaksin Shinawatra, suggested during a visit to the afflicted areas in Phetchabun that the government should identify water-flow routes and then relocate villages elsewhere (BBC, 2001). Thus, the regime tries to deal with the consequences of deforestation by removing the probable victims of the next floods.

The most pessimistic assessments note that the Thai government is more devoted to economic development and political compromises than to effective protection of the forests. As one analyst observed, the Thai government has only managed to provide "a series of fumbling piece-meal reactions to political crises while all the time hoping to sustain rapid economic expansion" (Hunsaker, 1996, p. 24). The key to the problem, if one factor can be singled out above all others, is "weak government control over private interests", within what Bello calls "fast-track capitalism" (Bello et al., 1998, p. 192).

On the positive side, the Thai government can claim a series of well-intentioned measures and policies to try to curtail deforestation, a logging ban which greatly reduced logging in some areas, a forestry bureaucracy which provides a good knowledge base and accurate assessments of the state of the forests, a number of reforestation programs, recent provisions for "community forestry" to try to see whether communities can actually conserve forests, and some responsiveness to the vigorous lobbying of NGOs and the resistance of some local communities to state programs.

But the political and bureaucratic complexities of the Thai political system and the considerable and often corrupt responsiveness of various agents of the state to local and regional business elites have facilitated the continuing – albeit slower – decline of the forests, and undermined the implementation of national policies designed to conserve forests. The floods, ultimately, were not a sufficiently severe threat to state legitimacy, or to the interests of the political elite.

CONCLUSIONS

The natural forests of both China and Thailand were seriously depleted during the 20th century. In both societies, deforestation was identified by scientists and forestry officials as a problem which could damage the country's economic base if it continued unchecked. The forestry bureaucracies in the two societies tried to deal with deforestation through regulations on logging, establishment of forest reserves, reforestation programs, and plantation forests. International organizations such as the World Bank eventually provided resources for some of these endeavours in each country. But neither society succeeded in stopping the continuing loss of natural forests. Both societies maintained a 'weak proactive' forestry regime – a collection of policies that had some impact, but were not sufficient to stop the depletion of natural forest.

Some of the reasons why these policies were weak in both societies are similar: a higher priority on economic development than on environmental conservation by officials and political leaders at all levels; the resulting insufficient allocation of funds for state agencies which were supposed to monitor and control illegal logging in forest reserves; local corruption and collusion between some officials and logging interests; and desire of both governments to avoid unnecessary conflict with ethnic minorities in some forested regions for the sake of political stability.

In both societies, an ecological disaster widely attributed to deforestation prompted a much stronger state response. The floods, loss of life, and destruction of property in Thailand in 1988, and in China in 1998, led to a ban on logging in both societies to try to prevent further disasters. This 'strong reactive' response has reduced the rate of deforestation in both societies well below the pre-disaster rate, and has also helped to focus the attention of the public, as well as of politicians and officials, on the problems which can result from continuing loss of forests. The logging bans have also pushed logging for the Chinese and Thai markets into poorer neighboring states such as Laos, Burma, and Cambodia where control over logging is looser and where state officials are more easily tempted by windfall gains from cutting natural forests.

However, there are important differences. First, China has managed to produce a net increase in forest cover over the past two decades, while Thailand saw a continuing decline in net forest cover, even after the ban on logging. Second, it appears from the available evidence that the ban on logging in natural forests in China has been more effective than the ban on logging in Thailand. I have not demonstrated this difference empirically, but it is my provisional conclusion after a review of information on the implementation of the logging bans in the two societies. If this conclusion is correct (and a much more detailed study in both countries would be needed to confirm it), then some further analysis of the reasons for these differences is warranted. I offer the following tentative analysis:

In both China and Thailand, the national commitment to economic development and the pursuit of profit by individuals and local firms has provided strong incentives for exploiting natural forests, evading rules, inducing official support through corruption, illegal or over-quota logging, and other practices which have made it difficult to implement restrictive state policies. But some factors suggest that Thailand should have been more successful than China in dealing with deforestation.

First, Thailand has been quite open to influence by international agencies and NGOs with conservationist agendas, and to lobbying by local conservationist and environmentalist NGOs and activists (Hirsch, 1997). Second, during most of the past ten years at least, Thailand has allowed vigorous scrutiny and criticism of officials and state policies by the mass media (Thitinan, 1997). Third, Thailand's political system during most of the past ten years has been democratic, and includes competition between several political parties during periodic elections (Hewison, 1997), a factor advanced by some theorists as a condition for better environmental policies and management (eg. Jacobs, 1991). In China, by contrast, there are no vigorous NGOs which are not linked to the government in some way and which are not constrained by the need to avoid criticizing government policy, the mass media are constrained by the same imperative, and there are no other political parties which could generate opposition to the regime's policies.

Hence, where economic development policies have led to unsustainable exploitation of the environment in the two countries, we might expect more vigorous opposition from various segments of civil society in Thailand than in China. One of the mechanisms by which 'ecological modernization' operates in open societies is the lobbying and publicizing of opposition groups and parties, which help to induce greater regulatory intervention by the state along with shifts in the practices and policies of enterprises. On the basis of these considerations, Thailand should be ahead of China on the path toward 'ecological modernization'.

However, there are some other considerations which would suggest that China would take more vigorous action than Thailand in the event of an ecological disaster attributable to failures in environmental policies.

First, the regime in China is able to act more forcefully than the regime in Thailand since there are no opposition groups which can threaten its rule, and since the control apparatus of the Party-State extends from the central government down through the provinces and counties into each village in the country. Local governments cannot easily evade policies which the central government has prioritized, and to which it is devoting extraordinary resources for implementation, monitoring, and enforcement. The government's fertility control campaign (the so-called 'one-child policy') has been implemented with this kind of resolute commitment, and has been extraordinarily successful in reducing fertility even in rural areas where fertility would otherwise be relatively high. The central government appears to equally determined to implement and monitor the logging ban, if we can judge by publicity, commitment of resources, and enforcement during the years after the 1998 ban, and continuing with the extension of the ban to seventeen provinces in 2000.

Second, logging interests in China are more closely linked to the state – whether as logging collectives or state farms or military-linked companies – and can be more easily coerced into adhering to state policies than in Thailand, where most logging is carried out by private commercial interests or by forest-dwelling communities.

Third, local officials in China do not depend on local business elites to get their positions. They do benefit from economic development and the resulting inflows of money into the local government coffers through licences, taxes, and other revenues from logging. But getting and keeping their positions as officials does not require spending money provided by business interests to win elections or buy votes. By contrast, the 'money-politics' of Thai electioneering (Hewison, 1997) makes local politicians more personally dependent on funds from local business cliques, who benefit from loose enforcement of logging restrictions and favorable allocation of permits, and expect to see the returns on their investments after elections.

Finally, the flooding in China in 1998 was much more costly, in economic terms, than the flooding in Thailand in 1988, and affected a much more densely populated region of the country. Thus, the potential threat to the regime's legitimacy, as the protector of the nation's heartland and the inheritor of the historical water-control function of the Chinese state, was much greater than in Thailand. From these two cases, then, I offer the following ideas for further analysis:

(1) Deforestation in developing countries will normally induce only 'weak proactive' policies. Ecological modernization may be occurring, but even where there are forestry bureaucracies with sufficient expertise, and even where international agencies have provided funds for reforestation, as in Thailand and China, the processes of ecological modernization are not vigorous enough to save natural forests, given the higher priority always placed on economic prosperity.
(2) Ecological crisis brought about by policy failures can precipitate 'strong reactive' responses which produce much more dramatic reductions in forest depletion than have been achieved with typical 'weak proactive' policies. Such actions will occur in proportion to the threat to a regime's legitimacy as a result of public perceptions that regime-incompetence is responsible for preventable economic damage and a substantial decline in national economic well-being.
(3) Neither democracy nor critical mass media nor activist NGOs are necessary for such a response to occur. Indeed, a polity may be hobbled, as seems to have occurred in Thailand, by the vigorous lobbying, resistance, or mutually beneficial collusion of a welter of competing interests and parties. By contrast, it seems that the government in China can sometimes produce a more vigorously implemented policy because the regime can mobilize a political and administrative apparatus which extends from the central government down to the level of counties and villages, and because countervailing forces are weak or absent.

Of course, there are many dangers in such a political system if a regime decides to implement badly conceived policies, as in the 'Great Leap Forward', and ecological modernization by no means eliminates the possibility that major policies will be implemented without a scientific consensus about their value. Indeed, the regime in China has suppressed debate on the massive 'Three Gorges Dam' project, even in the face of the doubts of many scientists and engineers about its long-term effectiveness and safety (Dai, 1998), and runs the risk that this suppression of debate will facilitate a future disaster, as some analysts have argued.

The floods and subsequent logging ban, however, are much less controversial, and the scientific consensus about the importance of the logging ban seems well-established. The processes of ecological modernization, which have occurred among the main scientific and technical institutions in Chinese society, can help to inform effective policy responses where there are strong scientific reasons for a policy, and a general consensus about what must be done.

As Heilbroner (1974) and Ophuls (1977) suggested several decades ago, it is possible that democracies are unable to produce the vigorous action and the severe restrictions on the pursuit of individual benefit which may be essential to avoid some kinds of longer-term environmental disasters. This suggestion has not been popular among environmentalist scholars and activists, who are generally committed to *both* environmentalism and democratic decision-making (Dobson, 2000). However, it is possible that sufficiently forceful state action will only occur in certain kinds of authoritarian states. Indeed, democratic states typically become more authoritarian during wartime, for the same reason. A corollary is that environment crises, in the future, may push some democratic societies toward more authoritarian modes of governance.

In the meantime, it seems that both authoritarian and democratic states among developing societies in the contemporary economic world-system are too committed to short-term economic goals to impose more than 'weakly proactive' environmentalist policies on their citizens. The most pessimistic conclusion is that more vigorous action will occur only when actual or impending environmental disaster threatens national economic well-being, and thus also threatens the survival of a regime.

In the case of deforestation, the problem even with this pessimistic scenario is that deforestation will not usually produce a highly visible local disaster which causes massive economic damage and loss of life. Floods due in part to deforestation can be devastating in China, and very damaging in Thailand, but they are not so important in most other societies where deforestation has occurred. Hence, it is difficult to see how a single environmental event could galvanize the regimes in most of these societies in the same way that the 1988 and 1998 floods have done in both China and Thailand. Most environmental degradation, including deforestation, attracts little attention, except by scientists and by people who find it more and more difficult to make a living from a disappearing resource. In the long term, continuing deforestation will produce a whole series of consequences which could be labelled 'disastrous', if viewed over time and across the full range of consequences. But these processes and outcomes will be much less dramatic than floods, and will probably not threaten regime-legitimacy.

Hence, to achieve strong-proactive policies in regard to deforestation in most developing countries, we cannot count on dramatic environmental disasters as a wake-up call to the state. Perhaps the exponents of ecological modernization can generate functional substitutes for environmental disaster by producing vivid images of the post-forest world, and offering those images to societies too busy making a living in the present to spend much time imagining the future. Of course, the success of such an enterprise would generate demands for resources from the international community, which would have to bear some of the costs of more strongly proactive policies. An obvious priority are the states in Southeast Asia which have become the 'forestry-hinterlands' of China and Thailand as a result of the relative successes of the logging bans in the two societies.

NOTES

1. My treatment of political legitimacy is not strictly conventional, and glosses the many debates about this concept. However, I can claim considerable agreement with some treatments and measurements of legitimacy. For example, 'good government' here overlaps with 'government performance' in Weatherford (1992), and with 'performance' in Alagappa (1995).

2. A regime has a number of choices in responding to a threat to one of the pillars of regime-legitimacy. A threat to public perceptions of good government (e.g. corruption scandals) could be met by addressing the particular problem (e.g. anti-corruption campaigns) or by increasing the strength of the other two foundations of legitimacy (e.g. by promoting economic development or enhancing perceived national power). The extent to which legitimacy is essential for political stability is also a factor in regime responses. If a regime is able and willing to use coercive force against the population, and if use of force is the easiest or cheapest response, threats to any or all of the three foundations of its legitimacy may only increase a regime's reliance on coercion.

REFERENCES

Alagappa, M. (Ed.) (1995). *Political Legitimacy in Southeast Asia: The Quest for Moral Authority*. Stanford, California: Stanford University Press.

Alford, W. P., & Shen, Y. (1998). The limits of the law in addressing China's environmental dilemma. In: M. B. McElroy, C. P. Nielsen & P. Lydon (Eds), *Energizing China: Reconciling Environmental Protection and Economic Growth* (pp. 405–429). Cambridge, Mass.: Harvard University Press.

Bangkok Post (1998a). Logging: warning for officials to get tough with loggers. *Bangkok Post*. 19 July.

Bangkok Post (1998b). Too much ginger: a recipe for disaster. *Bangkok Post*. 23 November.

BBC (2001). Thailand floods kill 70. *BBC News Online*. 12 August.

Becker, J. (1996). *Hungry Ghosts: China's Secret Famine*. London: John Murray.

Beijing Review (2000). Imported timber stock up. *Beijing Review*, *43*(25), 19 June, p. 27.

Bello, W., Cunningham, S., & Li, K. P. (1998). *A Siamese Tragedy: Development and Disintegration in Modern Thailand*. London: Zed Books.

Blakesley, D., & Elliott, S. (2000). Restoring conservation forests in northern Thailand and the monitoring of frugivorous birds: 1. *OBC* [Oriental Bird Club] *Bulletin*, *31*, June.

Brandt, L., & Zhu, X. (2000). Redistribution in a decentralized economy: growth and inflation in China under reform. *Journal of Political Economy*, *108*, 422–439.

Bryant, R. L., & Bailey, S. (1997). *Third World Political Ecology*. London: Routledge.

Cannon, T. (2000). Introduction: the economic reforms, demographic processes, and environmental problems. In: T. Cannon (Ed.), *China's Economic Growth: The Impact on Regions, Migration, and the Environment* (pp. 1–29). N.Y.: St. Martin's Press.

China Daily (2000a). When man and nature collide. *China Daily*, 26 January.

China Daily (2000b). Timber imports to grow. *China Daily*. 16 June.

Chongcharoen, P. (2001). Reserve loses large area to encroachers. *Bangkok Post*. 23 February.

Dai, Q. (1998). *The River Dragon Has Come! The Three Gorges Dam and the Fate of China's Yangtze River and Its People*. Armonk, N.Y.: M. E. Sharpe.

Dauvergne, P. (1997). *Shadows in the Forest: Japan and the Politics of Timber in Southeast Asia*. Cambridge, Mass.: The MIT Press.

Dobson, A. (2000). *Green Political Thought*. (3rd ed.). London: Routledge.

Economy, E. (1997). *The Case Study of China: Reforms and Resources: The Implications for State Capacity in the PRC*. Occasional Paper, Project on Environmental Scarcities, State Capacity, and Civil Violence. Cambridge: American Academy of Arts and Sciences and the University of Toronto.

Edmonds, R. L. (2000). Recent developments and the prospects for the Sanxia (Three Gorges) Dam. In: T. Cannon (Ed.), *China's Economic Growth: The Impact on Regions, Migration, and the Environment* (pp. 161–183). N.Y.: St. Martin's Press.

Elvin, M. (1998). The environmental legacy of imperial China. *The China Quarterly*, *56*, 773–756.

England, P. (1996). UNCED and the implementation of forest policy in Thailand. In: P. Hirsch (Ed.), *Seeing Forest for Trees: Environment and Environmentalism in Thailand* (pp. 53–71). Chiang Mai: Silkworm Books.

Fang, L. (1998). Dispatches from flood country. *Asiaweek*, 18 September, 1998, 62–65.

Frank, D. J., Hironaka, A., & Schofer, E. (2000). The nation-state and the natural environment over the twentieth century. *American Sociological Review*, *65*, 96–116.

Harkness, J. (1998). Recent trends in forestry and conservation of biodiversity in China. *The China Quarterly*, *56*, 911–934.

Heilbroner, R. (1974). *In Inquiry into the Hiuman Prospect*. N.Y.: Norton.

Hewison, K. (1997). Introduction: power, opposition, and democratisation. In: K. Hewison (Ed.), *Political Change in Thailand: Democracy and Participation* (pp. 1–20). London: Routledge.

Hewison, K. (Ed.) (1997). *Political Change in Thailand: Democracy and Participation*. London: Routledge.

Hirsch, P. (1997). The politics of environment: opposition and legitimacy. In: K. Hewison (Ed.), *Political Change in Thailand: Democracy and Participation* (pp. 179–194). London: Routledge.

Hunsaker, B. (1996). The political economy of Thai deforestation. In: B. Hunsaker, T. Mayer, B. Griffiths & R. Dayley (Eds), *Loggers, Monks, Students, and Entrepreneurs: Four Essays on Thailand* (pp. 1–31). DeKalb, III: Center for Southeast Asian Studies.

Jacobs, M. (1991). *The Green Economy: Environment, Sustainable Development, and the Politics of the Future*. Vancouver: UBC Press.

Jahiel, A. R. (1998). The organization of environmental protection in China. *The China Quarterly*, *56*, 757–787.

Jiang, W. (1999). Breakthrough made in forest protection. *Beijing Review*, *42*(31), 2 August, 16–19.

Laird, J. (2000). *Money, Politics, Globalisation, and Crisis*. Singapore: Graham Brash.

Lang, G. (forthcoming). Forests, floods, and the environmental state in China.

Liang, C. (1998). Flood investigations continue. *China Daily*, 2 November.

Liang, C. (2000). Sichuan farmers go against the grain. *China Daily*, 3 February.

Marchak, P. (1995). *Logging the globe*. Montreal & Kingston: McGill-Queen's University Press.

Mather, A. S., & Needle, C. L. (2000). The relationships of population and forest trends. *The Geographic Journal*, *166*(1), 2–13.

McDonald, H. (1990). Partners in plunder. *Far Eastern Economic Review*, 22 February.

McQuistan, C. (2000). Country profile: Thailand. *ITTO* [International Tropical Timber Organization] *Newsletter*. (retrieved 27/10/'01, at: http://www.itto.or.jp/newsletter/ v9n1/21.html)

Mol, A. P. J. (1995). *The Refinement of Production: Ecological Modernization Theory and the Chemical Industry*. Utrecht, The Netherlands: Van Arkel.

Muldavin, J. (2000). The paradoxes of environmental policy and resource management in reform-era China. *Economic Geography*, *76*(3), 244–271.

Murray, G. (2001). China combats illegal logging. Kyodo News, 10 March, 2001 (at: www.globalhemp.com/News/2001/March/china_combats_illegal.shtml)

Noikorn, U. (1998). Salween scandal: investigation starts after log books lost. *Bangkok Post*. 18 July.

OEPP (Office of Environmental Policy and Planning) (2000). *Thailand State of the Environment Report*. Government of Thailand. (retrieved, 10/8/'01, at: http:www.oepp.go.th/eng/soe2000_1.html).

Ophuls, W. (1977). *Ecology and the Politics of Scarcity: Prologue to a Political Theory of the Steady State*. San Francisco: W. H. Freeman and Co.

Pearce, F. (2000). Going, going . . . *New Scientist*, *166*(2242), 10 June), 16–17.

Poffenberger, M., & McGean, B. (Eds) (1996). *Village Voices, Forest Choices: Joint Forest Management in India*. Delhi: Oxford University Press.

Poffenberger, M., McGean, B., & Khare, A. (1996). Communities sustaining India's forests in the twenty-first century. In: M. B. Poffenberger & B. McGean (Eds), *Village Voices, Forest Choices: Joint Forest Management in India* (pp. 17–48). Delhi: Oxford University Press.

Pomfret, J. (1999). A heavy tide of corruption feeds floods on Yangtze. *International Herald Tribune*, July 31.

Prudhisan, J., & Maneerat, M. (1997). Non-governmental development organisations: empowerment and environment. In: K. Hewison (Ed.), *Political Change in Thailand: Democracy and Participation* (pp. 195–216). Routledge: London.

Rajesh, N. (2000). Thailand: State-owned forestry industry fuels controversy with forestry certification. World Rainforest Movement, Bulletin No. 41, December. (retrieved 23/9/'01 at: http://www.wrm.org.uy/bulletin/41/Thailand.html).

Ramitanondh, S. (1989). Forests and deforestation in Thailand: a pandisciplinary approach. In: *Culture and Environment in Thailand* (pp. 23–50). Bangkok: The Siam Society.

Rasmussen, J. N. et al. (2000). *For Whom and For What? Principles, Criteria, and Indicators for Sustainable Forest Resources Management in Thailand*. Danish Forest and Landscape Research Institute and Chiang Mai University.

Richardson, S. D. (1990). *Forests and forestry in China: Changing Patterns of Resource Development*. Washington, D.C.: Island Press.

Ross, L. (1998). China: environmental protection, domestic policy trends, patterns of participation in regimes and compliance with international norms. *The China Quarterly*, 56, 809–835.

Rozelle, S., Albers, H., Guo, L., & Benziger, V. (1998). Forest resources under economic reform in China. *China Information*, *13*, 106–125.

Rozelle, S., Huang, J., Husain, S. A., & Zazueta, A. (2000). *China: From Afforestation to Poverty Alleviation and Natural Forest Management*. Washington, D.C.: The World Bank.

Samabuddhi, K. (2001a). Illegal logging a tragic lesson. *Bangkok Post*. 10 May.

Samabuddhi, K. (2001b). Naked hills blamed for flash floods, mudslides: policy of tree-felling has led to tragedy. *Bangkok Post*. 20 August.

Schnaiberg, A., & Gould, K. A. (1995). *Environment and Society: The Enduring Conflict*. N.Y.: St. Martin's Press.

Schnaiberg, A., & Gould, K. A. (1994). *Environment and Society: The Enduring Conflict*. N.Y.: St. Martin's Press.

Suh, S. (1998). Under the unforgiving sky. *Asiaweek*, 21 August, 23–24.

Sukkasem, T. (2000). Troops join campaign to stop loggers. *Bangkok Post*, 7 November.

Thitinan, P. (1997). Thailand's media: whose watchdog? In: K. Hewison (Ed.), *Political Change in Thailand: Democracy and Participation* (pp. 217–232). London: Routledge.

Wang, L. (1996). Sustainable mountain watershed management in China. [in Chinese], *Journal of Beijing Forestry University*, *6*(2).

Weatherford, M. S. (1992). Measuring political legitimacy. *American Political Science Review*, *86*, 149–168.

Williams, M. (2001). The history of deforestation. *History Today*, *51*(7), 30–40.

Xu, M., Qi, Y., & Gong, P. (2000). China's new forest policy. *Science*, *289*, 22 Sept., 2049.

Yin, R. (1998). Forestry and the environment in China: the current situation and strategic choices. *World Development*, *26*, 2153–2167.

Zhang, P., Shao, G., Zhao, G., Le Master, D. et al. (2000). China's forest policy for the 21st century. *Science*, *288*, 23 June, 2135–2136.

MOTIVATING A CONFLICTED ENVIRONMENTAL STATE: COMMUNITY-DRIVEN REGULATION IN VIETNAM

Dara O'Rourke

> Without the support of the public, even the easiest task cannot be accomplished. With the support of the public, even the hardest task can be fulfilled.
>
> Vietnamese Communist Party slogan

INTRODUCTION

The Vietnamese government, like many countries, faces significant conflicts between developmental goals and environmental protection. Although the government has proclaimed a commitment to protecting the country's ecosystems, workers, and urban environments, and has recently created national environmental institutions and provincial enforcement agencies, Vietnam continues to experience problems in the implementation of its environmental laws. A lack of funds, trained personnel, and political influence severely constrain the effectiveness of state environmental agencies. More importantly, contradictions and conflicts within the state – between developmentalist and environmental concerns – create disincentives for enforcement of environmental regulations.

The Environmental State Under Pressure, Volume 10, pages 221–244.

ISBN: 0-7623-0854-0

While certainly common in developing countries (and many industrialized countries as well), these conflicts are particularly stark in Vietnam. Vietnam appears to combine the worst of both Soviet-bloc environmental callousness with East Asian development-at-all-costs. Beginning from a base of 1950s-vintage highly polluting heavy industry, adding the recent expansion of export-oriented light industry, and acknowledging the state's limited capacity for environmental regulation, the country seems destined for rapid urban and environmental degradation. Recent assessments of Ho Chi Minh City conjure an image of an ecological nightmare combining Warsaw with Bangkok; the worst of the socialist world as a starting point for unbridled capitalist development.

Local environmental bodies remain weak and conflicted. These agencies are rarely proactive, seldom technically competent, and even less often carry much weight in internal government debates. Agencies have inspectors who virtually refuse to leave their offices, staff who are getting rich off of kick-backs, and personnel who lack the basic technical capacities to conduct the inspections for which they are responsible.[1] Even committed staff face significant pressures against enforcement from other state agencies, powerful state enterprise managers, and foreign investors.

However, despite all of these weaknesses and conflicts, research conducted in Vietnam over the last four years indicates that local agencies (and in particular province-level regulatory bodies) do sometimes respond to public complaints and regulate industrial pollution. Under specific conditions, when they are appropriately motivated, environmental agencies can become effective regulators.

This paper examines the challenges (and anomalies) of environmental regulation against the odds. Specifically, I will try to elucidate what drives these regulatory processes, and more broadly, what motivates and constrains state actions around the environment in a rapidly developing country.

The evidence for this argument is based on an in-depth study of Vietnam's national regulatory system and local enforcement procedures for pollution control. Research involved semi-structured interviews with factory managers, workers, community members, and government officials. Media reports, environmental impact assessments (EIAs), inspection documents, fines, compensations, and other government actions were reviewed. The cases I will discuss provide a wealth of evidence regarding processes of state and community action around pollution issues, when these processes are effective, and why. Despite broad variation, the diverse cases point towards a number of interesting dynamics.

This paper both confirms the constraints and contradictions of state environmental enforcement in a developing country, and shows that certain processes can motivate state actors to take measures to control pollution. In the cases I will discuss, community pressures served to tilt the balance in conflicts around the environment, motivating local state responses to specific pollution incidents, pressuring environmental agencies to improve their monitoring and enforcement capabilities, leveraging different state agencies off against one another, and raising broader public and elite awareness of environmental issues. This paper seeks to explain these processes, and to advance an hypothesis about processes of "Community-Driven Regulation" in Vietnam. As I will explain, Vietnam's system of laws and institutions has fostered a dynamic in which local environmental agencies can be surprisingly responsive to community complaints. The challenge however, is motivating conflicted state agencies to act.

THEORIES OF STATE ENVIRONMENTAL ENFORCEMENT

Political scientists, policy analysts, economists, sociologists, and even environmental scientists have described the challenges of environmental enforcement around the world, and proposed theories of why states do, or do not, effectively implement environmental regulations (see Cohen, 1998 for one review). This literature ranges from simple assessments of state agency capacities, to more complex theories of bureaucratic behavior, to agency strategies for maximizing net political support.

At the most general level, environmental enforcement is considered simply a question of state capacity. Essentially does the state agency have the funds, trained staff, and technical capacity to monitor and enforce its laws? Studies in developing countries in Asia, Africa, Eastern Europe, and the Americas repeatedly discuss the problems of inadequate staffing and funding, lack of scientific knowledge, lack of professionalism, lack of institutional capacity, lack of coordination and cooperation, limited independence, and the over-centralization of environmental responsibilities in weak national environmental bureaucracies (Desai, 1998; Eder, 1996; Dwivedi & Vajpeyi; 1995, Sapru, 1998).

Capacity, however, is more than just staffing and funding. Other characteristics are also critical to environmental enforcement such as state coherence (the degree to which agencies and actors in the state agree to work toward shared objectives), autonomy (the extent to which the state can act independently of external forces), legitimacy (the strength of the state's moral authority), reach (the state's ability to get things done in society), and responsiveness (the extent to which polices meet the needs and grievances of citizens) (Barber, 1997).

Coordination and decision-making between agencies and departments can also be critical to the implementation of environmental policies. Decision-making authority can be both too highly centralized or too fragmented (Desai, 1998). Centralization can lead to problems when regulators don't fully understand problems on the ground, trade-offs that need to be taken at the local level, or the power of local vested interests. Rigid hierarchies are also less capable of learning from local experiences and experiments in implementation. On the other hand, completely localized policy implementation can lead to problems of limited capacities, corruption, and poor coordination between jurisdictions.

As numerous analysts have argued, the state is often an arena of competing interests seeking to advance different goals and objectives (Schnaiberg, 1994; O'Connor, 1994). Gould et al. (1996) argue that the state continually faces conflicting interests and goals around environmental issues. At the most basic level, the state must both facilitate capital accumulation and protect society's living conditions. This means both promoting industrial expansion and trying to protect air and water quality. Sometimes this takes on a "zero-sum" competition for access to natural resources (such as use of forests for timber companies and national parks). Other times the state simply is not capable of effectively enforcing environmental regulations in the face of powerful corporate interests. As Evans (2001) argues, "within any jurisdiction, and often cutting across them, agencies are divided by sector and function and have competing responsibilities and interests. The role of the state consists then of a variety of roles played out in contradictory ways." State action around the environment in Vietnam clearly shows this contestation.

THE ENVIRONMENTAL STATE IN VIETNAM

Vietnam is in the process of establishing essentially a command-and-control system of environmental regulation (although modified to the Vietnamese political context), with an extensive system of standards, monitoring, and enforcement. The Law on Environmental Protection (LEP), promulgated in December 1993, is the umbrella environmental law for Vietnam (SRV, 1994). Since the passage of the LEP, the government has issued a wide range of decrees, directives, and circulars that flesh out the law, and create implementation instruments to realize the goals of environmental regulation and enforcement. In 1995, the Vietnam Standards Institute within the Ministry of Science, Technology, and Environment (MOSTE) issued national environmental standards, including standards on: ambient air quality; maximum allowable concentrations of hazardous substances in ambient air; inorganic and organic industrial emissions; pesticide residues; surface water quality; coastal water quality; ground water quality; industrial wastewater discharge; and maximum permitted noise levels. While this list is impressive for its comprehensiveness, it may actually be too detailed for most agencies to implement. Local regulatory bodies simply don't have the equipment or training to monitor and enforce this range of standards.

An important component of Vietnam's system of environmental laws involves the rights of citizens to complain about environmental problems. Article 33 of the Law states that people who detect signs of pollution must immediately notify the local People's Committee. Article 43 states that the public has the right to complain or "denounce" state management of environmental problems. And Article 49 and 52 establish that polluters must compensate those people who suffer impacts from pollution. These statements of environmental rights, while still fairly vague, have served to legitimate public complaints and created a small window of opportunity for public participation in environmental issues.

The government has also passed a decree on environmental fines (known as Decree 26). However, actual implementation of this system of penalties varies widely in different locales, and the entire system of fines seems to have had little impact on pollution levels. As one factory manager explained, "Fines only serve as a kind of warning not to pollute," while a local government official complained that, "Fines go to the state treasury. Losses are born by the local communities" (personal interviews conducted July 1998). Based on their current levels, fines don't even appear to be much of a warning. The highest fine in 1997 and 1998 in the four provinces I studied was approximately $380 for a foreign firm and only $170 for a state enterprise. Clearly fines of this size have little economic impact on firms with multi-million dollar budgets.

While fines are extremely low, compensations to impacted communities are sometimes set high enough that they can influence firm decisions. Community demands for compensation have been increasing steadily since the passage of the Law on Environmental Protection. Communities now feel that they have legal rights not to be polluted, or at the minimum to be compensated for the economic impacts of pollution. The system of compensations, however, is hardly ideal. Compensations are usually only paid after economic damages have occurred, and only if the community members can prove that a specific factory caused the damage.

As I will discuss below, actual enforcement is usually more a matter of local politics and negotiation than a function of strict adherence to official policies. The Law on Environmental Protection grants local authorities the power of setting and enforcing local regulations. Implementation thus remains the critical issue.

Structures, Hierarchies, and Coordination

The National Environment Agency (NEA), within the Ministry of Science, Technology and Environment (MOSTE), is officially responsible for environmental management in Vietnam, and in particular for the implementation of the Law on Environmental Protection. However, the NEA and MOSTE are only two players in an extremely complicated patchwork of ministries, departments, and agencies operating at multiple levels who are responsible for regulating pollution. In each of the country's 61 provinces and its three largest cities (Hanoi, Ho Chi Minh City, and Haiphong), the government has established Departments of Science Technology and Environment (DOSTE), which are responsible for monitoring and enforcing the nations' environmental standards and regulations. These departments are largely responsible for influencing whether or not laws are implemented and whether or not the environment is protected. Table 1 lists some of the agencies involved in different aspects of environmental policy development and implementation.[2]

Table 1. Agencies Involved in Environmental Policy.

Environmental Activity	Government Organization
Policy Making	Communist Party of Vietnam Prime Minister National Assembly Provincial People's Councils National Environment Agency
Planning	Ministry of Planning and Investment Ministry of Finance Provincial Departments of Planning and Investment Line Ministry Planning Departments Ministry of Science, Technology, and Environment Universities and Institutes
Oversight	Ministry of Science, Technology, and Environment (MOSTE) National Environment Agency Provincial People's Committees Line Ministries
Implementation	National Environment Agency Provincial Departments of Science, Technology, and Environment (DOSTEs) Line Ministry Environment DepartmentsSource: Adapted from UNDP 1995.

Source: Adapted from UNDP 1995.

The Law on Environmental Protection also requires line ministries to establish their own environmental management divisions. Most ministries have thus created nominal environmental divisions, some of which are much stronger than others. The Ministry of Construction for instance, has a much more developed environmental unit than the Ministry of Industry. The Ministry of Agriculture and Rural Development now has expansive environmental programs under its control (primarily relating to green-side issues such as forestry and rural ecosystems). And the Ministry of Planning and Investment (MPI) now has a powerful environmental unit within its Department of Science, Education and Environment (DSEE). DSEE is the counterpart to NEA and MOSTE on foreign development projects which have environmental components. Figure 1 shows a basic schematic of the government structure on environmental management, and Fig. 2 shows the key ministries involved in environmental issues.

This dispersal of environmental responsibilities to the line ministries has both positive and negative implications. One major problem is the overlap of responsibilities and competition between ministries and agencies to control decision-making over environmental planning, EIA review, and policy formulation. This dispersal of responsibilities without attendant mechanisms for resolving inter-ministerial disputes remains a problem for many areas of environmental management.

The organizational relations between the central government and the provinces around environmental management is also quite complex. The NEA is a division of the Ministry of Science, Technology, and Environment (MOSTE). Ostensibly the Departments of Science, Technology, and Environment (DOSTE) are the provincial versions of the MOSTE. However, the DOSTEs do not report directly to, or take instructions from, the MOSTE. Rather, the DOSTEs are managed by the People's Committees of each province or city, which report directly to the Office of the Government and the Prime Minister. The NEA does attempt to guide the DOSTEs on implementation of national environmental policies, and occasionally hires them to carry out national inspection programs or EIA reviews. However, the DOSTEs remain primarily responsive to local People's Committees.

As Figs 1 and 2 should indicate, environmental institutions in general are organized along vertical hierarchical lines, and as such transmit information and orders up and down along these vertical chains of command. The different organizations and institutions responsible for environmental issues seldom pass information or coordinate action among institutions horizontally. So for instance, the provincial and city DOSTEs don't generally coordinate well with the National Environment Agency, and the NEA doesn't coordinate well with the Ministry of Planning and Investment's Department of Science, Education, and Environment.

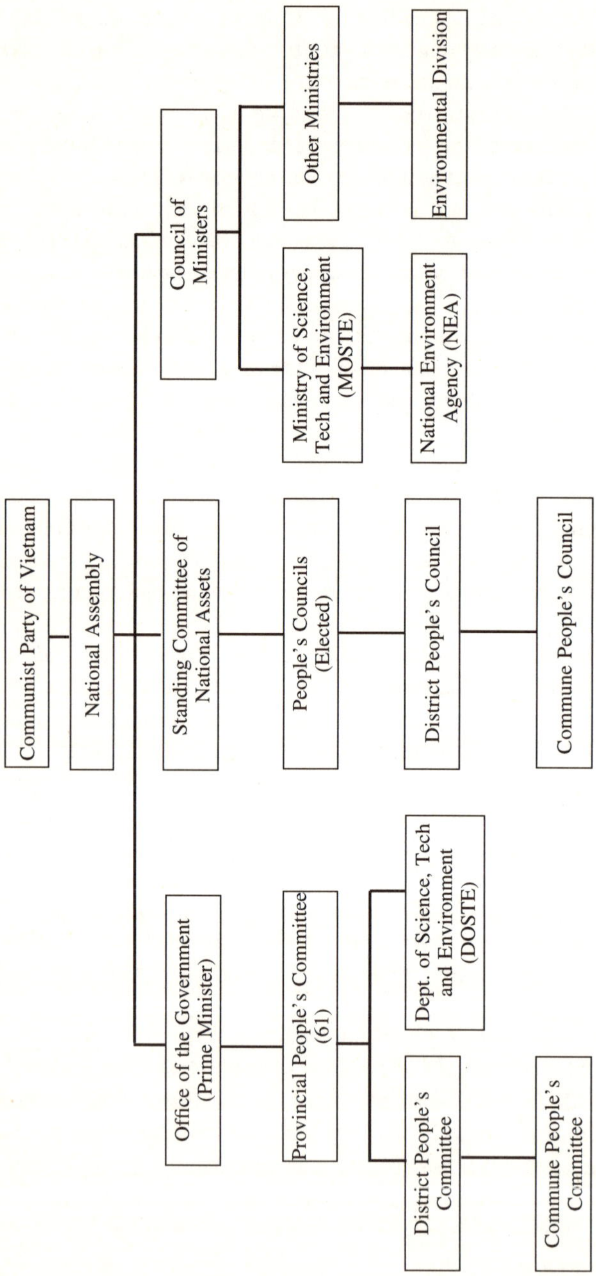

Fig. 1. Government Structure for Environmental Management.

Source: Adapted from UNDP 1999.

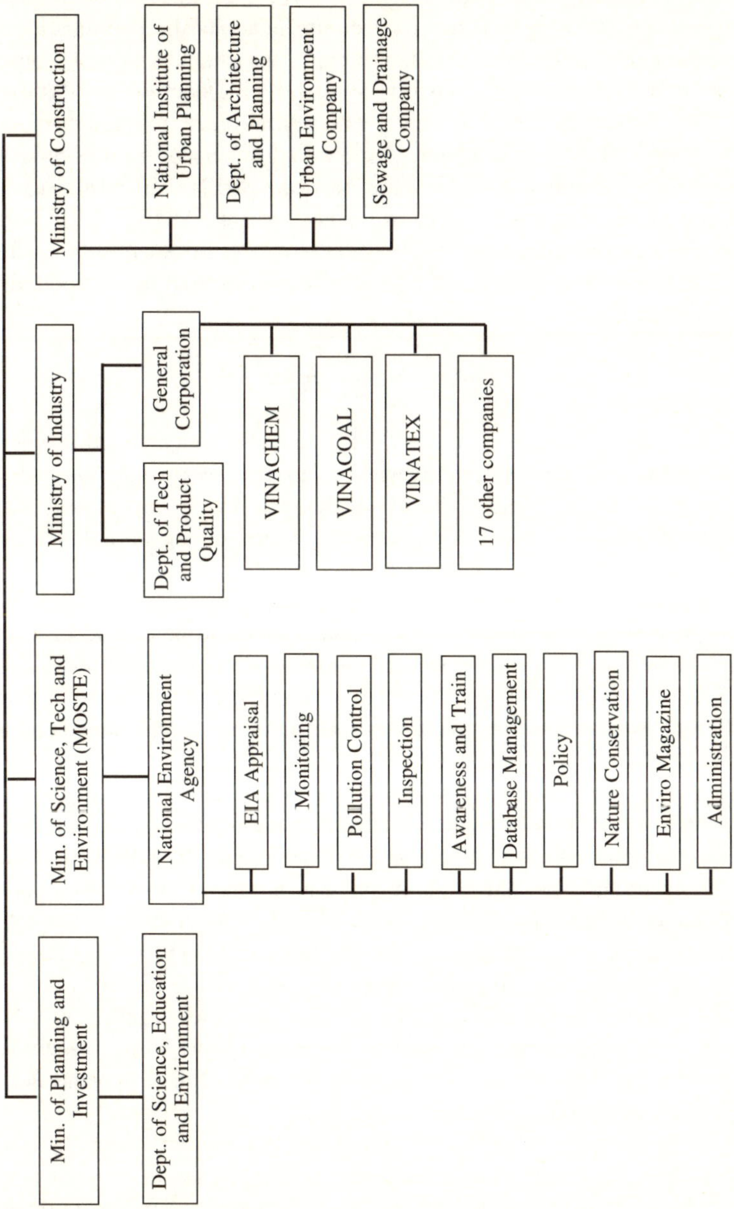

Fig. 2. Ministries Involved in Industrial Environmental Issues.

Source: Adapted from UNDP 1999.

In a multi-year study of environmental issues in Vietnam, the World Bank (1994) made one of its highest priority recommendations the coordination of environmental policy and implementation through "the establishment of a supra-ministerial body or council to be chaired by at least a Deputy Prime Minister with MOSTE serving as the secretariat." Three years later, in another report, the World Bank (1997, p. vii) again put the establishment of a cross-ministerial consultative committee to coordinate between MOSTE, the Ministry of Planning and Investment, the Ministry of Finance, and the Ministry of Industry as its top priority recommendation. However, to date, no such coordinating committee has been established, and lines of decision-making around pollution issues remain unclear.

Conflicts in the State

State agencies face a range of costs related to environmental enforcement, including the financial costs of building agency capacity and carrying out inspections, as well as the political costs of challenging factory managers, other government officials, and local constituencies. There are major political and economic costs associated with closing down a polluting factory (which is why it is so rarely done). On the other hand, there are also political costs to ignoring community complaints and allowing local environments to be degraded. In the long-term, government regulators face concerns about both "over-regulation" that scares off foreign investors or harms the economy, and "under-regulation" which allows destructive activities which undermine the local quality of life, resource base and political legitimacy.

These conflicts are particularly stark in regards to State-Owned Enterprises (SOEs). When the state is both the polluter and the regulator it is extremely difficult to overcome agency conflicts and advance regulation. The issue arises for example when the National Environment Agency has to deal with a pollution problem at a Ministry of Industry (MOI) affiliated factory. While the Ministry of Science, Technology, and Environment (MOSTE) is on the same administrative level as the other line ministries, NEA is not powerful enough to force the Ministry of Industry, or even the environmental department within MOI to do something it opposes. And as mentioned there is no established system within the Vietnamese government for arbitrating inter-ministerial disputes around environmental issues.

The example of trying to shut down factories is particularly telling. In 1995, NEA released a "black list" of 13 state enterprises it felt should be shut down because of the severity of their pollution. These firms were very clear polluters, with little hope of ever improving to the point of compliance. The reaction from other ministries and agencies however, was so strong that NEA's plans were completely blocked. To date, not one of the factories on NEA's black list has been shut down (UNDP, 1999).

COMMUNITY-DRIVEN REGULATION

In the face of these conflicts and contradictions, state agencies must be motivated to enforce environmental laws. From my interviews with government regulators it is clear that the vast majority of regulatory actions in Vietnam occur only after community complaints. For instance, staff at the Departments of Science, Technology and Environment (DOSTE) in three provinces – Ha Noi, Dong Nai, and Phu Tho – admitted that all inspections to date have been driven by community complaints.[3] Representatives of the National Environment Agency (NEA) similarly acknowledged that all of the inspections conducted between 1996 and 1998 were instigated after community complaints. Staffing weaknesses in environmental agencies, the current absence of a system for prioritizing inspections, and the strength of community demands, has led to this situation of Community-Driven Regulation.

In the six detailed case studies I examined, only when state actions were instigated by, and combined with community pressures, did a firm significantly improve its environmental performance. Without community pressure, existing policies achieved little in the way of environmental protection. Community actions that successfully drove a process of state legitimated regulation achieved environmental improvements. This process of Community-Driven Regulation (CDR) does not supplant so much as actuate and reinforce traditional regulation.

The frontline environmental agencies – the provincial Departments of Science, Technology, and Environment (DOSTEs) – face a continuous struggle to enforce Vietnam's environmental laws and decrees. Agency staff that are committed to enforcing the law face internal and external pressures against enforcement. Weaknesses in capacities and motivations of agency staff further impede enforcement. However, under certain conditions these barriers can be surmounted.

Successful cases of CDR follow a similar pattern: (1) communities identify priority environmental problems and instigate action to solve them – usually through complaint letters to a local government agency, letters to the firm, or protests; (2) the state responds by investigating, gathering data, and analyzing past performance and existing requirements on the firm; (3) the state may also set fines or require technical changes inside the factory; (4) the community monitors the state's actions and any changes in the performance of the firm (albeit through unscientific means); (5) if the pollution is not reduced the community escalates its pressure on the firm and challenges the state to fulfill its legal mandate, often turning to extralocal actors (such as the media or higher governmental bodies) to support their claims.

When the CDR process is successful, the community performs activities which complement state functions and actions. Community efforts to monitor factory performance, target problems, demand results, and verify improvements, actually support state efforts to establish and implement a broader legal framework. My cases show that while it is by no means perfect, CDR is functioning and is helping to realize the formal environmental regulations that are on the books in Vietnam. Bringing community action into the regulatory dynamic has achieved environmental gains where the state alone had not. The surprising success of community action in a largely unsupportive legal environment raises a series of questions about how these actions work.

The Dona Bochang Factory and the Dong Nai DOSTE

The Dong Nai province DOSTE (an industrial province just outside of Ho Chi Minh City) received roughly 60 complaints about pollution problems per year between 1994 and 1996. However, in 1997, the DOSTE inspection division reported receiving over 100 complaint letters in the first six months alone (personal interview, April 9, 1997). Complaints have streamed in at this rate ever since (UNDP, 1999). One community has been particularly vocal and persistent with their complaints about a factory called the Dona Bochang Textiles Plant.

Community members have argued in their letters that this Taiwanese joint-venture is an insult to the neighborhood, affecting peoples' daily lives, disrupting special occasions, and even defiling their center of worship – the local Catholic church. Pollution impacts such as respiratory problems, corroded roofs, and blackened plants have led to an escalation of community actions that have included regular complaint letters, throwing bricks at the factory, working with the media, and developing a long-term campaign to pressure the DOSTE to either regulate the factory or move it altogether.

As the Taiwanese managers and government officials soon found out, the people living around Dona Bochang are a tightly knit community. Approximately 95% of the population are Catholics who moved to the area in 1954, fleeing the Communist victory in the north. Many have been living in this area for over 40 years, long before a school was torn down to make room for the factory. The community's solidarity and internal social capital has been strengthened by over 40 years of church organizing. The residents along the factory's back wall live together, work together, socialize together, and worship together. Each time I went to interview an individual household, within a few minutes, 15 to 20 people would be gathered in the house telling their stories.

Locating a highly polluting factory in this community is a glaring example of unplanned urban development and the absence of zoning in Vietnam. The factory and the local residents are separated by no more than a three meter-high wall and a dirt road that runs along the perimeter of the factory. People live cramped together in small houses along the back wall of the factory. The community's church is located along another of the factory's walls. The factory's air emissions when not blowing across the back wall into the residential area, often blow directly into the church. Unfortunately for the parishioners, the church is an open air building with little more than a roof, an altar, and rows of pews.

In my interviews, one family stood out as leaders of community action. This family seemed fairly well educated and quite well off for the community, running their own small household enterprise finishing wood furniture. Living and working just a few feet away from the factory wall, the family had collected a thick file on the factory's pollution, including press clippings, letters they had sent to various government agencies, the responses they had received, and photographs of pollution impacts. They regularly drafted letters for others to sign. They had been on the official delegations to the factory and to government meetings. They had even made a video of the pollution.

After years of having their complaints ignored, an incident served to ignite community actions in 1993. On the day of a local wedding, air pollution from the factory coated trays of food laid out for the reception in a layer of black soot. Community members considered this the last straw and marched to the front gate and threatened to tear down the wall and shut down the factory if the manager did not come out to talk to them. Some young people went so far as to throw bricks at the factory, highlighting how serious the community was in their determination to force a response.

On that day a factory representative asserted that the factory was doing all they could and promised the problems would be solved. The community forced the manager to sign a statement attesting to the level of pollution. Photographs were taken. Several months later, when nothing had changed, the community brought their complaints, the pictures, and the signed statement, to the Dong Nai DOSTE and the media. After newspaper reports questioned the failure of the government to regulate the pollution, with headlines announcing "Dona Bochang Factory Continues to Generate Pollution," the DOSTE agreed to take action.

The DOSTE responded to the community complaints by organizing an inspection team and several meetings between community members and the factory. The community however, criticized the inspection process, charging that because it was a planned inspection, the factory was able to turn off the polluting equipment before the inspectors arrived. Community members argued that their daily experiences were more accurate than the data collected from the inspections. Later, when pollution levels resumed, the community sent more written complaints to the government and the media. This renewed pressure motivated more meetings, and finally resulted in the factory agreeing to install equipment to reduce its emissions.

The head of DOSTE's inspection division confirmed how important these public complaints are to their regulatory process, "If the complaints of a community are very strong, that factory will be inspected first. We have too many factories to inspect, so we prioritize based on complaints" (personal interview, June 9, 1997). The director of the environmental management division agreed, asserting that "Every normal inspection in Dong Nai is preceded by a complaint" (personal interview, August 1, 1998).

By the fall of 1997, the neighbors of Dona Bochang had achieved a qualified victory over the factory. Since the wedding party incident, the factory had made three changes to reduce its air pollution. First, it built a taller smokestack – the classic solution to local environmental problems. When this did not reduce the local impacts, the factory changed its practice of "blowing the tubes" from its boiler, which was a major source of the black soot people complained about. Finally, when this still had not resolved the problems, the factory installed an air filtration system to capture the pollution. This process took several years, but resulted in a significant reduction in air emissions.

The state's role in this case is complicated. As this is a joint-venture, the Dong Nai People's Committee owns 10% of the factory. Community action is thus in conflict with the short-term economic interests of the provincial People's Committee (which controls the DOSTE). The community's perception that they had to overcome this conflict of interest led them to look to extra-local actors such as the National Environment Agency and the media to help address their problems. It also strengthened the community's resolve to keep pressure on the factory and the provincial authorities. Community members did not trust the state to take action without repeated pressure. However, at the same time, the fact that the factory was majority foreign owned may have worked to the community's advantage. While the Vietnamese government is largely concerned with attracting foreign investors, individual agencies are also sometimes sensitive about public perceptions that the state is privileging foreign capitalists over common people.

The improvements at Dona Bochang appear to be due in large part to the strength, organization, and persistence of a tight-knit local community. However, the community on its own, was not able to change Dona Bochang. Direct letters and meetings with the factory did not result in pollution reductions. Success came through pressure on local and national government agencies, exerted both directly and through the media. The community's linkages to local government officials and extra-local reporters were critical to its success in motivating state action.

The Dona Bochang case represents a success of Community-Driven Regulation. A cohesive and connected community was able to pressure a state agency to take action on a polluting firm. The community sounded repeated alarms, and monitored state and firm actions. By using official complaint procedures, as well as unofficial tactics (protests, threats, media pressures), a tight-knit community was able to exert significant influence over pollution issues.

The Ba Nhat Factory and the Hanoi DOSTE

The Hanoi DOSTE receives over 1000 community complaints about pollution each year. One of the longest lasting of these controversies has focused on the Ba Nhat Chemical factory. Ba Nhat has been producing chemicals in this area since the 1960s, when three small cooperatives were merged into a city-owned company. The Hanoi Department of Industry owns the factory which employs 200 people. Over the years, output has grown, as has the pollution which rains down on the apartment buildings just 5 meters from Ba Nhat's walls.

Pollution has been serious since at least 1987 when the community began complaining in earnest about the impacts of the factory's production. During the last 12 years, community members have written over 100 letters to all levels of the government, including the National Assembly; submitted a letter to the courts, similar to a lawsuit demanding action on the factory; motivated journalists to write articles, and even written their own articles and paid to have them published. These actions have been coordinated by the "Committee Against the Pollution of Ba Nhat" which meets regularly to strategize about the factory, and is headed by a retired professor.

Community members were successful in pressuring the government to commission a study on the factory's pollution. The results of the study by another university professor found that 3000 people were adversely affected by pollution that included: carbon monoxide emissions 70 times higher than the legal limit, dust 10 times higher, sulfur dioxide 4 times higher, and other toxic gases 5 to 7 times the permitted levels (Nguyen, 1996). By the early 1990s, most people seemed in agreement that the factory was a problem. Every level of government imaginable had been contacted. Data clearly showed the factory in violation of environmental laws. Nonetheless, the factory continued with business as usual.

The community around Ba Nhat has a number of critical traits necessary to motivate action on environmental issues. They are cohesive, have high technical capacity, and have good connections to government officials. The community is the best educated of any I studied in Vietnam, made up of current and retired professors from the nearby Polytechnic University, as well as government employees. People are relatively well-off, solidly upper middle class in Vietnam. The community is in an urban area, close to the hallways of power. The community even has access to a wealth of damning environmental data. However, even with all of these critical characteristics, the community failed for year after year to win changes at Ba Nhat.

City government agencies are at the center of the Ba Nhat decision making. The Hanoi Department of Industry (DoI) owns and manages the factory. The Hanoi Department of Science, Technology, and Environment (DOSTE) is responsible for regulating Ba Nhat (although community members complain that responsibility for environmental management of the factory is not well defined). Both agencies report directly to the Hanoi People's Committee. Within this political system the DOSTE is much weaker than DoI. In fact, the DOSTE has not shut down or moved any of DoI's 200 factories, despite repeated promises to do so.

For years the community failed to find any leverage over the Department of Industry. For state-owned enterprises like Ba Nhat, environmental reforms necessarily involve one state agency pressuring another state agency to make a change. As the National Environment Agency does not have jurisdiction over city-owned factories, this case boils down to a political battle between the promoters and regulators of Ba Nhat within the Hanoi city government. Failing to motivate changes in the Hanoi bureaucracy, community members took their complaints to higher levels, petitioning the National Assembly and even the Prime Minister.

Finally, in late 1998, after more than 10 years of community complaints, the Hanoi government announced that it would physically move the factory out of the city to a rural area with an existing chemical complex. Department of Science, Technology, and Environment (DOSTE) staff explained in interviews that they had faced a series of battles over this decision. First, the DOSTE had to overcome the Department of Industry's resistance to moving the factory at all. When DOSTE finally won approval to move the factory, they then had to begin the process of working with suburban and rural government officials and community members to convince them to accept the factory. These efforts were blocked twice before a rural community with an existing chemical plant finally agreed to accept the plant. Continued (and escalated) community pressures from the Ba Nhat community were critical to strengthening the position of the DOSTE, and I believe, ultimately tipped the scales towards moving the factory. As one government official explained, "Pollution was the key issue on motivating the move. There were many complaints from the public, and the National Assembly representative worked to push forward the decision. Ba Nhat is the first factory in Hanoi to be moved by force because of public pressure" (personal interview – December 26, 1998).

The Ba Nhat case shows clearly that community capacity and cohesion alone are not enough, and at the same time illustrates the subtleties of linkages to the state. The community around Ba Nhat is by no means isolated, but its connections with the state were frustrated by other powerful interests for 10 years. With no autonomy and little capacity, the Hanoi DOSTE is almost powerless to regulate polluting state enterprises that provide jobs and tax revenues to the Department of Industry. Only extensive public pressure through the media, and connections to power above the Hanoi People's Committee, was ultimately able to overcome the recalcitrant position of the Department of Industry.

PATHWAYS TO ENVIRONMENTAL ENFORCEMENT

Vietnam now has essentially a complaint-based environmental protection system. Public pressures appear to be the primary means to motivate state agencies to pressure firms to reduce pollution. Because agency capacity is so weak, virtually the only time these agencies go out and actually enforce is when they are pressured by community members. Ironically, this public pressure also strengthens environmental agencies, giving them cover to regulate, and supporting their internal requests for more resources from the state.

Obviously, there are many weaknesses and problems with a complaint-driven inspection system. With little data and no training, community members often end up only complaining about pollution problems that they can see, smell, or feel. This results in a focus on localized, short-term, acute impacts of pollution. This type of pollution likely accounts for a significant percentage of industrial pollution in Vietnam at present. Nonetheless, this focus severely limits the range of environmental issues that become priorities for state action. With no knowledge of technical alternatives, communities tend to push for pollution control rather than prevention simply because their main concern is stopping local emissions. Another potential problem with this dynamic is that stronger communities may force factories to clean up or move, and scare off dirty factories from siting in their area, gradually shifting pollution to areas with the weakest communities.

The clear limits of community capacity and the potential equity implications of a system driven purely by community pressures, underscores the importance of strengthening the capacity and roles of allies within the state apparatus. At present, environmental agencies at all levels in Vietnam are very young and very weak. Strengthening basic environmental procedures at the national level, such as national ambient environmental monitoring of visible and invisible pollutants, national collection of environmental data, and state-sponsored research on environmental priorities, thus remains extremely important. More fundamental however, is the political position of environmental agencies within the state. Simply put, in internal government battles, environmental agencies generally lose. One of the optimistic implications of a community-driven model is that community actions may actually help state environmental agencies to overcome these weaknesses.

As I have mentioned, a somewhat unusual feature of Vietnamese environmental institutions is that the provincial DOSTEs have very weak formal ties to the Ministry of Science, Technology, and Environment or the National Environment Agency. This is particularly unusual because all of the other line ministries have formal relations with the equivalent departments at the provincial level (e.g. the Ministry of Agriculture to a provincial department of agriculture). As it turns out, this is actually a critical institutional factor for environmental policy implementation in Vietnam.

Some communities have been able to advance their interests for better environmental protection within this institutional structure. There appear to be a number of reasons for this. First, because the DOSTEs report directly to provincial People's Committees, which report directly to the Office of the Government and the Prime Minister, complaints that make it to the DOSTE and PC, can have a much greater effect on government action than if they went through the MOSTE bureaucracy on their way to top decision-makers.

Second, while MOSTE is in theory equal to other ministries, in fact it is much weaker and generally loses debates in the Council of Ministers which affect the interests of the Ministry of Planning and Investment (such as foreign investors) or the Ministry of Industry (such as State-Owned Enterprises). MOSTE is thus rarely able to advance environmental concerns through the political structure. As I have noted, the NEA and MOSTE for instance, are not powerful enough to shut down a factory. However, provincial and city DOSTEs have been successful in getting factories shut down or moved by pressuring local People's Committees. This seems to be due to the fact that the NEA and MOSTE have more potential blockages on their way to policy implementation.

Third, the NEA and MOSTE are much less responsive to public complaints and concerns than are local officials. Sitting in Hanoi, the NEA and MOSTE are largely insulated from local political pressures. DOSTEs are better "targets" for local complaints. Local community members can complain directly to local officials, going to their offices, or writing letters to officials or to local newspapers, and hounding officials to implement the laws. And so even though the DOSTEs may have less capacity and official power than the NEA, because of their responsiveness to local demands, and their connections to provincial decision-makers, they are more likely to enforce environmental regulations than national officials.

The vulnerability of local government officials to public critique and the broader struggle of the state for legitimacy has opened up space for community action around environmental issues. Vietnam's socialist legacy has essentially provided a window of opportunity for community participation, and civil society more broadly, to play a constructive role in pollution issues. And through this small window, many Vietnamese community members have jumped. As Roodman (1999b) argues, and my research confirms, "two main sources generate public pressure on industrial polluters and the officials who regulate them: citizen complaints and media coverage."

Vietnamese citizens now literally file thousands of complaints against industrial polluters each year, and journalists produce hundreds of stories (Roodman, 1999). The Ho Chi Minh City's DOSTE reports receiving over 1000 complaints per year. As mentioned, the Hanoi DOSTE similarly receives around 1000 complaints per year, while Dong Nai receives approximately 200 complaints per year. The DOSTEs also appear particularly sensitive to media criticisms for failures to enforce pollution laws. Perhaps it is because these critiques conjure an accusation of corruption and incompetence that DOSTEs respond to these media reports.

The passage of the Law on Environmental Protection was a critical step in creating a legal opening for community complaints and demands. But even before the LEP was passed, citizens were granted the right "to lodge complaints and denunciations with the competent State authorities against illegal doings of State organs, economic bodies . . . or of any individual" under Article 74 of the Vietnamese constitution (SRV, 1992). The constitution made clear that a "person who has suffered loss and injury shall be entitled to damages for any material harm suffered." This provision was translated into an environmental context via Article 43 of the LEP, which states that "Organizations, individuals have the right to complain, denounce to the State management agency for environmental protection or other competent State agencies about activities in breach of environmental protection legislation." As Roodman (1999) points out, this right of "complaints from people living near factories, along with media pressure, have perhaps played at least as significant role as conventional regulatory measures in driving industrial pollution reductions in Vietnam."

This opening and the right of citizens to criticize the government does of course have limitations. Community members allude to unstated lines that must not be crossed. For example, people generally avoid accusing high level officials of corruption directly or publicly. And the LEP itself is quite restrictive in how the public can participate in environmental decisions, essentially allowing only complaints after pollution has occurred, rather than broader public participation in development decisions.

CONCLUSIONS

The Vietnamese state has been undergoing major institutional and administrative changes over the last 10 years (Fforde & de Vylder, 1996, World Bank, 1993, 1994). And although the Communist Party continues to affirm its sole control over the government, the roles and capacities of the state are nonetheless being transformed. Most importantly for this analysis, the state is being forced to develop new mechanisms and processes for dealing with industrial pollution problems. Based on recent high level policy statements, it appears that the state recognizes a number of weaknesses and problems in its environmental protection efforts. The government is thus working to shore up its environmental agencies and authority, and to move gradually toward more effective protection policies. However, this is a long and slow road.

At present, environmental agencies at all levels in Vietnam have very limited capacities for environmental regulation, and have limited political powers in internal government battles and day-to-day negotiations with other government agencies. Corruption among poorly paid inspectors only adds to the challenges of regulation. However, public and media pressure around environmental issues is gradually raising the profile, and the bargaining power of environmental agencies. Community pressures have helped to overcome agency resistance to implement laws that impact other state actors (such as the Ministry of Industry). Community pressures are motivating inspectors to do their jobs, a not insignificant feat as most inspectors are overwhelmed by their tasks, under-trained for their duties, and under-paid. Community action is also helping to shine light on local-level corruption, and increasing transparency in all state environmental actions.

Vietnam now thus has essentially a complaint-driven environmental protection system, what I have termed Community-Driven Regulation. Both inspections and sanctions are motivated largely by community demands. The state has played a central role in creating the legal structure for this system, and, perhaps accidentally, for creating the institutional arrangements which make the DOSTEs an effective target for public pressure. To their credit though, these agencies have worked (since their creation in 1995) to build their own capacity to gather environmental information and to monitor compliance with the country's new laws and regulations. Several DOSTEs are now fairly effective in responding to specific community complaints when they feel impelled.

On the ground, when pressured to act, the DOSTEs can work to effect environmental enforcement. Sanctions, compensation, and compliance schedules are all being implemented, albeit through negotiated processes. Of course, Vietnam's complaint-driven, negotiated regulation looks much different in practice than the legal mandates for environmental regulation look on paper. Although official regulatory processes remain largely ineffective, some community and state actors have hit upon alternative mechanisms and pathways to enforcement.

This process seems to work because of the institutional structure of DOSTE reporting and responsibility, and because of both the DOSTE's and individual firm's sensitivities to public criticisms. Media reports and public letter writing campaigns raise the implication of corruption or incompetence within the DOSTEs. This pressure from below, combined with the pressure from the hierarchy above, which reaches all the way to the Prime Minister and the Office of the Government, can serve to squeeze the DOSTEs into action. At the end of the day, the DOSTEs must respond to both competency concerns and larger questions of state legitimacy.

The two case studies presented (and four others from a larger research project – O'Rourke, 2001) point to a number of general conclusions about the role of the state in this complaint-driven process. First, state agencies need a certain level of autonomy from industrial actors, otherwise economic interests take precedence over environmental concerns. If the state is too "close" to a firm, regulation becomes virtually impossible. This can occur in both state-enterprises and joint-ventures. Second, state agencies need a certain level of connectedness with communities affected by pollution. There needs to be some form or process of connection for communities to successfully impart their complaints and goals. Here again, this is why the local environmental agencies rather than the National Environment Agency seem to be so much more effective in environmental enforcement.

Community complaints and organized pressures are the key driver of this process. It should be noted however, that the state is by no means always happy to respond to community demands for stricter environmental protection. Despite positive examples, state agencies do regularly attempt to block community action. Essentially all protests in Vietnam remain illegal, and most state enterprises continue to exist above the law. The range of community actions is thus circumscribed by state decrees and the unwritten rules protecting state enterprises. Vague legal rights create barriers for communities to complain and demand action against a firm.

However, if specific state agencies can be motivated to respond to community demands, Community-Driven Regulation can boost the capacity and effectiveness of local environmental regulators. In several of my case studies, state agencies played pivotal roles in supporting and legitimating community demands for pollution reduction. Successful community actions responded to these openings and focused pressure on the right actors within the state. With so many pressures against enforcement, Community-Driven Regulation may hold out the best hope for advancing environmental protection in Vietnam.

NOTES

1. This critical assessment is based on direct work with officials in four government agencies over a four year period.
2. These institutional arrangements continue to evolve with the political and economic reforms underway in Vietnam.
3. There is one recent exception to this pattern. The National Environment Agency instigated a nationwide program in 1997 to "inspect" firms for compliance with the EIA law. This program was simply an attempt to assess how many firms had conducted EIAs, and whether firms were complying with the terms of their EIAs.

REFERENCES

Afsah, S., Benoit, L., & David, W. (1996). *Controlling Industrial Pollution: A New Paradigm.* Washington, D.C.: World Bank.

Barber, C. V. (1997). The Case Study of Indonesia. In: *AAAS Project on Environmental Scarcities, State Capacity, and Civil Violence.* Washington, D.C.: Committee on International Security Studies.

Carew-Reid, J. (1998). Assessing Progress in Sustainable Development in Vietnam – A Discussion Paper. *Vietnam Capacity 21 Project.* Ministry of Planning and Investment, Hanoi.

Cohen, M. (1998). *Monitoring and Enforcement of Environmental Policy.* Unpublished manuscript available on the Internet at www.worldbank.org/nipr/

Desai, U. (Ed.) (1998). *Ecological Policy and Politics in Developing Countries.* Albany: State University of New York Press.

Dwivedi, O. P., & Dhirendra K. V. (1995). *Environmental Policies in the Third World: A Comparative Perspective.* Westport: Greenwood Press.

Eder, N. (1996). *Poisoned Prosperity – Development, Modernization, and the Environment in South Korea.* Armonk, NY: M. E. Sharpe.

Evans, P. (2001). *Livable Cities: The Politics of Urban Livelihood and Sustainability*. Berkeley: University of California Press.

Evans, P. (1997). The Eclipse of the State? Reflections on Stateness in an Era of Globalization. *World Politics*, *50*(1).

Fforde, A., & de Vylder, S. (1996). *From Plan to Market – The Economic Transition in Vietnam*. Boulder: Westview Press.

Gould, K., Allan, S., & Adam, W. (1996). *Local Environmental Struggles: Citizen Activism in the Treadmill of Production*. New York: Cambridge University Press.

Hettige, H., Mainul, H., Sheoli, P., & David, W. (1995). *Determinants of Pollution Abatement in Developing Countries: Evidence from South and South-East Asia. Policy Research Department*. Washington, D.C.: World Bank.

Kolko, G. (1995). Vietnam Since 1975: Winning a War and Losing the Peace. *Journal of Contemporary Asia*, *25*(1), 3–49.

Laplante, B. (1995). Industrial Pollution Control: Role of Public Information. Presentation to the *Economic Development Institute Workshop on Industrial Pollution Prevention in Vietnam*. Washington, D.C., Sept 13th.

Nguyen, D. K. (1996). Report on the Environmental Management Practices of Hanoi's DOSTE. Paper presented at the *VCEP Seminar on Environmental Management*, Hanoi, August 20–23, 1996.

O'Connor, J. (1994). Is Sustainable Capitalism Possible?. In: M. O'Connor (Ed.), *Is Capitalism Sustainable? Political Economy and the Politics of Ecology*. New York: Guilford Press.

O'Rourke, D. (2001). Community-Driven Regulation: Towards an Improved Model of Environmental Regulation in Vietnam. In: P. B. Evans (Ed.), *Livable Cities: The Politics of Urban Livelihood and Sustainability*. Berkeley: University of California Press.

Roodman, D. M. (1999). Vietnam: The Paradox of Public Pressure. *Worldwatch Magazine*, *12*(6), November/December. Washington, D.C.: Worldwatch Institute.

Roodman, D. M. (1999b). Regulatory Framework for Industrial Pollution: Constraints and Opportunities. Paper presented at the Conference on Sustainable Industrial Development, Ministry of Industry, Ministry of Science, Technology, and Environment, and World Bank, Hanoi, June 10–11.

Sapru, R. K. (1998). Environmental Policy and Politics in India. In: U. Desai (Ed.), *Ecological Policy and Politics in Developing Countries*. Albany: State University of New York Press.

Schnaiberg, A. (1994). The Political Economy of Environmental Problems and Policies: Consciousness, Conflict, and Control Capacity. *Advances in Human Ecology*, *3*.

Socialist Republic of Vietnam (SRV) (1995). *Viet Nam National Environmental Action Plan*. Hanoi, Draft April 20, 1995.

Socialist Republic of Vietnam (SRV) (1994). *Law on Environmental Protection*. Hanoi: National Political Publishing House.

Taylor, B. R. (Ed.) (1995). *Ecological Resistance Movements: The Global Emergence of Radical and Popular Environmentalism*. Albany: State University of New York Press.

Thanh, N. C. (1993). *Vietnam Environment Sector Study*, Manila: Asian Development Bank.

United Nations Development Program (UNDP) (1999). *A Study on Aid to the Environment Sector in Vietnam*. Ministry of Planning and Investment, Hanoi, Vietnam.

United Nations Development Program (UNDP) (1997). *Incorporating Environmental Considerations into Urban Plannin*. Vietnam Capacity 21 Project, Hanoi, May.

United Nations Development Program (UNDP) (1995). *Incorporating Environmental Considerations into Investment Decision-Making in Viet Nam*. Hanoi, December.

United Nations Industrial Development Organization (UNIDO) (1998). *Incentives for Pollution Prevention and Control in Dong Nai. Report to the project* VIE/95/053, August 6, 1998.

World Bank (1997). *Vietnam – Economic Sector Report on Industrial Pollution Prevention.* Agriculture and Environment Operations Division, Washington, D.C.

World Bank (1994). *Vietnam – Environmental Programs and Policy Priorities for an Economy in Transition.* Agriculture and Natural Resources Division, East Asia and Pacific Region. Washington, D.C.

World Bank (1993). *Viet Nam – Transition to the Market.* Washington, D.C.: World Bank.

THE ENVIRONMENTAL STATE IN CONSTANT TRANSITION: DECENTRALIZATION AND ECONOMIZATION IN RUSSIA

Olga Aksenova and Valeriy Nedelkov

1. INTRODUCTION

This article aims at analyzing environmental policy-making in Russia, especially in the Vologda region. The study is focused on the following processes ongoing in Russian environmental policy:

- the decentralization of a highly centralized and bureaucratic state environmental administration system established at the end of the 1980s;
- the emergence of an environmental market and new actors in environmental policy;
- the development of privatization and economization processes in environmental policy-making.

Our main goal was to reveal eco-modernisational trends in the regional environmental policy.

Our understanding of the eco-modernization theoretical approach and the possibilities of its application to a transitional state is described in section two

The Environmental State Under Pressure, Volume 10, pages 245–267.

ISBN: 0-7623-0854-0

of the article. Section three contains a description of Russian environmental policy at the federal, regional and local level and an analysis of the transformations, which have taken place during the last decade. The organization of environmental management in industrial enterprises is described in the fourth section. The fifth section includes an analysis of the regional environmental market, and the emergence of new actors and organizational structures in Russian environmental policy during environmental reform. The main conclusions are summarized in the final section.

Methodology

This article is based on two sociological investigations, carried out between 1997 and 2000. The first one is a study of regional environmental policy and environmental NGOs in nine regions of the European part of Russia. The second is a study of ecological modernization processes in the Vologda region (North of Russia).[1] The choice for a regional level for analysis was not accidental. The economic, social and even cultural differences between Russian regions are very high. Regional authorities have significant room for shaping their own strategy and policy-making system. The investigation of state environmental politics at the federal level could show only the general framework of the policy process and official policy rules and statements that frequently do not coincide with the real activities of regional social actors.

The methodology of investigation was determined by the realities of the Russian regional environmental policy domain. Non-stop change, frequent restructuring, and the absence of established organizational space with a clear functional task division characterizes the modern situation in Russian environmental management. Under these circumstances the qualitative methods of sociological research such as case studies, in-depth interviews, and sociological interventions were used in both field studies.

The Vologda region has an average level of industrial development typical for Russian provinces. The organization of the state environmental policies and industrial eco-management and its ongoing transformations in that region were analyzed in detail. The environmental authorities at regional and local levels were analyzed and the emerging new environmental market and its actors were examined. Identification of the regional environmental management network was carried out with the aim of defining the position of different actors and their interactions. The documents of regional environmental protection organizations were analyzed for the period of ten years since 1988, when the modern system of central state management was established. It was necessary to reveal more or less stable tendencies in an unstable situation.

The data received in the Samara region (in-depth interviews with heads of state nature protection structures and ecoNGO leaders, official documents and media publications) were also used. The Samara region (Volga River area) has much more advanced industry, a denser communication network and stronger state positions in environmental policy than the Vologda region. We assumed that eco-modernization processes could be more developed there. Therefore, some data from Samara and Vologda regions were compared to verify our conclusions on perspectives of Vologda environmental policy developments. Several illustrative examples of the environmental policy of Nizhniy Novgorod region, Briansk region and Karelia Republic were also included.

Brief Description of the Vologda Region

The Vologda region is situated at the North of European Russia. The city of Vologda (capital of the region) is an ancient Russian cultural and historical center; the whole region is a very attractive place for tourism. Most regional industries are of middle and small size. There are two big paper plants in the city of Sokol but both of them practically closed after the financial crisis of 17 August 1998.

The only big industrial center now is the city of Cherepovets. This center enjoys a favorable economic treatment in the region. There are three huge industrial companies in the city: two chemical corporations ("Azot" and "Ammofos") and one steel company "Severstal". The latter company includes a number of plants (full cycle of steel production). "Severstal" is one of the most successful Russian companies which never suffered seriously from the economic crisis and stagnation.[2] It used to provide all the industries of the European part of Russia with steel, but now it is working mainly for Western and Asian markets.

"Severstal" became the main political force in the region. Representatives of the company occupy all the key positions in the executive authority bodies and compose a powerful lobby in the regional parliament. "Azot" and "Ammofos" do not have such political influence as "Severstal". Only the economic and political activities of "trans-regional" gas and energy monopolies provide a concurrent set of interests. These competitive interests provide a possibility for alternatives in development and 'democracy' trends in regional politics, contributing to a more pluralistic way of modern environmental decision-making.

The pollution level in the cities of the region is high, despite the economic crisis, and it is extremely high in Cherepovets. During a long period, ecoNGOs have insisted on the necessity of giving this city the status of an "environmental disaster zone". At the same time, there are huge distances between cities, towns and settlements of the region, and the communication network is not very dense. This makes environmental risks more local than in such highly industrialized regions as Samara.

The present research is the first step and the first attempt to analyze eco-modernization aspects in the changes in environmental management and policy-making in Russian regions. It should be followed by a more extensive and in depth comparative research in different Russian regions. Our objective is to present a first analysis and understanding of ongoing regional environmental policy transformation processes that continue to be "white spots" even for Russian sociologists.

2. ECOLOGICAL MODERNIZATION AND TRANSITIONAL STATES

The ecological modernization concept, developed by Western environmental sociologists (e.g. Weale, 1992; Mol & Spaargaren, 1993; Mol, 1995), is used by us as a theoretical base for the analysis and evaluation of transformations in Russian environmental policy. Therefore, an explanation of our understanding of ecological modernization processes in Russia is necessary. Ecological modernization (EM) has been considered as a process of pro-ecological restructuring of all institutions of modern industrial society without de-industrialization or other radical economic or social transformations (Mol, 1995). EM is expressed in changes of the role and position of different actors (state structures, corporations, ecoNGOs, and other) in environmental politics, in rising interests of economic actors in environmentally sound policy. It is also characterized by the shift from bureaucratic state policy to more self-organization, a switch to market mechanisms in eco-management, and a move from curative and reactive environmental policy to a preventive one. EM is conceptualized in the form of sociological theories as well as political strategies of the state, political parties and environmental movements. We also consider EM as a stage in the development of modernity, especially related to the industrial dimension of modern society, and characterized by the emancipation of the environmental sphere (cf. Mol, 1995). EM changes are significantly triggered by economic-technological developments, which create environmental risks, and at the same time, provide organizational and technological means for risk minimization or prevention.

The main question dealt with in this article is: could ecological-modernization-like transformations emerge in the transitional Russian society whose industrial as well as institutional structure was created in the Soviet period? And how would these changes look like? Of course, the Soviet system was rather different from Western modernity. In Russia, a developed industry with a prevalent military sector had been created, which strongly contributed to entering into the 'risk-society phase' before Perestroika. (cf. Yanitsky, 1998). Therefore, at least the technological base of Russian (militarized) industry was sufficiently advanced to provide the means for environmental risk prevention. Besides that, several developments in Russia create the institutional and organizational conditions for the emergence of eco-modernization transformations. The main factors that could catalyze such transformations are:

- the transition towards a market economy and democratic society, followed by deep institutional and organizational changes and restructuring processes in industries;
- the country's entrance into the globalization processes that provide transmission of Western methods, style and type of policy-making and management over all spheres of social life;
- the economic growth started in many Russian regions.[3]

The main social structures related to Russian environmental policy were established at the beginning of the 1990s. Among them were federal environment protection structures, their regional branches, research and educational institutions, environmental departments of companies, and ecoNGOs. The latter continued their activities even in conditions of economic crisis and developed further (see Khaliy, 2000). The population was extremely active in the arena of environmental policy during Perestroika but after the collapse of the USSR citizens' activity decreased (see Yanitsky, 1996). The environmental awareness and activism of the whole society remained very low during the last decade of economic crisis and stagnation. According to our in-depth interviews with politicians, state officers and members of ecoNGOs in nine Russian regions environmental issues are still not a priority for politicians and ordinary people.

At the same time state environmental protection structures, ecoNGOs, industrial companies and other social actors are now facing the growth of environmental risks and it is becoming increasingly obvious that an environmental strategy relevant to new political, economic and social conditions has to be developed and implemented.

Our research clearly show that there is no eco-modernization as a formulated policy expressed in strategies, concepts, long-term programs of state structures, political parties or environmental movements in Russia, both at the federal and regional levels. In the meantime, deep and quick changes are going on in the regional environmental policy sphere now. Against this background the paper focuses on the transformations of Russian environmental policy that could be interpreted as being in line with the eco-modernization idea, even if the actors contributing to such a policy do not realize this. We assume that the process of economization, decentralization, the emergence of new actors and organizational change ongoing in Russian environmental policy could contain such eco-modernization realities.

3. RUSSIAN ENVIRONMENTAL POLICY: DECENTRALIZATION AND CONSTANT RESTRUCTURING

Russian environmental policy over the last decade has been unstable and permanently changing. Before concentrating on decentralization tendencies and the crucial role of finances in environmental policy, we first provide a brief description of the federal environment protection structure.

The Federal Context of Environmental Protection

In Soviet times, the environmental protection system was part of centralized bureaucratic planning. Environmental protection functions were distributed among various ministries and departments. For example in the building industry requirements of environment protection were included in the Construction Norms and Rules (so called CNaR) elaborated for projects and construction works (see chapter "Environment Protection" in "Construction Norms and Rules", 1986). Departments of engineering organizations and the State Committee on Building Affairs made an assessment of a project's compliance to CNaR.

For a considerable time there were only two specialized organizations whose activities were primarily related to environmental protection. The first one was the Sanitary-Epidemiological Oversight Authority of the USSR Ministry of Health (below 'Sanitary Authority'), whose task was monitoring and control of all the factors which could harm human health. The second was the Hydro-Meteorological Center (now 'Center for Monitoring of Environmental Pollution') that had only monitoring functions.

The present system of state environmental protection organizations was created at the end of the 1980s, when the State Committee on the Environment was established which later transformed into the Ministry of Ecology. During the subsequent ten years this Ministry was renamed and restructured many times. Now it is called the Federal Environment Protection Committee (further EPC) that has regional and local departments. The position of the federal EPC inside the federal government is weak. Environmental problems are not the priority of state policy during the current crisis. This is confirmed by regular transformations in EPC and other environmental protection structures, all leading to a weakening of the state environmental policy. The main functions of the Committees are the following: monitoring environmental quality, controlling the use of nature resources, developing expertise of all activities related to environmental impacts, and execution of economic regulation in environmental protection (see e.g. Osipov & Lvova, 1996).

Several other committees are responsible for controlling the use of particular resources (forest, minerals, water, etc.). All of them have regional branches. Their structure also has been changing and restructuring all the time. Thus, for example, the Water Control Committee was united with the Geology Committee in a new organization, named the Nature Resource Committee. The activities of the latter are focused more on the exploitation of nature resource than on nature protection. The environmental protection function of the newly structured water control department was quite restricted. Thus the Nature Resource Committee of Karelia Republic promotes the environmentally dangerous project of vanadium mining in Zaonezhie which is a famous part of Karelia for tourism. The Water Control Committee was against this project when it was an independent organization. Now as a part of Nature Resource Committee this structure strongly supports the mining project. (see Aksenova, 2000)

The Ecofund System

Environmental management in industry was and still is traditionally based on a state direct regulation system. Increasingly, however, economic regulation is introduced, based on permits and licenses and on different forms of payments for environmental pollution. This regulation is also changing permanently. The main organization that gives permission to use natural resources (in the form of yearly agreements, passports, licenses, etc.) is EPC: its federal, regional and local branches (depending on the level of company activities). Permission from the Sanitary Authority and a license of the Water Control Committee also are required to start production.

All payments for pollution are collected in the ecofunds system. There are federal, regional and local ecofunds. Each payment is divided between the three levels in the following division: 10% (Federal ecofund), 30% (Regional ecofund) and 60% (local ecofund) (see Lukianchkov, 1998). The ecofund system is a main source of financing the activities of the Environmental Protection Committees. The principal items for expenditure are monitoring, pollution prevention measures in industry (sponsorship of technological innovations, construction of filter systems, etc.), maintenance of Committee equipment, investigations, and environmental education.

Only the three level fund structure (federal, regional and local) and the percentage of payments are common elements of the ecofund system throughout Russia. The role and position of funds in environmental policy, their management, and use of resources differ among regions and levels. For example, a regional ecofund can be a part of a regional government budget or it can be an independent financial structure. In the Vologda and Samara regions the ecofund is integrated into the regional budget. In all cases, the expenditures of the fund depend first of all on decisions of regional (and local) authorities.

The ecofund size depends greatly on the regional economic situation and capability of enterprises to pay for pollution. But there are factors that influence the supply of payments into ecofunds and determine who control and distribute fund resources. Among them there are the peculiarities of regional political games, and personal activities of regional environmental political leaders, and their personal ties with regional administration. Thus, regional EPCs control regional ecofunds in Vologda and Samara. The situation is different in the Nizhnii Novgorod region where the regional ecofund is under the responsibility of the Environmental Department of regional administration. This happened due to the innovative activity of the first director of the Environmental Department and the high environmental awareness of the former governor of the region who was an ecoNGO leader in the past. They decided to create a managerial structure, which could be more effective than the regional EPC.

Political influence of any environment protection structure in the region is closely related to ecofund resources and possibilities to control them, while the key persons in Vologda and Samara regional eco-policy are the heads of EPCs. The director of Environmental Department is the most influential person in Nizhni Novgorod environmental policy. The Nizhnii Novgorod environmental policy is determined by Environmental Department and not by EPC.

The Decline of Federal and the Emergence of Regional Environmental Policy

The dangerous environmental situation in Cherepovets and the awareness created by the environmental movement of these problems in this city forced the central government to give special attention to Vologda environmental policy during Perestroika. Significant investments were made in environmental protection in the region. The regional structure of environment protection had been created before the 1998 economic crisis started. But the federal financing of regional departments of EPC was restricted during the period from 1991 up to the middle of 1990s. Only the salaries of the staff were paid from the federal budget. All activities of the organization, including execution of its functions and implementation of environment protection programs, started to be financed from the regional budgets and regional ecofunds.

As a result, the regional EPCs in Vologda and other regions began to lose their function as independent federal controller because financially it became more and more dependent on the regional budget. Committee politics depends now on the regional authority's position and interests towards powerful economic structures such as "Severstal" company in Vologda region, which strongly influence regional authority decisions. The same thing happened with other controlling bodies, with the exception probably of the Sanitary Authority: it still preserves its vertical hierarchy, and it is dominantly financed from the federal budget. The local monitoring points of the Center of Environmental Pollution Monitoring are also sponsored by regional or local budgets. In the Samara region several monitoring points were closed because local authorities and owners of industrial plants stopped financing them to hide real pollution levels (see Aksenova, 1999).

At the same time, regional authorities are faced more seriously with the necessity of resolving regional pollution problems than the federal government. As was mentioned the environmental risks in Russia are comparatively local. "Severstal" pollution is dangerous for the city of Cherepovets and Vologda region first of all. This problem remains on the political agenda of the local and regional authority. As a result the position of the Vologda region EPC inside regional government is stronger politically than the position of the Federal EPC inside federal government.

Consequently, the Vologda authorities made an attempt to establish their own nature protection organizational structure and to create their own regional environmental strategy. One of the main obstacles for such a strategy was the absence of coordination between different environment protection bodies. The Sanitary Authority, EPC and the numerous regional state structures that control different resources were acting independently from each other. They never formed any joint policy community or even a looser network. Regular interactions existed only between these organizations when economic regulations and the financing of environmental policy were concerned.

Economic regulation was functioning effectively in the Vologda region even during the economic and financial crisis. Enterprise managers tried to make all payments for pollution in time, as otherwise their tax declaration could not be approved by the Tax Inspection. These payments collected in the regional ecofund provided the resources and possibilities for creating and maintaining a regional environmental policy system when the federal institutions became powerless. The regional administration also established a Regional Environmental Protection Department in 1992 for coordinating the activities of all governmental environmental organizations. Such departments were organized in many other regions as well. These new structures created a regional legislative framework for environmental policy-making, developed economic regulations in the field of environment, and elaborated and implemented regional environmental strategy.

Regular meetings and consultations with heads of federal environmental committees, environmental officials of "Severstal" and other big companies were organized. Besides these organizations, regional research institutions and universities were involved in elaborating a regional environmental program. The environmental policy network started its emergence with a core formed by the Environment Protection Department of regional administration and EPC. Directors of regional branches of federal environmental structures are not obliged to participate in these meetings and consultations. Formally they are working under a federal subordination system. But in reality they became rather regional than federal organizations, due to the restricted federal financing. In the Samara region, for instance, authorities never constructed new state bodies such as environment protection department. The regional EPC became an organizational center for elaborating and implementing regional environmental protection programs relatively independent from the federal system, and thus functioned practically as a regional ministry.

Regional authorities have enough room for maneuver for shaping also a regional system of economic regulation in the field of environment. This can be seen even more clearly in Samara region where the regional government and parliament elaborated a regional law for tax exemptions of enterprises if they re-use waste. Environmental authorities of both Samara and Vologda regions reduced payments for pollution if enterprise administrations implemented pollution prevention measures.

Serious problems for regional environmental policy development are related to the absence of standardized monitoring schemes. All federal organizations have among others a monitoring function. The Center for Environmental Pollution Monitoring is specialized in monitoring and has a dense network of monitoring points. The Sanitary Committee also has such a network. All organizations have their own monitoring methodology and their own criteria for data evaluation. As a result there is no possibility to compare data and even interpretations are difficult. Often a very strange and contradictory data set of environmental pollution in the region appears, which is of course an extremely poor foundation for environmental program elaboration. Regional authorities never had a responsibility for the elaboration of any standardized monitoring system. But they tried to organize a Regional Monitoring Agency to elaborate and implement a methodology that would make it possible to compare all data and unify the results of different measurement networks. This work was started but not finished. The Regional Monitoring Agency stopped functioning as an environment protection organization and began dealing with the exploitation of natural resources.

Regional Environmental Policy Systems Under Pressure

In Vologda region a regional environmental program was created but after the August 1998 crisis its implementation stopped due to lack of financial resources in the region. The Regional Administration Department, responsible for implementation, was closed. Only the position of the vice-governor, responsible for environment protection, remained. During a period of time, EPC played the role of "regional ministry" of environment. But the activities of the regional government in the field of environmental policy were decreasing step by step. Environmental issues were moved away from the regional political agenda.

Thus the attempt to create a regional environmental policy system that could replace to a major extent the federal one failed. Nevertheless, the attempt marked a strong decentralization tendency present in Russian environmental policy. This kind of decentralization doesn't mean a change of direct state regulation into more self-regulatory systems. It just means replacing federal centralized regulation with regional regulation.

In explaining this failure of regionalisation in environmental policy the majority of our respondents referred to the financial crisis of August 1998. But during that crisis one cannot speak of a total economic disaster in the region. The "Severstal" company and some other enterprises preserved their economic positions. Moreover, we could state that economic growth started at that time in the Vologda region as in many other Russian provinces. It was hidden and latent,[4] and it was detected at the federal level only in spring 1999 (Vishnepolskiy, 1999). But this means that the regional budget deficit could not to be very high at that time.

Probably the main reason for regional environmental policy destruction was not so much an economic crisis, but rather growing economic interests of companies and authorities who are trying to move all obstacles for industrial growth, including requirements of environment protection.[5] This process is common in almost all the nine regions investigated. As the head of Briansk EPC openly said: "Industries are not interested in additional control" (Soloviov, 2000, p. 17).

At the same time, the relation between the Federal EPC and its regional departments became almost invisible. Only a few of the staff of regional Committees had the status of "state officers" and received their salaries from the federal budget. Other employees could work as "technical personal" or could be fired (by the decision of the head of the Committee). The Committee had to search for other sources for financing its staff (e.g. municipal budget, foreign grants). As a result, a very strange situation emerged after August 1998. There was no federal environmental strategy, and the implementation of regional environmental policy stopped. The relations between the central office and regional departments of EPC existed only in the form of regular payments to the federal ecofund and annual reports to the federal office. At the same time, the regional Committee retained a core role in economic regulations, as it controlled this structure and was thus supplied with financial resources into the regional ecofund. Thus the Committees remained strong organizations in the absence of both federal and regional environmental policy. Economic regulation and the collection of finances became the main function of the Committee, but the organization continued to execute other functions (control pollution level, monitoring, expertise, etc.).

Local Level Environment Protection

The ongoing restructuring processes at a local level are very similar to the regional ones. Local departments of EPC are closely related to local authorities for economic reasons. Their activities are mainly financed from local ecofunds, whose resources can be spent only in agreement with local authorities. The Regional Committee significantly reduced financial support to local organizations. Recent events have confirmed this tendency. The regional EPC left local Committees to the responsibility of local authorities.

The principal difference between ongoing processes on regional and local levels of state regulation is an even larger shortage of local budgets in comparison with regional ones. Only Cherepovets authorities have enough resources from the municipal budget and the ecofund for implementation of a city environmental policy due to profitable enterprises. The Vologda City municipal ecofund does not have such a strong financial base as Cherepovets, because there are no large industrial companies in the city. At the same time, the Vologda City government is searching for possibilities to implement environmental protection projects related first of all to industrial water pollution control. As it does not have any powerful administrative or economic instruments for direct control and enforcement, it has to find new methods and strategies for policy-making. According to our research, the Vologda municipal Environment Protection Committee is now playing a major role as municipal administration department. But there are more changes and innovations. In 1998, the mayor of Vologda started negotiations and consultations with different actors including representatives of Vologda ecoNGOs (Committee on Ecology of Suhona River Basin), deputies of the city parliament, representatives of commercial organizations and industrial enterprises. During these negotiations the possibilities, advantages and disadvantages of fundraising and close cooperation were discussed, involving non-state actors more into the core of policy-making and implementation activities. Participants decided to elaborate a program of small river protection and made a preliminary task division. Such methods of policy-making reminds us of political modernization tendencies (cf Jänicke, 1993) and are new phenomena for Russian environmental decision-making processes, even at the local level.

4. ENVIRONMENTAL PROTECTION STRUCTURES OF INDUSTRIAL COMPANIES

All big companies in the region under study are developing environmental management schemes and activities. "Ammofos", "Azot", and "Severstal" companies in Cherepovets, as well as the two paper plants in Sokol have environmental departments. The main reason for this environmental activity of industries is state environmental regulation and the necessity to reach limits of pollution determined by state organizations for avoiding large payments for pollution (Lukinachikov, 1998). Another important factor is related to environmental requirements of Western countries if the company is to supply goods for the Western market. In-depth interviews with heads of these enterprise environmental departments show that a green image is not so important inside the country as it is for the foreign market. Next to state and market pressures, in several cases the influence of civil society on polluters proved significant. For example, during a long time "Severstal" company was under pressure from not only Cherepovets ecoNGOs, but also from the (federal) Russian environmental movement. Direct actions of radical NGOs were conducted in 1995 against the company. All these factors forced the company to make investments in pollution prevention activities and resulted in a changing style of interaction with other social actors. Since then, the environmental management staff of this corporation demonstrates what we could label a Western style of environmental management: openness and a willingness to negotiate and cooperate with different actors, including ecoNGOs. To a major extent it should be understood as symbolical behavior rather than a real conviction of the company top management, as all internal policy and strategic investment decisions of the company remain closed. Nevertheless, this relative openness can be considered as some progress in comparison with previous situations, in which company administrations entered into open struggles with ecoNGOs and denied the existence of any pollution problem. We consider this as a small step towards the establishment of eco-modernization relationships between companies and ecoNGOs.

Another factor, which influenced company eco-management, was the absence of any branch or regional structure supporting enterprise environmental management in a major part of Russian industries. Former cooperation between enterprises (either sectoral or regional) was destroyed following the move to a capitalist development path and the consequent deep structural transformations in managerial systems of Russian industries. The ties between environmental departments of industrial companies that began to develop at the end of eighties were broken and informational exchange between enterprises of the same branch stopped. Such internal interactions remain now only in state-owned industries of the energy and transport sector (e.g. railways, Gazprom). As a result, there is no standard scheme how to organize environmental management in companies. Industrial companies have to create their own eco-management structure based on previous experiences, the overall managerial structure of the company and innovative ideas of their leaders. Only a few principal elements are common in environmental management structures of big companies: control of pollution, elaboration and implementation of protective measures (technological, organizational, etc.), elaboration of the system of internal administrative and economic sanctions against polluting subdivisions of the company.

Recently, a tendency to the re-establishment of inter-industrial cooperation and informational flows in the field of environmental management has been emerging. Company environmental managers are very interested in these relationships. All of them told us about the necessity of reestablishing ties between single branch companies, as it could provide them with information on organizational and technological know-how. Especially regional environmental policy is now playing a crucial role in shaping industrial eco-management because of the absence of a well-functioning branch system. In several cases a network has been formed between environmental managers of plants of different branches (chemistry, metallurgy, machinery, etc.) situated in one region.

Enterprise Environmental Departments

Big companies usually face all of the described above types of environmental pressures (state regulation, requirements of Western partners, pressure of ecoNGOs). They have enough resources to implement comparatively effective environmental management to avoid major conflicts and receive some benefits (e.g. wider access to the Western market). Usually, some kind of environmental department coordinates all environmental activities of the company, elaborates an environmental policy and implements it. Such departments are responsible for water and air pollution control as well as waste management. The status of environmental department chief is considered high. Thus the head of the environmental protection department of "Severstal" has the position of vice-director of the company. Top environmental managers of Cherepovets companies play an active role in the regional and city environmental policy-making process.

Environmental departments of big companies of Cherepovets City have also established relationships with European environmental protection organizations (state and educational structures) that provide them information and training in modern pollution prevention methodologies and implement cleaner production projects, influencing the re-orientation of the company environmental management towards a more preventive form.

But only big companies have such environment protection structures. Small and medium-sized enterprises (such as Vologda Electro-Mechanical Plant, Sheksna Woodwork Plant) have only one staff member as environmental manager, and this position is often just a formal one. The person responsible for environmental protection at the plant usually has no real influence on enterprise decision-making processes. Their director or chief-engineer (the second position in Russian plant management structure) makes all the decisions on environment protection. This does not mean that small and medium sized enterprises do not implement environmental measures. But they do not have resources for maintaining constant activities in this field, and can only implement some environmental measures from time to time (e.g. building of local filters, substitution of toxic substances in production process, etc.). The leadership of the Electro-Mechanical Plant even had to search for foreign grants for constructing a water recycling system. As finances are very limited, each decision related to cost is highly important and can be made by top managers only. They prefer to invite experienced experts from Russian state and non-state organizations specializing in environmental management if they need to implement any improvement. As a result these companies catalyze the development of the environmental market in the region and the emergence of new actors in environmental arena.

5. GAME WITHOUT RULES: THE EMERGENCE OF NEW ACTORS IN ENVIRONMENTAL REFORM

Despite economic stagnation a market of environmental services has developed in most regions. The ecoNGO pressure for public environmental evaluation of industrial projects created growing demand for environmental experts. Cooperation of industrial companies and enterprises with Western partners increased the need for ecoaudit services. The absence of resources for expensive equipment for air and water cleaning at the enterprise or municipal budget created a necessity for small filter and sewage treatment systems and experts to install them. But the most important factor in market demand is formed by the economic incentives of pollution prevention and consists of the enforcement of acceptable norms and standards for industries. The key principle of economic regulation is the following: industrial enterprises must determine the limits of acceptable levels of pollution (e.g. acceptable norms for water or air pollution). They should pay for the pollution within these standards, they should pay twice as much for pollution that exceeds the acceptable level and also twice as much if they do not determine acceptable norms.

Enterprise managers must prepare a so-called "project of norm" which should be approved by the Sanitary Authority and the Water Control Committee (if it concerns water pollution) and subsequently it should be investigated and approved by the EPC. Only environmental departments of big companies can elaborate such standards by themselves. Other enterprises have to delegate the fulfillment of this work to (private) organizations specializing in such activities. The preparation of the "project of norm" includes an analysis of all production and storage facilities of the enterprise, the determination of acceptable limits of pollution and the elaboration of pollution prevention options and measures that are discussed with plant managers and then should be included in enterprise development plans.

The Environmental State Going to the Market

All regional Committees have legal possibilities to run commercial activities because the federal law that determines their activities is not clear and strict. When the Vologda region EPC leaders faced a necessity to survive, they organized the Center of Environmental Program in the framework of the Committee. It is purely a commercial organization working in the regional environmental market. Similar processes are going on in other Russian regions too. Thus, the Samara EPC also established commercial organizations, but the Samara

Committee continues to be involved in the realization of regional environmental strategy and continues to play the role of regional environmental ministry. This region has a more developed industrial network than the Vologda region. Larger risks of accidents and of social-ecological conflicts force the Samara government to keep the environmental situation better under control and to implement environmental policy to some extent.

Vologda EPC is transforming into an economic agent step by step, due to the weakness of the federal center, the lack of finances and the disappearance of a regional environmental strategy. The commercial activities can contradict the control functions of the EPC. One of the former officers of the Committee says: "It is a big contradiction when you are working as experts for an industrial company and continue to control the pollution level of this company. As an expert you have to defend the interests of your client, as state controller you must sometimes act against these interests". The interests of environment protection are moving away to the periphery in this game.

In the beginning of the 1990s, only state institutions were involved in the project activities (departments of Universities, groups in engineering institutes, commercial units created by state environment protection organizations, see above). This situation changed in the middle of the 1990s. The work with regional industry requires a high level of expert mobility and flexibility, which could not be provided by the state bureaucracy. Several organizations or individuals working on the "project of norm" began to act independently. At the same time, a significant part of them did not hurry to change their official status as state organizations or NGOs. First of all, this situation is related to an inappropriate tax system. The legalization of these activities in separate enterprises could be really dangerous for small ventures due to the enormous pressure of taxes. So in most cases this work is carried out within a state organization, while the persons doing the work form at the same time an independent unit. This possibility exists due to many factors, among which cash payments for work, friendly relations with managers, informal agreements on use of organizational bank account, etc. The clients never ask for permission at the formal organization, as they are only interested in a personal license of specialists in audits and 'norm projects'.

The absence of clear rules of the game in the emerging market is also a significant factor for "shadow" work. For example, there is no Western style marketing system in this field. Directors of enterprises will never trust presentations or advertisements in the media. Only long personal relations, intensive negotiations, and recommendations from managers of other plants could help such environmental companies to get a client. State or former state agencies have an advantage in this.

Another problem is the information required for the elaboration of 'norm projects'. The data of water or air quality monitoring are necessary ingredients. State structures such as EPC are ready to sell this information but there is no established and regulated market for this information and the prices are extremely high now. The overall price of 'norm projects' would increase enormously if these data were offered and bought on such an unregulated market. Therefore, small groups have to search for information using personal relations or even steal data.

The history of organization of "ArtEco" Engineering Center is very typical for the developments in regional environmental markets. EPC organized a research group from its own employees for investigations on water pollution in the region. The specialists who conducted these investigations received very small fees and limited salaries but they acquired a large database that was useful for conducting water norm projects. The group left the Committee and began to work on projects for regional small and medium-sized enterprises. For more than two years it had to function as part of the principal Vologda City ecoNGO "Committee on Ecology of Suhona River Basin". The group could change its official status into the independent "ArtEco" Engineering Center only after reaching financial sustainability and an image of a skilled and reliable partner.

Some of the environmental firms and consultants that have started their work with "project of norm" extend their activities towards ecoaudit, environmental impact assessment or small sewage treatment projects. The number of such groups in a region is limited by the size of the environmental market. There are approximately 15 firms in the Vologda region and only a few of them have a favorable position in the market. Many specialists of these firms came to the idea of cleaner production. For example, the Environment Protection Committee required the construction of a water cleaning system for the enterprise "Vologodskoe", but experts invited by the enterprise staff insisted on the implementation of a set of cleaner production measures to be implemented. As these experts have no knowledge of Western cleaner production methodologies, the necessity and possibility of preventive management seems to have emerged as an obvious measure.

The Center of Environmental Programs of the Regional EPC became the strongest competitor for small environmental business in 1999. It held all information on enterprises which needed norm projects and on their financial situation and capability to pay for the project, and it monopolized all key monitoring data. More important is the fact that this organization, being part of a state controlling structure, has instruments to influence companies to carry out an audit or "project of norm". The modern regional environmental market is being governed first of all by the system of economic regulation and second by decisions of EPC.

But small environmental firms survive even under these circumstances. As was mentioned above market activity requires a high degree of flexibility. Small ventures are very mobile and flexible. The staff of these firms is usually young, skilled, and ready for innovations and changes. But the main reason for their survival is that the regional market became divided between Center of Environmental Programs and other environmental businesses. The Center is working with big projects for relatively large-scale enterprises, while small environmental firms are dealing with small and medium-sized industries.

The environmental market and the new actors in the arena of regional environmental management transform the overall organizational structure of regional environmental policy, making it more complex (because new actors and new relations and resource dependencies appear) and more flexible. This comes close to our understanding of eco-modernization principles.

The emergence of new actors complements the existing configuration of policy network members in the regions. At the end of the eighties, such a network included only state organizations and industrial firms, and the relationships between those actors were mainly administrative. The contemporary network core is formed by organizations that execute economic regulation of environmental protection, environmental businesses, and industrial producers: the regional EPC, Water Control Committee and Sanitary Authority, small and medium-sized enterprises that survived after the crisis, big companies (such as "Severstal", "Azot", "Ammofos"), and small environmental ventures. Two groups or policy communities can be distinguished inside the core of this network. The first consists of leaders of big companies, regional departments of the federal bodies listed above, Cherepovets EPC, and a few environmental ventures working in close cooperation with the regional EPC. The second includes top managers of small and medium-sized enterprises, independent environmental ventures, and the municipal EPCs (except the Cherepovets Committee). Interrelations exist between these two sub-communities, but internal ties are stronger.

6. CONCLUSIONS

Summarizing the analysis of transformations in regional environmental policy we can state that there are two, partly contradictory, tendencies in the Vologda region. First there is a decline of state environmental policy, related to limited finances of state environmental organizations and environmental programs, both at federal and regional levels. Initially, such restrictions were caused by the economic crisis and budget deficits. But more recently with the advancement of Russian 'capitalism', the industrial development and orientation on economic growth without any limits became the main reason for the decrease in regional environmental finances and thus in environmental policy-making, implementation and enforcement.

At the same time and secondly, there is a tendency in the field of environmental policy towards decentralization, economization and privatization processes. Decentralization in the Vologda environmental policy shows a transfer of steering capacity of the state from the federal level to the regional and local level and the development of self-organization and self-regulation in the sphere of environmental management.

Arguably, the transformation of the managerial role of the state in regional environmental management and the commercialization of the EPCs can be interpreted as a tendency of ecological modernization. While on the one hand, these phenomena do not correspond to ecological modernization as the latter supposes the combination of strong state management with self-organization processes, on the other hand the weakening of the state and the emergence of its commercial activities catalyzed a process of "economization" of regional eco-management in industry. This forced the development of economic regulation and an environmental market in the region.

As illustrated, the decentralization and commercial activities of state organizations generated the creation of private or independent environmental ventures. These environmental businesses are playing a key role in environmental reforms in Vologda industries. The emergence of these actors in the environmental policy arena proves a vital factor for eco-modernization developments, as these firms have a direct economic interest in environmental innovations and can function as a catalyst for eco-modernization developments. They are already trying to promote and implement pollution prevention methods and strategies in industries and to convince both state structures and companies of the necessity to do so. Equally, decentralization processes lead to similar forms of interaction, negotiations and consultations between representatives of state environmental organizations, regional and local authorities, ecoNGOs, industries, and businesses at the local level. These kinds of communications are often put forward in eco-modernization literature, and move beyond the traditional Russian environmental decision-making routines, in which for instance authorities never trusted NGOs and always tried to avoid any contact with them (see e.g. Khaliy, 1996).

Despite various and perhaps even dominant destructive trends that exist in regional environmental policy, the above innovations and developments can be interpreted as signs of the emergence of ecological modernization transformations, be they of a specific Russian kind. It is difficult to make any predictions on the progress, stabilization or decline of ecological modernization in the Vologda region, or on the entire Russian territory. The future of environmental reforms strongly depends on changes in the overall political, economic and social conditions in the region and in the country.

Epilogue: The Instability of Russian Ecological Modernization

The drastic administrative transformations that started in Russian politics as a whole – and environmental policy in particular – during the period of preparation of this paper are indicative of the instability of ecological modernization tendencies. For our investigation the most important changes are the following. First, in 2000 the Putin government started to make a serious attempt to stop decentralization processes and restore federal power by limiting the power of regional governors. Second, the state environmental policy system is under strong restructuring. The federal Environment Protection Committee and Forest Committee have been closed recently. The activities and mandates of both organizations have been transferred to the Nature Resource Committee, which is responsible for the use of natural resources.[6] Third, the eco-fund system is under reorganization.

These reorganizations confirm our conclusions that the focus on economic growth is the main reason for the decline of (regional) environmental policy. President Vladimir Putin openly states that now the first aim of the state is economic growth on the base of natural resource exploitation. Environmental protection is considered an obstacle for such growth and should be postponed to the future (see Putin, 2000).

It is difficult to assess the real and final consequences of these governmental actions and plans on environmental reforms. Restoration of the central state power could easily destroy the self-organization structures which have emerged in the regions, and closing EPC could significantly change the developments analyzed and described in this article. But these political processes are not finished. Instability may be the stable factor in Russian environmental protection for some time to come.

NOTES

1. The first research was conducted by the group "Social-Ecological Problems of Russian Province" of Institute of Sociology RAS (Moscow), and the second by above research group and Engineering Center "ArtEco" (Vologda), a regional NGO specialized on industrial eco-management. One of the principal goals of both studies was to reveal developments towards ecological modernization in Russian environmental policy. The results of the research are regularly publishing in almanac "Uchastie" ("Participation", Social Ecology of Russian Regions), published in the framework of the first project.

2. See Grishankov and Shmarov (1998 and 1999) and Arseniev (1998) on the rating of the largest industrial companies in Russia.

3. See Bessonov, Gurova and Ivanter (1999). *Expert*, *Dengy* (Money), and *Vlast* (Power) are Russian weekly journals of current events in politics and economy.

4. The administration of the companies hide all figures related to growth of production in order to avoid taxes (Vishnepolskiy, 1999).

5. It is necessary to stress that there was not any significant economic growth before the August crisis. Some experts state that modern economic development was triggered by the financial crisis, which restricted the access of Western competitors to the Russian market making their production too expensive for Russian consumers (see Vishnepolskiy et al., 1999). Anyway orientation towards economic growth has become an ideology of regional and federal authorities now. It could be confirmed by the position of president Putin who openly declared the priority of economic growth under environmental protection (see Putin, 2000).

6. See newspaper *Prirodnoresursnie Vesty*, N11, June 2000.

ACKNOWLEDGMENTS

The authors profited from discussions on regional environmental policy issues with our colleague Irina Khaliy (Institute of Sociology RAS). We are especially grateful to Arthur Mol (Wageningen University) for interest and attention to our work. His advice helped us to improve this paper greatly. We are very grateful to Juriy Bazanov (chairman of Vologda Regional EPC), Aleksey Yakunichev (Mayor of the city of Vologda, the capital of Vologda region) and Igor Litvinov (chairman of Commission on environment protection, Spatial Planning and Land Use of Vologda city Council). We thank Oleg Leontiev, vice-chairman of the Committee on Ecology of the Sukhona River Basin, and the staff of "ArtEco" Center for support in organizing the present research. Consultations on the Samara region environmental policy with Gennadiy Ardakov (Volga River Territorial Center on Environmental Pollution Monitoring), Valery Safronov and Valeriy Tsikalo (Samara Nature Protection Committee) were very helpful. We express our gratitude to the Embassy of the Kingdom of the Netherlands in Russia, and the Dutch ecoNGO Milieukontakt Oost-Europa for financial support.

REFERENCES

Aksenova O. (1999). The Regional Environmental Policy. *Uchastie* (Participation), Issue 1, Russian Sociological Society, Moscow, 21–26 (in Russian).

Aksenova, O. (2000). The Open Struggle With Shadow. *Uchastie* (Participation), Issue 5. Russian Sociological Society, Moscow, 19–24 (in Russian).

Arseniev V. (1998). Rating of the Biggest Industrial Companies in Russia. *Dengy* ("Money"), *N 29*, 10–25 (in Russian).

Beck, U. (1992). *Risk Society. Towards a New Modernity*. London: Sage Publications.

Bessonov, V., Gurova, N., & Ivanter, A. (1999). Unexpected Happiness. Russian Economy is Growing. *Expert, N 17*, 10–15 (in Russian).

Construction Norms and Rules (1986). Moscow: State Committee of USSR on Building Affairs.

Grishankov, D., & Shmarov, A. (1998). Rating of the Biggest Industrial Companies in Russia. *Expert, N 36,* 44–74 (in Russian).

Grishankov, D., & Shmarov, A. (1999). Rating of the Biggest Industrial Companies in Russia. *Expert N 38,* 11–51 (in Russian).

Jänicke, M. (1993). Über ökologische und politieke Modernisierungen. *Zeitschrift für Umweltpolitik und Umweltrecht*, 2, 159–175.

Mol, A. P. J., & Spaargaren, G. (1993). Environment, Modernity and the Risk-Society. The Apocalyptic Horizon of Environmental Reforms. *International Sociology*, *8*(4), 431–459.

Mol, A. P. J. (1995). *The Refinement of Production. Ecological Modernization Theory and the Chemical Industry.* Utrecht: International Books.

Khaliy, I. (Ed.) (1996). *Actions of Environmental Movement.* Moscow: Russian Academy of Sciences (in Russian).

Khaliy, I. (2000). *The Public Guard Nature and Environment in Russian Regions.* Moscow: Milieukontakt Oost-Evropa, Woman Assosiation "EcoSociology" (in English).

Lukinachikov, N. N. (1998). *Economic and Organizational Mechanisms of Environmental Management and of Nature Resource Use*. Moscow: NIA-Priroda (in Russian).

Osipov, Y. B., & Lvova, E. M. (Ed.) (1996). *Nature Protection Management in Russia Federation.* Moscow: NIA-Priroda, (in Russian).

Putin, V. (2000). The role of mineral resource exploitation in the strategy of the Russian economy. In: N. N. Marfenin (Ed.), *State of Russia in the Surrounding World: Analytical series World* (pp. 18–28). Moscow, Moscow University of Ecology and Politology, (in Russian).

Soloviov, V. (2000). Problems of Environmental Protection of the Briansk Region. *Uchastie* (Participation), *4*, 11–17 (in Russian).

Vishnepolskiy, K. et al. (1999). How Did Russian Enterprises Reach Economic Growth? *Dengy* (Money), *N 17*, 12–17 (in Russian).

Weale, A. (1992). *The New Politics of Pollution.* Manchester/New York: Manchester University Press.

Yanitsky, O. (Ed.) (1998). *Risks and Dangers of the Transitional Society*. Moscow: Institute of Sociology RAS (in Russian).

$ 90-95